HIGH SCHOOL FEMINIST STUDIES

Compiled by Carol Ahlum and Jacqueline Fralley

Edited with an Introduction by Florence Howe

The Feminist Press
Box 334
Old Westbury, New York 11568

The Clearinghouse on Women's Studies

Contents

3: INTERDISCIPLINARY

Introduction

By Florence Howe

The energy, imagination and information in this book respond to a deep-felt need to improve the heart of the high school curriculum—literature and language, history and social studies. We read literature, as one student put it, "to find out what to do with our lives." We read history to learn about the past so that we may understand the present and plan for the future. But what if women are omitted from the history recorded in textbooks? What if, as a study by Mary Beaven has indicated, the portraits of women provided in the high school literature classroom are harmful to students?[1] The high school years are critical for the future of females and males alike, not only for what they enable students to understand about human relations between women and men and among members of families, but also for what they enable students to envision of the world of work. For many students, these are the last years of required schooling, the years preceding important choices: marriage, vocation or college. Half don't or can't choose college, and a larger proportion of the talented who don't go on are women. Who controls those choices? What influence could or should the high school curriculum have on those students? Directly or indirectly, the courses described in this volume answer those questions.

The development of these courses—now known as high school women's studies—can be attributed to a number of complex factors, the most important of which is the women's movement. Like most social movements, it has been a teaching movement, aimed to tell masses of people about significant discoveries, that, acknowledged and acted upon, will change lives. The women's movement has taught us to look at, think about and act on principles affirming the dignity of women, including their right to study and to work, to run for political office, even to remain unmarried and childless if they should so choose. Perhaps as significant as its large messages, its mass organizations and publications, has been the women's movement's chief teaching tool—the small consciousness-raising group. In such groups, women share experiences: they attempt to analyze the conditions of their lives and to discover strategies for changing those conditions that are unsatisfactory. By 1976, in most major cities, one can also find men's consciousness-raising groups. By 1976, a substantial proportion of women and some men have come to understand the dynamics of "sexual politics," can define "patriarchy," "sex object," "sexism." Some of them have begun as well to consider the connections between those social realities and the educational system through which we all pass.

By the end of the sixties, the women's movement had begun to reach faculty and graduate students on college campuses and in professional associations. Studies of the status of women faculty led directly to charges of widespread discrimination, all of which have been, since that time, upheld in the courts and through the passage of such federal legislation as Title IX and the Women's Educational Equity Act. Such studies, broadened to include the attrition rates of women in graduate schools, for example, and the percentage of bright women who chose not to go to graduate school at all, led to other kinds of queries. Men and women sit side by side in the same classroom, but are they receiving equal education? Why are aspirations so different for each sex? Why don't bright women pursue the same careers as their male counterparts?

With such questions in mind, researchers turned to the curriculum, in elementary and secondary schools as well as in colleges. In junior high, when boys were sent to shop and girls to cooking, they were receiving distinct messages about their futures. Obviously discriminatory, such practices have now been dealt with by the law. But far more subtle are the messages propounded in most other classrooms. There, as study after study indicates, women are depicted consistently as different from and inferior to men. In early readers, for example, mothers are not bright enough to get a balloon out of a tree, but suggest that their children wait until daddy comes home—to use the kitchen ladder to solve the problem. As the two studies we include in this volume indicate, women are left out of history texts entirely and are present only in demeaning, minor portraits in literature offered to the high school student. Most significantly, women are mothers and housewives in all texts, not working people, not social or political leaders, not writers, inventors, artists, factory workers, bus drivers—despite the reality of the twentieth-century world.

The response to this male-centered and male-biased curriculum was women's studies—or feminist studies, as it has also come to be called. It is an area for study and research; it is also an alternative curriculum with several distinctive goals:

1. to raise the consciousness of students about the sexist curriculum and the wider society;
2. to compensate for the omission of women from the curriculum;
3. to develop the knowledge—through research—necessary to broaden the curriculum;
4. to recover the lost or neglected history and culture of women of all classes, races, nationalities.

The ultimate purpose of women's studies hearkens back to its primary source—the women's movement: to improve the status of women in the society, to render to women the dignity and social justice due them.

A women's studies program on a campus in 1976 may resemble a mini-college, with course-offerings in every disciplinary area and in many interdisciplinary ones as well. There are nearly 200 such programs on college campuses, most of them degree-granting or offering "minors" or "second majors." There are also graduate programs at more than a dozen institutions. And on more than half the campuses in the country, one can find at least a few individual women's studies courses, typically in departments of English, history or sociology. Courses called "Images of Women in Modern Literature," "Women Writers," "Women in U.S. History," or "The Sociology of Women" are commonplace, even on the most conservative college campuses. There are four scholarly journals, a national newsletter, and, in 1976, a national professional association will be launched.[2] Despite moves toward retrenchment in most colleges across the country in the mid-seventies, women's studies has continued to grow at a rate that has astonished even its adherents.

It has also grown off the college campus—most importantly, as this volume indicates, in the high school. No one knows when the earliest high school feminist course was given, or where. No one knows how many such courses have been given, or how many are being given today. But one of the courses in this collection was taught as early as 1970, two others beginning in 1971, nine beginning in 1972 and six in 1973. In the years since this volume has been projected, we have heard from hundreds of high school teachers interested in its contents.

The twenty-three syllabi or descriptions of curriculum included in this volume are not, in any statistical sense, representative. They are, to describe them most simply, the best that we have received—without attempting a national competition. That the geographical distribution is skewed in favor of the eastern seaboard north of Washington D. C., is a direct result of our own location and of a decision to spend only very limited funds on travel. On the other hand, the twenty-three contributions come from twelve states, six of them away from the east coast: Ohio, Wisconsin, Minnesota, Colorado, California, Oregon. While most are from senior rather than junior high schools, and most from public rather than private schools, from middle-class suburban rather than urban schools, the range includes an alternative school for working class students (The Group School in Cambridge, Massachusetts) and at least two high schools with large black and/or Puerto Rican populations (Dwight Morrow High School in Englewood, New Jersey and Adlai Stevenson High School in New York City).

We have divided the selections in this book into three categories: history, literature and interdisciplinary. The group we have named "interdisciplinary" resembles somewhat either college courses in "The Sociology of Women" or those introductory courses often required of the women's studies major. These are the least traditional courses, the most free-wheeling, the most difficult to describe or pigeon-hole. Though they are taught usually by members of social studies departments, they are organized topically rather than chronologically. Occasionally, one of the topics is history. These courses focus on the lives of contemporary women, on the issue of sex-role stereotyping in all aspects of life, including the media, the classroom and work. One of the most exceptional of these courses, developed by The Group School, focuses entirely on "Women and Work," and is comparable to college courses that draw materials from economics, history, sociology and literature into a single course.

It is only fair to add that all women's studies courses are, by their very nature, interdisciplinary, since they must begin by convincing students of their *raison d'etre*. Thus, history and literature courses, like the ones we include here, may open with a consciousness-raising unit on women's "roles" or "status," or a week's work on prejudice, or an analysis of a textbook's bias. But the general thrust of the course will move students quickly into either the study of literary works or the study of a chronological sequence of events.

The history courses illustrate new directions among scholars in women's history: the need to reperiodize history (beyond wars and revolutions); the use of autobiography as an important source, especially for the lives of women; and the inclusion of class and race as additional key factors in describing the history of women. Similarly, the literature courses include a variety of women writers not ordinarily to be found on high school reading lists: Zora Neale Hurston, Edith Wharton, Alice Childress, Charlotte Perkins Gilman, Margaret Walker, Kate Chopin, Agnes Smedley, Susan Glaspell, Sylvia Plath, Doris Lessing, just to name a few.

Not unlike those at the college level, high school feminist studies courses are demanding and reading assignments are typically heavy. Writing or action projects emphasize independent and thoughtful investigation and analysis, whether students report their own family's history or analyze the portraits of women and men offered in a group of TV situation comedies. The teacher's job is to provide the opportunities for students to seek answers to questions and to report their findings. Thus, these women's studies courses also follow in the rich tradition of innovative teaching at the high school level.

Perhaps the most important questions about high school feminist studies remain to be answered. Will such courses spread in the forms presented here, and in the manner of college courses—from school to school—as supplementary "electives" added to the senior high curriculum? Or will teachers attempt to patch feminist segments onto their standard curriculum? Or is "our real task," as one teacher writes, a much more difficult one—"to incorporate women, and black and working people into our entire curriculum"? And what of other aspects of the high school curriculum not touched on here—foreign language, economics, science, health, home economics, even mathematics and business?

Regardless of approach, we will need local and national efforts to support high school teachers who do not have the time (or the time off) for the preparation of new courses or for scholarly research that college teachers take for granted. In addition, high school teachers are not expected to be curriculum developers or researchers. But as everyone teaching women's studies knows, to do so requires being both curriculum developer and researcher as well as innovative classroom teacher. High school teachers will need time off and support not only for inservice courses, but for summer institutes and sabbatical study. College women's studies programs ought to plan special offerings for high school teachers, including evening courses, intensive summer programs and year-long internships or assistantships. Only with such cooperation can we look forward to revising educational programs to meet the human needs of students during the years of critical life choices.

Notes

1. Mary H. Beaven, "Responses of Adolescents to Feminine Characters in Literature," *Research in the Teaching of English,* Spring 1972, pp. 48-68.
2. *Feminist Studies* (417 Riverside Drive, New York, N.Y. 10027); *Women's Studies: An Interdisciplinary Journal* (Queens College/CUNY, Flushing, N.Y. 11367); *Signs: Journal of Women in Culture and Society* (Barnard College, New York, N.Y. 10025); *Women's Studies Newsletter* (The Feminist Press, Old Westbury, N.Y. 11568). For further information about the National Women's Studies Association, write to The Clearinghouse on Women's Studies at The Feminist Press.

Textbook Analysis

WOMEN IN THE HIGH SCHOOL CURRICULUM:
A REVIEW OF U. S. HISTORY AND ENGLISH LITERATURE TEXTS
By Phyllis Arlow and Merle Froschl

Women in High School History Textbooks

In a thorough analysis of twelve popularly used textbooks, Janice Trecker summarizes the traditional treatment of women in these books:

> Women receive a few paragraphs of extravagant praise as essential to America, their high position in our culture is stressed, and a few are even mentioned. For the other ninety-nine percent of the book, women are ignored.[1]

Concerned about the inclusion of women in the secondary school's social studies curriculum, we are interested in locating those aspects of women's lives that have been most neglected in standard history texts and in assessing the quality of such information that is included.

We began this study by examining fourteen currently used textbooks for the following:[2] the listings of women in the index and the table of contents; the choice of women included; the selection and number of illustrations portraying women; the representation of minority women; the use of language. Finally, we looked in-depth at four key areas—the colonial period, the rights and reform movements, women and work and contemporary America—in order to assess how textbooks portray women's contributions to history.

We then correlated our findings with those of other surveys and studies. In all, our report compiles research on thirty-six textbooks and attempts to create a portrait of the treatment of women in high school history.

Omission of Women

One fact became immediately apparent—that was the omission of women from the general framework of history. In indexes we found separate listings for "women," which usually amounted to no more than a sentence or two in the text. Women's lives are usually relegated to special, secondary categories of concern, such as "Social Life in Victorian England" or "Women's Rights Movement—see Suffrage." There are no separate headings for "men."

The typical U. S. history textbook devotes one out of its 500 to 800 pages to women, their lives and their contributions. Where women are included, they appear under separate headings, in special sections, even on different colored paper. They are made to appear supplemental—as postscripts to history rather than an integral part of it.

To be sure, there are a few prominent women included in standard history texts. However, it is interesting to note which women are consistently included and which are consistently ignored. Included are usually Pocahontas, Anne Hutchinson, Susan B. Anthony,

Elizabeth Cady Stanton, Lucretia Mott, Amelia Bloomer, Harriet Beecher Stowe, Jane Addams, Dorothea Dix, Carry Nation, Sacajawea, Clara Barton, Frances Perkins, Eleanor Roosevelt and Harriet Tubman. Granted that history texts are necessarily selective, one wonders, nevertheless, about the basis for selection: Why Harriet Tubman and not Sojourner Truth? Who decides that Carry Nation is more important than Margaret Sanger? Why are such reformers as Clara Barton and Dorothea Dix more significant than Rose Schneiderman and Mother Jones? Where are Mary McCleod Bethune, Margaret Fuller, Elizabeth Blackwell and hundreds of others? Janice Trecker supplies an explanation for the selectivity of texts:

> Although it is tempting to imagine some historical autocrat sternly de-
> creeing who's in and who's out . . . the omission of many significant
> women is probably not a sign of intentional bias. The treatment of
> women simply reflects the attitudes and prejudices of society. Male
> activities in our society are considered the more important; therefore
> male activities are given primacy in the texts. There is a definite image
> of women in our society, and women in history who conform to this
> image are more apt to be included.[3]

Many women are omitted by virtue of the topics chosen for inclusion in textbooks. As though by design, those areas in which women have traditionally achieved recognition—the arts, theater and dance—are generally omitted.

Pictures, photographs and paintings are almost exclusively of male subjects. Few women appear in illustrations (one in seventeen is average), and where they do they are often subordinate to or "the wives of" important men. For example, the only mention of Eleanor Roosevelt in one text occurs beneath a picture captioned "President and Mrs. Franklin D. Roosevelt, 1935."[4]

When women are the central figures in illustrations, they are often treated humorously, supplying comic relief to the more serious story of man's achievements. In one book, a photograph demonstrates how "Two beautiful Gibson Girls could set a man's head spinning."[5] Another photograph shows a well-dressed woman talking on the telephone in an immaculate, modern kitchen with the naive caption, "Electric kitchens liberated many women from the drudgery of housework."[6] Both photographs appear in a section entitled "The United States Becomes an Industrial and Urban Nation."

Recently, the women's movement has begun to supply editors with new "humor" for illustrations. In one book, the movement appears as a photograph of a "Women's Lib" march in which women are shown carrying placards that protest against their role as "unpaid slave laborers." The editors felt the need to balance this point of view with Hugh Hefner's statement: "These chicks are our natural enemy. It is time to do battle with them."[7] The book's intention to amuse is obvious; nowhere are the serious issues and concerns of the women's movement discussed.

The minority woman is almost completely absent from history textbooks. We found no mention of American Indian, Chicana, Puerto Rican or Asian women. It is as though they never existed. Significantly, the inclusion of black history in texts has not made room for the black female, except for the briefest mention of Harriet Tubman. One text's discussion of "Negro Suffrage" does not explain its extension to black males only, nor does the same text mention, in its special section dealing with "The Negro in America," black women at all. When texts include slavery in America, it is with little awareness of the rich cultural heritage of Africa that slavery destroyed, and no insight into the special problems and achievements of the black slave woman. There is no word of the struggles of such black women as Katherine Ferguson and Sarah Douglass to set up schools for black children. Such women as Sojourner Truth, Mary Church Terrell, Mary McCleod Bethune, Ida Wells Barnett, to name but a few, are rarely included. Missing also are portraits of contemporary black women as well as their special problems of employment in contemporary U. S. society.

A more subtle manifestation of sex bias can be found in the language of history texts. Language is not merely a means of communication; it is also an expression of values and behavioral models. The overwhelming male bias of the language of social studies textbooks is evidenced by an exclusive use of male pronouns and generic terms, the inclusion of demeaning terms for women and the perpetuation of the image of women as fragile and timid.

Masculine forms (he, man) in our language are commonly used as though they referred to all people, male and female. In fact, however, such terms used in texts operate to exclude females. When told that "men" headed West, or that "man-made" improvements have raised America's standard of living, the reader does not form a mental image that includes females. Consider this passage on colonial America:

> Men had to do things for themselves or with the aid of a few scattered neighbors. . . . In the end men and their institutions were adjusted to the demands of the American continent.[8]

The hypothetical person in texts is always male: the "man" of tomorrow, for example, or "These are the times that try men's souls." Females are typically referred to as the wives or mothers of males. Women are also seen as appendages, as in "The pioneer took his family West." Elizabeth Burr, Susan Dunn and Norma Farquhar conclude:

> Authors tend to blur man with people in general. . . . At the same time, they are not willing to blur women with people in general. One never sees a picture of women captioned simply "farmers" or "pioneers." Linguistic failure to permit women to be "people" mirrors a long tradition of male supremacy and a socially induced need to keep women in a separate and unequal category.[9]

Acknowledgment of Women's Contributions

To assess how textbooks portray women's contributions to history, we looked at four key areas—the colonial period, the rights and reform movements, women and work and contemporary America—all areas in which an abundance of information is available to historians.

In her research for the Education Task Force of the Lexington Chapter of NOW,[10] Selma Williams uncovered a great deal of primary and secondary source material about women during the colonial period of history: cases of Indian tribes that were both matrilineal and matrilocal, the trial transcript of Anne Hutchinson, first-hand references to Elizabeth Poole, the poetry of Anne Bradstreet. Colonial women participated in a variety of activities including medicine, farming, business and arms-bearing. Yet there is little information in most texts concerning the woman in early America. In textbooks we find that America of the colonies was a "man's" world. Typical of the masculine image is this passage from a popular text:

> The farmer's lot was not an easy one. He and his sons had to get up at daybreak—and even earlier in the winter—to milk the cows, bring in the firewood for the stoves, feed the hens and pigs, and fill the water for the livestock.[11]

Notable women of the period are not discussed in terms of their contributions to American history, but are given minimal coverage in parenthetical asides. This point is illustrated by the following excerpts from several texts:

> Then around 1612, John Rolfe (who later married the Indian Pocahontas) learned how to grow and cure tobacco.[12]

> Lewis and Clark benefited by having with them a young Shoshone, Sacajawea, wife of the interpreter Dorion.[13]

> Other exiles from Massachusetts, among them Mrs. Anne Hutchinson, soon started other settlements along the shores of Narragansett Bay.[14]

The only woman of the colonial period mentioned in one history book is Abigail Adams. There she is not noted for her writings and letters on reform, but as "Abigail Adams, wife of John Adams and mother of John Quincy Adams."[15]

Nowhere is there a picture of the lives of women during this period in history. No book points out that women made a considerable contribution to colonial life as community builders and apprentices in trades and professions. Often they worked side by side with men in a society that needed all the available skilled hands. Probably women were never so "free" again in the New World. Their story should be told.

Much more information about women appears in sections on women's rights and in general sections on the reform movement of the late nineteenth century. Yet even here a full page on suffrage is a rarity, and the treatment is generally superficial. Consider the following excerpts, the only coverage given in those texts to women's rights:

> Hence in 1848 Lucretia Mott and Elizabeth Cady Stanton called a women's convention, which met in Seneca Falls, New York. The delegates resolved that all men and women were created equal and endowed with certain inalienable rights.[16]

> Agitation for women's rights culminated in the Seneca Falls Convention of 1848 and a Declaration of Sentiments couched in the phraseology of the Declaration of Independence.[17]

> Dorothea Dix, a resolute Quaker and a teacher, undertook prison reform and in particular a more humane treatment of the insane. Lucretia Mott, Elizabeth Cady Stanton, and Margaret Fuller began an agitation that women, though they were daughters or wives, should have property rights or even the right to vote.[18] .

In one book, no reference is made to the Seneca Falls Convention, yet three paragraphs are used to describe the Bloomer costumes.

Interpretive and summarizing statements about women as reformers or about reform movements tend to be simplistic, uninformed, or overtly male-biased, as in the following examples:

> Reformers believed that women had as much to contribute to reform as men.[19]

> The organized feminist movement arose earlier in the United States than in any other nation not because American women enjoyed so few privileges but because they had so many that they demanded more.[20]

> The essential demands of the abolitionists, the feminists, the educational reforms and the labor unions were all eventually fulfilled.[21]

> After the vote, American women now assumed an unquestioned role in shaping the production of goods—material, humanistic, literary and artistic. They were the chief spenders of money.[22]

> The patriotic services rendered by women during World War I quickly broke down resistance to the idea of women voting.[23]

Nowhere do the textbooks give a balanced picture of the continuing roles of women during the era of rights and reforms. We find undue emphasis on the lengths of women's skirts rather than information on their struggle for civil rights; the characteristics of the Gibson Girl rather than the activities of feminists; the fashions of the flapper rather than the social changes between the wars.

Textbooks almost totally neglect the whole question of women's work and women's role in the early labor movement. Instead, the story of labor is limited to the introduction of women workers into the textile mills in the 1820's. In some cases, authors clearly show their prejudices against women's participation in the labor force, as in the following:

> The ranks of labor were so constantly diluted by immigrants and women that the artisans were alarmed over their declining status.[24]

> Unionization was pursued so rapidly and widely as to include even seamstresses and cloak makers.[25]

Few texts mention the fact that women and children were among the most overworked and underpaid workers in America, and none consider the effect of such labor on family and community life. Most texts, however, do mention the Lowell mills—usually with a brief and wholly complimentary description of the working conditions for young farm women.

In general, the sections on labor in textbooks follow a familiar pattern in regard to women: women workers are given little space, very few are mentioned by name and fewer still are quoted. Most books give women and work no more than three entries of a few lines each.

It is difficult to understand how women in labor can be dismissed with so few lines of text when, in 1890, at least one million women worked in factories. They outnumbered the men in clothing factories and made up about half the labor force in textile mills and tobacco factories. In addition, women organized strikes and supported male unions under the most extreme hardships and fought to end child labor abuses and the inhumane conditions of the nation's factories.

Today, more than half of all women between the ages of eighteen and fifty-five spend at least part of each year working for pay. Yet discussions of contemporary labor problems tend to neglect women, just as do historical accounts. Texts avoid discussion of those forces that have kept women in the lowest paid work. Nor is unpaid housework mentioned. One text summarizes the contemporary position of working women as follows:

> As of the early 1950's one out of every four married women were in the labor market. This came largely as a result of conveniences in homemaking which gave women extra time.[26]

An accurate picture of the women who make up forty percent of the American work force is given by Robert Smuts in *Women and Work in America:*

> The picture of women's occupations outside the home has changed since 1890 in only a few essentials: a sharp decline in the relative importance of manual work on farm, in factory and in household service occupations; and sharp increases in the importance of clerical and sales work, teaching and nursing, and nonhousehold service jobs. There are still relatively few women in managerial positions and in the traditionally male professions.[27]

In all mention of work in history texts, only "man's work" is considered worthy of description. But working women have a story to be told as well. Where are the farm women who, throughout history, rose before the sun and spent their days as active partners in the family's common work? Or the thousands of frontier women who homesteaded and claimed property without the help of a male partner? Or the women who, during the Civil War, worked as cooks, laundresses, adventurers, spies, scouts and guides? (Of all of women's activities during the Civil War, women's entry into nursing is the only one regularly noted in history texts.) Or the women who took in boarders, sewing and washing to provide for the necessities of the household? Or the women whose volunteer efforts made possible hospital reforms and community organizations? Or the women writers, artists and dancers who have contributed to our cultural heritage?

If in textbooks the treatment of women throughout history is inadequate, the examination of women's contemporary lives is equally incomplete. Even texts that include sections on the terms of Presidents Kennedy and Johnson still give the impression that the passage of the nineteenth amendment solved all the problems of discrimination against women.

There is little or no information on the current legal challenges to discriminatory laws, nor any discussion of how the law affects women in general.

In addition, one of the greatest battles of the early twentieth century, the crusade for birth control, is glaringly omitted. Considering its continued impact on women and society, Janice Trecker asks:

How many students know that men and women were jailed for advocating birth control? That books were seized, that clinics were raided by the police? That desperate birth control leaders went on hunger strikes to plead their case?[28]

Our rapidly changing social conditions make such topics as sex-role socialization an important issue for social studies texts. Young people should understand the forces that shape the concepts of masculinity and femininity not only to understand themselves, but to understand the social and political structures of society.

A Look to the Future
Based on the information in these commonly used texts, one might summarize the history and contribution of the American woman as Janice Trecker reasonably does:

Women arrived in 1619. They held the Seneca Falls Convention on Women's Rights in 1848. During the rest of the nineteenth century, they participated in reform movements, chiefly temperance and were exploited in factories. In 1920 they were given the vote. They joined the armed forces for the first time during the Second World War and thereafter have enjoyed the good life in America.[29]

So little has been included that when one is asked what is missing, one is tempted to answer, "everything." It is not only that students need to learn about the lives of more women "achievers," but that they need to know about the lives of ordinary women as well: diaries, letters, journals and newspapers are a rich source of information about women who have either been excluded from historical accounts or who were recorded only in their stereotyped feminine roles. No one who has read personal accounts of the women of the western frontier can believe the textbook picture of the idealized pioneer women. No one who has read narratives of the Triangle Fire of 1911 will be satisfied with a scanty reference to women workers. No one who has read the lives of Margaret Sanger, Alice Paul or Isadora Duncan will believe that the Flapper was the most important woman of that era.

Women and men students both have a right to learn about the achievements of women in history and about the process through which women have worked to change their status. Since texts are notably biased, students will have to rely, at least for the next decade or two, on supplementary materials to present a true picture of history.

Women in High School English Literature

The literature which is taught in secondary schools is used not merely as a tool for improving reading, written expression and general information. To a great degree, literature defines values and reality. The effect of reading material on the beliefs of students is immediate. While all are not in agreement, at least one study using reading content as a means of changing attitudes has demonstrated that these attitudes change in a positive direction with positive character presentations, and in a negative direction with negative character presentations.[30] Considerable evidence supports the fact that not only are females portrayed differently from males in secondary school literature, they are portrayed as inferior, less capable or less significant beings. It is therefore important for educators to recognize the messages which secondary school literature is transmitting to adolescents.

While a number of studies have already clearly established the sex-bias of high school English texts, we decided to review these theses and as many of the most widely used books as possible, with the aim of writing our own report. We examined for evidence of sexism those anthologies now in use in the secondary school English curriculum,[31] and those textbooks which according to the National Council of Teachers of English were the most widely used in secondary school English classes in the United States.

Our main focus was on the portrayal of female character in these anthologies. We examined the number of male and female authors in the anthologies now in use, the overall focus of the books, the language and editorial comments describing them, and the inclusion of minority women in selections.[32] Finally, we correlated our findings with other surveys and studies which included both anthologies and other supplementary reading selections.[33] Our report is a compilation of the research that reflects the most recent thinking about the portrayal of women in literature presently in use in the secondary school English curriculum.

The Maleness of Literature

As our study of secondary school literature progressed, it became clear that we could not begin to discuss the female image in literature without first noting the overall "maleness" which characterized every anthology we examined. Most of the literature taught in high school classrooms, whether in anthologies or in supplementary readings, is male-centered in imagery, theme and characterization. Literature which focuses around the endurance and courage of men is plentiful, while almost no literature presents women who are physically strong or courageous. Stories about male athletes are abundant; those about female athletes are rare. Similarly, men who are successful in their work outside the home are portrayed often in the literature examined, while almost no literature presents women who are engaged in work outside the home. The fact that one-half of the adult female population is presently in the labor force, and that many women are responsible for the support of their families is almost totally ignored.[34] Women are still portrayed as perennial cake-bakers, too fragile and dependent to do the important work of life. Even in their role as wife and mother, women are not portrayed in these books as people capable of intelligently caring for and guiding the lives of children.

Our study of secondary school literature corresponds with the findings of such researchers as Broverman, Reisman, Griffin, Maccoby and Horner, who have shown that the traits identified as feminine are valued less than those considered to be masculine.[35] According to these psychological studies, the masculine image is synonymous with that of the healthy adult person—independent, aggressive, competitive, task-oriented, assertive, innovative, active. The feminine image—passive, fragile, yielding, dependent, empathetic, nonaggressive, supportive and graceful—is antithetical to that of the healthy adult.[36]

The language used in anthologies is also male-centered. The editor assumes the reader is male, rather than both male and female. The allegedly generic "he" and "man" are used consistently in editorial comments, questions to students and in chapter divisions. For example, in the introduction to one eleventh-grade textbook, masculine imagery prevails:

We begin by assuming that literature is controlled energy. The energy is man's need to express himself. . . . Control . . . is a successful football player's use of his strength . . . a painter communicating his feelings . . . a Grand Prix driver winning his race, and a writer achieving his goal through the controlled use of his medium.[37]

Another anthology divides its contents into two sections, "This Man, This World" and "Man's Destiny, Man's Choice."[38] In another text, published in 1974, the editor refers to the author as "he" throughout, whether the particular author being discussed is male or female.[39]

A disproportionately small number of female authors appears in anthologies currently in use. This is true whether the content is limited to twentieth-century fiction, or expanded to include European and American literature from its beginnings to the present day, and whether the book was published in 1974 or earlier. The Oregon Curriculum, for example, includes sixty-nine male authors and three female authors in one volume; and sixty-two and nine in another. In *Adventures in Appreciation,* there are sixty-three male authors and four female authors. Other studies revealed similar findings. A NOW survey of 171 anthologized selections counted 147 male authors to twenty-four female authors.[40] The most comprehensive survey involved 400 selections: of these, 306 were written by males, ninety-four by females.[41]

It is not uncommon for textbooks to include the same popular women writers—for example, Emily Dickinson and Willa Cather—while more contemporary female writers like Doris Lessing or Mary McCarthy rarely, if ever, appear. Yet, many unknown or undistinguished male writers like Mickey Mantle, George Freitag or Clifford Simak comprise a large part of the majority of anthologies. Furthermore, no attempt is made to represent women writers in various historical eras. *Adventures in Appreciation* includes four women writers (out of sixty-seven authors) who lived at approximately the same time (1830-1933) despite the fact that this book includes European and American literature from its beginnings to the present day.

The woman writer herself is regarded as an aberration. She is often depicted as a recluse, a mad woman, childless and unfulfilled. In one anthology, a page devoted to Gertrude Stein sums up her career in the following manner: "Miss Stein's experiments make her unintelligible to the general public."[42] Her most important contribution to literature is described as the stimulus she gave to other writers, notably Ernest Hemingway and Sherwood Anderson. Despite the fact that this page bears a portrait of Stein upon it, and that a few sentences are initially about her, the real subject of praise is Hemingway, whose achievements are discussed in great detail. Of course, the selection that follows is by Hemingway only.

Characterization is also male-dominated. In many stories, there are no female characters at all, and in the majority of selections, there are no female main characters. Females may appear briefly, but they are not developed as whole persons, and they are not integral to the plot. Often, the categories which are chosen (sports, war, nature) are those which have traditionally excluded female participation. For example, out of the eight divisions of one book, five of them (Survival, Spaceways, Mystery, Decision, Battleground) contain no female characters at all.[43]

In order to determine whether this male-centered pattern is balanced by supplementary readings, we consulted Scarvia B. Anderson's comprehensive study of the major works most often assigned in high school.[44] According to this 1964 survey conducted in 691 high schools throughout the United States, the most frequently assigned books are *Macbeth* and *Julius Caesar,* followed by *Silas Marner, Great Expectations, Tale of Two Cities, Pride and Prejudice, Return of the Native, Our Town, Red Badge of Courage, The Scarlet Letter* and *Huckleberry Finn.* This rather extensive reading list is hardly representative from any point of view. Almost all of the main characters are male, all the authors but two (Jane Austen and George Eliot) are white males, and only one item was written in the twentieth century. With the exception of *Our Town,* this list could have appeared seventy years ago as well as today. Why, for more than a half century, these Shakespearean plays and nineteenth-century novels have been read consistently in high schools throughout the United States is a matter worthy of scrutiny by educators. (*Silas Marner,* for example, was a daring choice once when the Harvard-Yale reading list for the year 1887 required a *modern* novel.) Whatever the original reasons, much of the literature now being taught in our schools is not necessarily useful to adolescents today.

Portrayal of Female Character

Women are relegated to secondary status in the literary curriculum not so much because they are omitted, but because of the distasteful way they are included. Female chracters are stereotyped either by the roles they fulfill or by the personality traits with which they are endowed. The majority of the stories in anthologies depict women in the traditional roles of wife and mother. Their roles are secondary ones—they are supportive of the male main characters. Often, they are the servers bringing in the tea or dinner. In "Alone at Sea" by Hannes Lindeman, for example, an adventure story of a man's struggle against the elements, the only female appears at the beginning in her role as server:

> Now Ruth is preparing breakfast for me. Fried eggs, sunny side up, on an ocean of butter, to give me more energy before taking off.[45]

In another story, "Astronaut Away" by Russell A. Apple, Lt. Walker mentally reviews telling his wife and daughter about his mission:

> His daughter Peggy would be home from play, dinner would be cooking; he could talk to both of them. And what seemed more important; he would like them to hear his voice at least once more.[46]

In this story, the wife, Beth, and the daughter, Peggy, receive virtually the same treatment, so that one must constantly check names to be certain if the author is referring to the wife, or to the little girl. For example, a statement like, "Beth had waved from the window as usual when he left home," could apply either to the adult female or the child.[47]

In "Leaves from a Surgeon's Journal," a story by Harvey Cushing, women appear only in the following sentence: "Red Cross nurses were serving them hot soup and other things, ending up with the inevitable cigarette."[48]

"Papa and the Bomb" by William Iverson tells the story of a father who is a mad genius constantly having "brainstorms." The contrast among the interests of father, son and mother is noteworthy—the son is telling the story:

> For instance, the other night I'm sitting in the kitchen doing my
> geometry homework, and my mother is also in the kitchen baking
> a honey cake, when he comes up from the cellar with this expression
> on his face, and I could see he had another brainstorm.[49]

Only one mother was encountered who was not a "server," but she was a cruel, twisted individual. Indeed, some of the most interesting women in the curriculum seem to bear out the "witch" stereotype which is well-recognized in fairy tales. In "The Rocking-Horse Winner," D. H. Lawrence describes this atypical mother:

> Only she herself knew that in the center of her heart was a hard little
> place that could not feel love, no, not for anybody. Everybody else
> said of her: "She is such a good mother. She adores her children."
> Only she herself, and her children themselves, knew it was not so.
> They read it in each other's eyes.[50]

Although most women are not depicted as malevolent beings, many are seen as detrimental to progress. Over and over again, women's helplessness in the face of disaster is evident. They are unable to cope—they panic, they are anxious, worried, overprotective, maudlin. The men, on the other hand, generally know how to behave during disasters—they are calm, competent, in control.

In "Fire in the Wilderness" by Benedict and Nancy Freedman, the wife is concerned with her husband's safety during a fire, but quite unnecessarily:

> ..."What about you? Mike—I'm so frightened you won't be careful!"
> ..."I'm fine, you know that. You do just what I tell you Kathy. Don't
> be frightened, don't get panicky, and don't leave the river."[51]

Unfortunately, despite Mike's advice, Kathy does suffer burns, and it is Mike who tells her about them, as if she could not feel her own wounds—"You got second degree burns on that pretty face of yours," Mike states.[52]

Even little children in these stories can see how silly the fears of the average adult woman are. In "Dawn of the Remembered Spring" by Jesse Stuart, the little boy declares: "I love to kill snakes. I'm not afraid of snakes. I laugh to think how afraid of snakes Mom was . . . ."[53]

In only one of the stories surveyed did a woman actually know more about a natural disaster than a man. In Walter van Tilburg Clark's "Why Don't You Look Where You're Going?" a woman has an excellent knowledge of the water's depth and, therefore, the ability to save the lives of the passengers aboard a ship. However, she is no "normal" woman—she is cruel and unfeminine. In fact, she has no real name, but is simply called "the masculine lady" as in the following illustration: "The masculine young lady disagreed . . . . The other passengers rebuked her heartlessness with silence."[54]

A frequent theme in literature portraying female character is the search for a marriage partner. Here can be found a variety of unwholesome women, from nagging mothers to females who are status-seeking, pushing, interfering, sarcastic and jealous. Most of these characters appear in connection with "romantic" stories which are grouped either by theme ("Relationships") or by genre ("Short Story"). The anthology selection "Sunday Costs Five Pesos," a one-act "comedy" of Mexican village life, is filled with stereotypic man-trappers who compete with each other to achieve their ultimate goal—marriage. Berta is described as "very pretty, but unfortunately she has a very high temper, possibly the result of her red hair."[55] She is never described in terms of her aspirations, abilities or intellect. Salome is introduced to the reader even more distastefully: "She is twenty-eight, and so many years of hunting a husband have left her with an acid tongue."[56] These women are bitter, ugly, competitive. They tell adolescents that woman's central goal is to find a man and to get married: the process itself is ugly, but if not successfully achieved, unmarried women become empty, hateful creatures, unfulfilled in every way.

When women are not being manipulative in such love fiction, they are being manipulated. They are often viewed as sex-objects—vain, silly creatures who, nevertheless, become desirable fantasies for the smitten male. In "The Chaser" by John Collier, Alan has approached an old man in order to obtain a love potion. The old man describes the benefits of his potion and, at the same time, a rather perverse definition of love evolves:

> "For indifference," said the old man, "they substitute devotion.
> For scorn, adoration. Give one tiny measure of this to the young
> lady . . . and however gay and giddy she is, she will change altogether.
> She will want nothing but solitude and you."
>
> "I can hardly believe it," said Alan. "She is so fond of parties."
>
> "She will not like them any more," said the old man. "She will be
> afraid of the pretty girls you may meet."
>
> "She will actually be jealous?" cried Alan in a rapture. "Of me?"
>
> "Yes, she will want to be everything to you. . . . You will be her sole
> interest in life."
>
> "That is love!" cried Alan.[57]

In another selection, "Love is a Fallacy" by Max Shulman, a young law student, who had observed that lawyers married beautiful, gracious and intelligent women, finds that the object of his affection almost fits these specifications perfectly. Although his love-object was not yet of pin-up proportions, the young man is certain that time would supply the lack. His most serious problem, however, was that she was not intelligent, but even here, he believed she could be molded more suitably:

> "Intelligent she was not. In fact, she veered in the opposite direction.
> But I believed that under my guidance, she would smarten up. At any
> rate, it was worth a try. It is, after all, easier to make a dumb girl smart
> than to make an ugly girl beautiful."[58]

The only females who are occasionally successful in escaping from the stereotyped pattern are the nonconforming "tomboys" or the tough, proud grandmothers. This bears out the notion advanced in one study that interesting female characters are generally not within their childbearing years, but are either premenstrual or post-menopausal.[59] Such females are not needed in their role as "server" to the male, and are therefore not threatening, and more free to do as they wish. Sometimes, however, because of their nonconformity, such characters suffer emotionally—such as Scout in *To Kill a Mockingbird,* Frankie in *A Member of the Wedding* or Emily in "Bad Characters." However, they are dynamic personalities, who have an identity separate from the family or the males in their lives. They have goals and interests of their own, and unquestionably, they represent the most wholesome females in the curriculum.

Implications

It is apparent from the study that the anthologies used in high school English classes depict life unrealistically. Women are not being supplied with admirable role models, and both males and females are learning harmful lessons which accentuate prejudices and preferences for a white, male-dominated culture.

Most of the literature surveyed depicts women in the traditional roles of housewife and mother, but even here, they are characterized as inferior people. Often, women are portrayed as cruel, competitive with each other, or as passive and childish creatures. Only "tomboys" or grandmothers reveal positive personality traits, and they are often considered to be outside of the "mainstream" of life.

One of the most serious implications of the study of secondary school literature is the contribution of such texts to the underachievement of the adolescent female. Most researchers are in agreement with Anne Grant West, who has stated that it is in the junior and senior high school that students idealize the sex roles prescribed by our culture, and it is, significantly, in these years that girls start to underachieve.[60] According to a study by Shaw and McCuen:

> There is evidence that girls who are underachievers in high school usually begin to be so about the onset of puberty, while for boys underachievement in high school usually has an earlier outset. This contrast is a further indication that the achievement drop-off among girls as they reach maturity is linked to the adult female sex role.[61]

A study conducted by Mary Beaven, which sought to discover which female characters students could positively identify with, revealed that there were few, if any, admirable role models present in the curriculum.[62] Girls wrote unfavorable comments which pointed to the dearth of favorable women characters in literature. They stated either that they could not recall reading anything at all about females, or that they were unimpressed with those they had read about. One male student commented: "We have read about so few women in English class that they are hardly worth mentioning. The few we have read about I wouldn't care to have for a wife or mother."[63]

It is highly significant that most girls could not recall reading about any women they could admire and those who did, did not wish to resemble any of the characters they had read about. When they did name admirable characters, highest on the list of characters girls *could* admire were Hester Prynne, Scarlett O'Hara and Juliet. Although all of these women were victims in one way or another, they were singled out because at least they were main characters. In the conclusion of her study, Mary Beaven remarks:

For the most part, women in the literature read and discussed in high school English classes play minor, unpleasant roles. The few major feminine characters tend to be either passive and insipid or vicious. And the result of the survey indicated that boys and girls can relate to few of these feminine characters.[64]

It is clear that adolescents, especially, are very much in need of the feminine contributions to consciousness and women and men need to understand and value the nature of these contributions. We need to read about what is happening to us in the context of realistic life situations and to provide learning experiences which are meaningful to our lives. Since the present texts are overwhelmingly biased, we will have to provide, for the next decade or two, supplementary materials which express the experiences of our lives with greater accuracy.

Notes

1. Janice Trecker, "The Amazing Invisible Woman," p. 2.
2. For a complete list of textbooks used in this study, see bibliography.
3. Janice Trecker, "Women in U. S. History Textbooks," p. 133.
4. Lewis P. Todd and Merle Curti, *Rise of the American Nation,* p. 683.
5. Richard C. Brown et al., *The American Achievement,* p. 520.
6. Brown, p. 518.
7. Richard Hofstadter et al., *The United States,* p. 841.
8. Avery O. Craven and Walter Johnson, *American History,* p. 223.
9. Elizabeth Burr et al., "Equal Treatment of the Sexes in Social Studies Textbooks: Guidelines for Authors and Editors," p. 7.
10. Education Task Force, National Organization for Women, "Putting Women in Their Place: Report on American History High School Textbooks," p. 13. The technique of using excerpts to illustrate points about the treatment of women was used effectively in this review of thirty U.S. history textbooks.
11. Todd and Curti, p. 47.
12. Todd and Curti, p. 21.
13. John W. Caughey and Ernest R. May, *History of the United States,* p. 147.
14. Todd and Curti, p. 32.
15. Ruth Wood Gavian and William A. Hamm, *United States History,* p. 188.
16. Alexander Desconde et al., *United States History,* p. 228.
17. Samuel E. Morison and Henry S. Commager, *The Growth of the American Republic,* p. 525.
18. Caughey and May, p. 200.
19. Irving Bartlett et al., *A New History of the United States,* p. 249.
20. Robert C. Cotner et al., *Readings in American History,* p. 381.
21. Henry W. Bragdon and Samuel P. McCutchen, *History of a Free People,* p. 287.
22. Bragdon and McCutchen, p. 590.
23. James A. Frost et al., *A History of the United States—The Evolution of a Free People,* p. 398.
24. Morison and Commager, p. 507.
25. Morison and Commager, p. 509.
26. Richard Hofstadter et al., *The United States—History of a Republic,* passim.
27. Robert W. Smuts, *Women and Work in America,* p. 35.
28. Trecker, "The Amazing Invisible Woman," p. 4.
29. Trecker, "Women in U. S. History Textbooks," p. 125.
30. Sarah Zimet, "Does Book Reading Influence Behavior?"
31. For a complete list of anthologies used in this study, see bibliography.
32. Most of the literature we surveyed was not only sexist, it was racist as well. The selections reinforce the American preference for a white, middle-class, male-dominated culture. Of the few female authors included in the anthologies in our survey, only four were black poets.

When minority women are included as characters in literature, there is little awareness that strategies which may be appropriate for one group are wrong for another. There is an over-emphasis on dialect, and a tendency to assume that all low-income families are the same. According to a NCTE Task Force on Racism and Bias in the Teaching of English, educational materials now suffer from the following deficiencies:

a. The inadequate representation of literary works by members of nonwhite minorities in general anthologies which serve as basic texts, and in basal readers and other language arts kits, including audio-visual materials, in most elementary, secondary and college English courses.

b. Representation of minority groups which is demeaning, insensitive or unflattering to the culture.

c. The inclusion of only popular and proven works by a limited number of "acceptable" writers, resulting in a mispresentation of the actual range of the group's contributions to literature.

d. Biased commentaries which gloss over or flatly ignore the oppression suffered by nonwhite minority persons.

e. The inclusion of commentaries in anthologies which depict inadequately the influence of nonwhite persons on literary, cultural and historical developments in America.

Although we have not here attempted to document racist attitudes found in the English high school curriculum, we acknowledge that sexism is intrinsically linked with racism. We are concerned not only with stereotypes assigned to white, middle- or upper-class women, but to those attributed to working-class women, as well as to all minority women.

33. For a complete list of studies used, see bibliography.
34. Francine Blau, "Women and Economics," pp. 48-50.
35. Eleanor Maccoby, ed., *The Development of Sex Differences,* p. 31.
36. Inge Broverman, et al., "Sex-Role Stereotypes and Clinical Judgments of Mental Health," pp. 1-7.
37. Albert R. Kitzhaber, ed., *Literature V,* p. 2.
38. Leo B. Kneer, ed., *Compass.*
39. Albert R. Kitzhaber, ed., *Viewpoints in Literature.*
40. Gayle Hurst, "Sex Bias in Junior High Literature Anthologies," passim.
41. Susan L. Wiik, "The Sexual Bias of Textbook Literature," p. 228.
42. Robert C. Pooley, ed., *The United States in Literature,* p. 246.
43. Leo B. Kneer, ed., *Perspectives.*
44. Scarvia B. Anderson, "Between the Grimms and 'The Group': Literature in American High Schools."
45. Kneer, *Perspectives,* p. 139.
46. Kneer, *Perspectives,* p. 210
47. Kneer, *Perspectives,* p. 210.
48. Kneer, *Perspectives,* p. 376.
49. Kneer, *Perspectives,* p. 412.
50. Kneer, *Exploring Life Through Literature,* p. 93.
51. Kneer, *Perspectives,* p. 160.
52. Kneer, *Perspectives,* p. 164.
53. Kitzhaber, *Viewpoints in Literature,* p. 74.
54. Kitzhaber, *Viewpoints in Literature,* p. 158.
55. Kneer, *Focus,* p. 33.
56. Kneer, *Focus,* p. 34.
57. Kitzhaber, *Viewpoints in Literature,* p. 7.
58. Kitzhaber, *Viewpoints in Literature,* p. 166.
59. Hurst, p. 12.
60. Anne Grant West, "Women's Liberation or Exploding the Fairy Princess Myth," p. 6.
61. Maccoby, p. 31.
62. Mary H. Beaven, "Responses of Adolescents to Feminine Characters in Literature," pp. 48-68.
63. Beaven, p. 56.
64. Beaven, p. 55.

Textbooks Reviewed

U. S. History

Bartlett, Irving; Fenton, Edwin; Fowler, David; and Mandelbaum, Seymour. *A New History of the United States.* New York: Holt, Rinehart and Winston, Inc., 1969.

Bragdon, Henry W., and McCutchen, Samuel P. *History of a Free People.* New York: The Macmillan Company, 1961.

Brown, Richard C.; Lang, William C.; and Wheeler, Mary A. *The American Achievement.* Morristown: Silver Burdett Company, 1966.

Caughey, John W., and May, Ernest R. *History of the United States.* Chicago: Rand McNally & Company, 1964.

Cotner, Robert C.; Ezell, John S.; and Fite, Gilbert. *Readings in American History.* Vol. II. New York: Houghton Mifflin Company, 1964.

Craven, Avery O., and Johnson, Walter. *American History.* Boston: Ginn & Company, 1961.

Desconde, Alexander; Dante, Harris; and Current, Richard. *United States History.* Glenview: Scott, Foresman and Company, 1967.

Frost, James A.; Brown, Ralph A.; Ellis, David M.; and Fink, William. *A History of the United States—The Evolution of a Free People.* Chicago: Follett Publishing Company, 1968.

Gavian, Ruth Wood, and Hamm, William A. *United States History.* Lexington, Mass.: D. C. Heath and Company, 1960.

Hofstadter, Richard; Miller, William; and Aaron, Daniel. *The United States.* Englewood Cliffs: Prentice-Hall, Inc., 1972.

————, *The United States—History of a Republic.* Englewood Cliffs: Prentice-Hall, Inc., 1961.

Knowsler, Allan O., and Frizzle, Donald B. *Discovering American History.* Vols. I & II. New York: Holt, Rinehart and Winston, Inc., 1967.

Morison, Samuel E., and Commager, Henry. *The Growth of the American Republic.* Cambridge: Oxford University Press, 1959.

Todd, Lewis P., and Curti, Merle. *Rise of the American Nation.* Vol. II. New York: Harcourt, Brace & World, Inc., 1966.

English Literature Anthologies

Fuller, Edmund, and Kinneck, Jo. *Adventures in American Literature.* Vol. I. New York: Harcourt, Brace & World, 1963.

Kitzhaber, Albert R., ed. *Viewpoints in Literature.* New York: Holt, Rinehart and Winston, 1974.

————. *Literature IV* (The Oregon Curriculum). New York: Holt, Rinehart and Winston, 1974.

————. *Literature IV Teacher's Guide.* New York: Holt Rinehart and Winston, 1970.

————. *Literature V* (The Oregon Curriculum). New York: Holt, Rinehart and Winston, 1970.

Kneer, Leo B., ed. *Perspectives.* Glenview: Scott, Foresman and Company, 1963.

————. *Compass.* Glenview: Scott, Foresman and Company, 1971.

————. *Accent: Each His Own.* Glenview: Scott, Foresman and Company, 1972.

————. *Focus.* Glenview: Scott, Foresman and Company, 1969.

————. *Exploring Life through Literature.* Glenview: Scott, Foresman and Company, 1973.

Perrine, Laurence; Jameson, Robert; Silveri, Rita; Harrison, G. B.; Gurney, A. R., Jr.; Pritchett, V. S.; Loban, Walter; and Folds, Thomas. *Adventures in Appreciation.* Vol. I. New York: Harcourt, Brace & World, 1968.

Pooley, Robert C., ed. *The United States in Literature.* Glenview: Scott, Foresman and Company, 1963.

Bibliography

Anderson, Scarvia B. "Between the Grimms and 'The Group': Literature in American High Schools." Princeton: Cooperative Test Division, Educational Testing Service, 1964.

Baumrind, Diana. "From Each According to Her Ability." *School Review,* February 1972.

Beaven, Mary H. "Responses of Adolescents to Feminine Characters in Literature." *Research in the Teaching of English,* Spring 1972.

Blau, Francine. "Women and Economics." In *51% Minority.* Connecticut Conference on the Status of Women, 1972.

Broverman, Inge K.; Broverman, Donald M.; Clarkson, Frank E.; Rosenkrantz, Paul S.; and Vogel, Susan R. "Sex-Role Stereotypes and Clinical Judgments of Mental Health." *Journal of Consulting and Clinical Psychology,* February 1970.

Burr, Elizabeth; Dunn, Susan; and Farquhar, Norma. "Equal Treatment of the Sexes in Social Studies Textbooks: Guidelines for Authors and Editors." Los Angeles: Westside Women's Committee, 1972.

Cornillon, Susan Koppelman, ed. *Women's Liberation and Literature.* Bowling Green: Bowling Green University Popular Press, 1972.

Council on Interracial Books for Children, Anne Grant, collaborator. "Testing Texts for Racism and Sexism." *Scholastic Teacher,* February 1973.

Education Task Force, National Organization for Women, Lexington, Massachusetts. "Putting Women in Their Place: Report on American History High School Textbooks." Manuscript, n.d.

Federbush, Marcia. "Let Them Aspire." Report on the Ann Arbor School System, 1971.

Ferguson, Mary Anne. *Images of Women in Literature.* Boston: Houghton Mifflin Company, 1973.

Fowler, Lois Josephs. "Women in Literature & the High School Curriculum." *English Journal,* November 1973.

Frazier, Nancy, and Sadker, Myra. *Sexism in School and Society.* New York: Harper & Row, 1973.

Gordon, Linda; Hunt, Persis; Pleck, Elizabeth; Scott, Marcia; and Ziegler, Rochelle. "Up from the Genitals: Sexism in American Historiography." Somerville: Radical Historians Caucus, n.d.

Hartman, Joan E. "Part II: Editing and Publishing Freshman Textbooks." *College English,* October 1972.

Howe, Florence. "Identity and Expression: A Writing Course for Women." *College English,* May, 1971.

————. "Sexism, Racism, and the Education of Women." *Today's Education,* May 1973.

Hurst, Gayle. "Sex Bias in Junior High Literature Anthologies." St. Louis: St. Louis National Organization for Women, n.d.

Jacobs, Jo. "Report of the Selected Social Studies Task Force." The Committee to Study Sex Discrimination in the Kalamazoo Public Schools, 1973.

Kagan, Jerome. "The Emergence of Sex-Differences." *School Review,* February 1972.

————. "Check One: Male-Female." *Psychology Today,* July 1969.

Kelly, Ernece B., ed. *Searching for America.* Urbana: National Council of Teachers of English, 1972.

Lerner, Gerda. "About Women's Studies: Mainly for High School Use." In *Female Studies V,* edited by Rae Siporin. Pittsburgh: KNOW, Inc., 1972.

————. *The Woman in American History.* Menlo Park: Addison-Wesley, 1971.

Lysne, Ruth, and Warner, Margo. "A Woman's Place: What's Cooking in Junior High School English Anthologies." *Minnesota English Journal,* Fall 1972.

Maccoby, Eleanor E., ed. *The Development of Sex Differences.* Stanford: Stanford University Press, 1966.

Maccoby, Eleanor E. "Women's Intellect." In *The Potential of Woman,* edited by Seymour M. Farber and Roger H. Wilson. New York: McGraw-Hill Book Company, 1963.

MacGregor, Molly. "Ronnie, Bruce and Betsy Ross in the Summer of '72." *California Social Studies Review,* Fall 1972.

Minuchin, Patricia. "The Schooling of Tomorrow's Woman." *School Review,* February 1972.

Mullen, Jean S. "Freshmen Textbooks." *College English,* October 1972.

The National Council of the Social Studies Task Force on Curriculum Guidelines. "Social Studies Curriculum Guidelines." *Social Education,* December 1971.

National Education Association. *Checklist for Selecting and Evaluating U. S. History Textbooks.* Washington: NEA, 1973.

Oetzel, Roberta. "Annotated Bibliography." In *The Development of Sex Differences.* Stanford: Stanford University Press, 1966.

Schmidt, Dolores Barracano. "Sexism in Education." In *Female Studies V,* edited by Rae Siporin. Pittsburgh: KNOW, Inc., 1972.

Schmidt, Dolores Barracano, and Schmidt, Earl Robert. "The Invisible Women: The Historian as Professional Magician." In *American Women and American Studies,* edited by Betty Chmaj. American Studies Association, 1971.

Scott, Anne. *The American Woman—Who Was She?* Englewood Cliffs: Prentice-Hall, Inc., 1971.

Scott, Foresman and Company. "Guidelines for Improving the Image of Women in Textbooks." Glenview: Scott, Foresman and Company, 1973.

Showalter, Elaine, ed. *Women's Liberation and Literature.* New York: Harcourt Brace Jovanovich, Inc., 1971.

Showalter, Elaine. "Women and the Literary Curriculum." *College English,* May 1971.

Sloan, Irving. "Treatment of Labor in U. S. History Textbooks." *American Teacher,* October 1973.

Smuts, Robert W. *Women and Work in America.* New York: Schocken, 1971.

Trecker, Janice. "Women in U. S. History Textbooks." *Social Education,* March 1971.

Trecker, Janice. "The Amazing Invisible Woman." Manuscript, n.d.

U'Ren, Marjorie B. "The Image of Woman in Textbooks." *Woman in Sexist Society,* edited by Vivian Gornick and Barbara K. Moran. New York: Basic Books, 1971.

Warren, Barbara. *The Feminine Image in Literature.* Rochelle Park: Hayden Book Company, 1973.

Wells, Nancy. "Women in American Literature." *English Journal,* November 1973.

West, Anne Grant. "Women's Liberation or Exploding the Fairy Princess Myth." *Scholastic Magazine,* November 1971.

Wiik, Susan L. "The Sexual Bias of Textbook Literature." *English Journal,* February 1973.

Zimet, Sarah. "Does Book Reading Influence Behavior?" Presentation to Colorado Library Association Annual Conference, December 1972.

Acknowledgments

Almost as soon as The Clearinghouse on Women's Studies began to publish lists of college teachers and courses, Carol Ahlum began to collect the names of high school teachers similarly occupied. Her vision must be acknowledged, in addition to the support of Shirley McCune and the Resource Center on Sex Roles, whose grant from the Ford Foundation helped Carol Ahlum and Jacqueline Fralley to begin the task of persuading high school teachers to report their work in women's studies. Unlike college teachers, high school teachers do not usually produce syllabi for their students. We appreciate the efforts of many contributors to describe their teaching in significant detail. We appreciate also the willingness of Merle Levine and members of The Group School to allow us to print sections of their forthcoming larger works.

I should like to acknowledge Merle Froschl's editorial skill, and to thank her, Sheila Blanchard, Paul Lauter and the staff of The Feminist Press for their support—and patience.

F.H.

1

History

Martha Beauchamp
Social Studies
Shanti High School
Hartford, Conn./1973-74

WOMEN IN AMERICAN HISTORY

Course Outline—Part I

1. Discussion of theory of patriarchy.
   Questions: Why study women's history? Name some important/famous women.
   Read: Chapters 1 and 2, *Century of Struggle,* Eleanor Flexner (Harvard Univ. Press).

2. Discussion of summary of history of women up to 1840's; comparison between colonial and present families; changing of spheres in religion (witches) and education.
   Questions: What were the roles of women in colonial and pioneer families? Were these women oppressed?
   Read: Article on Grimké sisters, "Struggling into Existence," Ellen Dubois (New England Free Press, 60 Union Sq., Somerville, Mass. 02143); chapter 3, *Century of Struggle.*

3. Discussion of Angelina and Sarah Grimké as abolitionists turned feminists; beginning of organization among women; Frances Wright, Female Labor Reform Association.
   Questions: Why did the Grimké sisters begin addressing themselves to rights of women? Why did women begin organizing in the mills? What were they seeking?
   Read: "Declaration of Sentiments," excerpted in chapter 5, *Century of Struggle.*

4. Analysis/discussion of "Declaration of Sentiments" with comparison to present demands of women.
   Questions: Have women achieved their goals as set forth in this document?
   Read: First 17 pages of *Sisters in Struggle,* Debby Woodroote (Pathfinder Press).

5. Discussion of beginnings of women's rights movement.
   Questions: Why would experiences in women's daily lives lead many of them to feminism? And today? What was the significance of the 14th and 15th amendments for the suffrage movement?
   Read: Chapters 7 and 8, *Century of Struggle; Women: A Journal of Liberation* (Spring 1970, special issue on Women in History).

6. Discussion of lives of various women important in the period from 1840-1872, most particularly Elizabeth Cady Stanton, Sojourner Truth, Susan B. Anthony, Harriet Tubman, Elizabeth Blackwell, Victoria Woodhull.
   Questions: Did educational opportunities for women increase during this time? Why or why not? What was women's role during the Civil War?
   Read: Chapters 10, 11, 15, 20 and 21, *Century of Struggle.*

7. Discussion of progress in women's suffrage, 1872-1920.
   Questions: Why did it take so long to get the vote? Was this an achievement, or settling for less again? Why was vote given first to women in the West?
   Read: Chapter 15, *Century of Struggle;* finish *Sisters in Struggle.*

8. Discussion of Reform Era during move for suffrage.
   Read: Chapter 22, *Century of Struggle.*
9. Discussion of opposition to suffrage.

Course Outline—Part II

1. Brief questionnaire from American History workshop. Reading of *Women's Work Is Never Done* (a play by Boston women, available from Ann Froines, Women's Studies Program, U Mass/Boston, Boston, Mass. 02116).
   Questions: What is women's work?
   Read: "American Women: Their Use and Abuse," New England Free Press.

2. Discussion of conditions of working women (past and present), their attempts to organize, and the importance of raising the consciousness of working class women.
   Read: "Hidden History of the Female," Martha Atkins (New England Free Press); conclusion of *Century of Struggle.*

3. Discussion of period of suffrage—1840-1920.
   Questions: Why did it take so long to get the vote? Was the effort successful in terms of the original goals of the women (see "Declaration of Sentiments")? Did the vote improve the conditions of working class women?
   Read: "Traffic in Women," Emma Goldman (Times Change Press, Penwell Rd., Washington, N.J. 07882); "Marriage and Love," Emma Goldman (Times Change Press); "Margaret Sanger—the Mother of Birth Control" (reprinted from *Coronet* and distributed by Planned Parenthood).

4. Discussion of Emma Goldman and Margaret Sanger.
   Questions: How did each of these women strive to improve conditions of women? Why were they persecuted?
   Read: "Women and Socialism," (reprinted from *Red Papers 3* and distributed by New England Free Press).

5. Discussion of women in socialist countries.
   Questions: How could the condition of women be changed under socialism?
   Read: Chapters 1-3, 9, 10 and 12, *The Feminine Mystique,* Betty Friedan (Dell); at least two modern women's magazines (*Better Homes and Gardens, McCall's,* etc.).

6. Discussion of women's role during war; change from worker to housewife.
   Questions: Analysis of women's magazines. What sort of woman reads these magazines? What information/stimulation does she receive? How did advertising media help return woman to her house? What were your reactions to these readings?
   Read: Chapter 14, *The Feminine Mystique.*

7. Discussion of the feminine mystique (continued).
   Questions: What are the alternatives open to women?
   Read: "Towards a Woman's Revolutionary Manifesto" in *Masculine/Feminine,* Betty and Theodore Roszak, eds, (Harper and Row); "Redstockings Manifesto" in *Sisterhood Is Powerful,* Robin Morgan, ed., (Vintage).

8. Discussion of condition of women today.
   Questions: What are the hopes of women today? Equal Rights Amendment: Why are people in favor of it? Why are they against?

Peggy Brick
Social Studies/Behavioral Science
Dwight Morrow High School
Englewood, N.J./1973-74

AMERICAN STUDIES: WOMEN IN AMERICAN HISTORY

Purpose

To help students understand the social history of the United States by studying the lives of women and the role they have played in the development of American society. Special emphasis will be given to the importance of class and race in determining women's roles and on the changes in role and status brought about by westward expansion, industrialization, urbanization, development of mass media, technological development and feminism.

Behavioral Goals

Students will demonstrate:

—an understanding of historical point of view by doing a content analysis of the treatment of women in one or more history books or by comparing the presentation by several historians of a person or event.

—the ability to utilize the biography or autobiography of one woman to investigate roles and life styles in one particular era of history.

—the ability to use a time line by recording the major events affecting the role and status of women.

—an awareness of the interaction between changing attitudes, social movements and laws by analyzing the cause and effect of major legislation affecting women.

—an awareness of the importance of social values and attitudes in determining behavior by analyzing primary sources for reactions to women who did not fulfill the traditional expectations of the woman's role.

—an understanding of the importance of social class in determining behavior patterns by examining the life styles of women of different classes at specific points in U. S. history.

—an understanding of the importance of regional economy to total life style by comparing laws, behavior and values concerning women in different areas of the nation.

—an ability to read and understand tables, graphs and charts by analyzing the changing economic status of women in various industries and professions.

—an understanding of the process of passing a constitutional amendment by discussing the process by which the 19th amendment was fought for and adopted.

—an awareness of how historical knowledge affects attitudes and feelings on a subject by taking and analyzing a personal attitude questionnaire at the beginning and at the end of the unit.

—the ability to use periodical literature in the study of history by analyzing newspapers and magazines for evidence of woman's role, status, and how these changed during the nation's history.

—an awareness of the continuity and the change in woman's role by doing role-play of situations at different times in history.

—an understanding of the importance of technological development by comparing everyday life styles during specific periods of history.

Content

   I. Overview
      A. What is history? How can it be understood? Why study history?
      B. Major events, movements in U. S. history

  II. The Role of Women
      A. Examination of the student's own attitudes and stereotypes
      B. Women as presented in traditional history texts
      C. Institutional support of woman in certain roles: family, church, government, economy

 III. Women in Early America
      A. Status and role of women in different regions: New England, Middle Atlantic states, the South
      B. Role played by women in different social classes, races, ethnic groups

 IV. Major Social Changes Bring Change in Role of Women During Late 1800's
      A. Feminist movement grows from abolition movement
      B. Effects of the Civil War in increasing roles of women
      C. Industrial Revolution increases role of women outside the home
      D. Effects of the great migrations: westward movement, immigration, urbanization
      E. Educational expansion

  V. Twentieth-Century Technology Affects Women
      A. Changing household technology
      B. Mass media influences life styles, values and expectations through radio, movies, women's magazines, advertising, television
      C. The automobile and the move to suburbia

 VI. Biography: in-depth study of one woman's life by each student

VII. Today's Women's Movement: examination of change and resistance to change in current history.

Further Suggestions

Unit on black/white experience prepared by Richard A. Kasschau. Available free from *Periodically,* ABA Clearinghouse on Precollege Psychology and Behavioral Science, 1200 17th St. N.W., Washington, D.C. 20036. Many exercises can be easily adapted for exploration of male/female experience. Ideas are useful generally for women's studies. (Subscriptions are free.)

Born to Win by James and Jongeard. A description of transactional analysis with gestalt experiments that are invaluable in exploring feelings about self.

Foundation for Change (1841 Broadway, New York, N. Y. 10023) produces (free) pamphlets on racism which are, again, adaptable to work on sexism. I use *Racism Rating: Test Your Textbooks* to examine sexism in history textbooks. Another useful title is *Black Women Are Proud.*

Leonard W. Ingraham
Bureau of Social Studies
NYC Board of Education
Brooklyn, N. Y./1972-73

TWO HISTORICAL THEMES IN WOMEN'S STUDIES

I. Women's Role in America

A. How women played an important role in early America
 1. Indian women and their role
 2. With explorers and early settlers
  a. At Jamestown: Pocahontas, "Tobacco Brides"
  b. On the Mayflower and at Plymouth

B. What was women's status in colonial days?
 1. As colonial farmer's wife
  a. Life and activities
  b. Some female proprietors
 2. Dissenters: Anne Hutchinson
 3. Lack of opportunities
  a. Legal, social and political restrictions
  b. Educational discrimination
 4. Indians and blacks

C. How American Revolution started women on the road to freedom
 1. Women's first great cause
 2. As colonial politicians without the vote
  a. Use of courage, wiles and ingenuity
  b. Boycott of Tories and British goods
 3. Case studies of: Abigail Adams, Mercy Otis Warren
 4. Women in the war

D. How women went West
 1. Some who went West
 2. Pioneer farms: a partnership of man and wife, women's responsibilities
 3. Case study: Sacajawea

E. How women fought against slavery
 1. Women in slavery
 2. Abolitionists
  a. Black: Sojourner Truth, Harriet Tubman
  b. White: Grimké Sisters, Harriet Beecher Stowe
 3. Women's struggle for rights of others

F. What were the effects of Civil War on women?
 1. Impact of the war on women and family structure
 2. New tasks, responsibilities and occupations
  a. Paid employment as female clerks, bookkeepers, secretaries

b. Government service: nurses, hospital attendants and cooks

c. A few women served as soldiers, spies, scouts, guides and saboteurs

3. After the war: black and white women as teachers in freedman's schools, pension claims agents, rehabilitation workers with soldiers and refugees

4. Case studies: Clara Barton, Dorothea Dix, Charlotte Forten

Understandings and Related Concepts

Understandings

1. Women contributed to development of America.

2. Women were in the forefront in the fight for human rights and freedom.

3. Women were discriminated against in early America.

4. Women made their mark in war and peace.

5. Black and white women fought slavery.

6. Women showed strength in managing and caring for their families during wars.

7. Women demonstrated courage.

Concepts

1. Societies draw upon ideas from other cultures.

2. Change is an inevitable condition of life.

3. Democratic governments provide protection for the rights of individuals and minority groups.

4. The environment in which a person lives greatly affects opportunities for personal growth and development.

5. All persons are born free and equal in dignity and rights.

6. Change at variance with goals has also taken place.

7. Human beings are much more alike than different.

Suggested Learning Activities

1. Persons to identify and terms to define:

Addams, Jane
American Woman Suffrage Association
Anthony, Susan B.
Atkinson, Ti-Grace
Barton, Clara
Bethune, Mary McLeod
Bloomer, Amelia
Coeducation
Dix, Dorothea
Fifteenth Amendment
Fourteenth Amendment
Garrison, William Lloyd
Grimké Sisters
Howe, Julia Ward
Lyon, Mary

Miner, Virginia
Mott, Lucretia
Mott, Lydia
National Woman Suffrage Association
Nightingale, Florence
Oberlin College
Pankhurst, Emmeline
"The Revolution"
Roosevelt, Eleanor
Sanger, Margaret
Second-class citizen
Stanton, Elizabeth Cady
Stowe, Harriet Beecher
Steinem, Gloria
Thirteenth Amendment

Persons to identify and terms to define (contd.):

Truth, Sojourner
Tubman, Harriet
Vassar College

Willard, Emma
Wollstonecraft, Mary
W.C.T.U.
Wright, Frances

2. Topics for debates or panel discussion:
   a. *Resolved,* That the objection of indelicacy and impropriety, which is often brought against woman when she addressed a public audience, comes with a very ill-grace from those who encourage, by their attendance, her appearance on the stage, in the concert, or in feats of the circus.
   b. *Resolved,* That woman has too long rested satisfied in the circumscribed limits which corrupt customs and a perverted application of the Scriptures have marked out for her, and that it is time she should move in the enlarged sphere which her great Creator has assigned her.
   c. *Resolved,* That it is the duty of the women of this country to secure to themselves their sacred right to the elective franchise.
   d. *Resolved,* Marriages and motherhood for girls, education and careers for boys.

3. Prepare a set of biographical sketches or radio scripts on women spies in: American Revolution, Civil War, World War I and II.

4. Compare:
   a. Position of women living in (1) Plymouth Colony (2) Virginia Colony (3) Revolutionary era (4) Civil War period (5) Frontier days (6) Covered wagon days
   b. Attitude of women toward marriage in seventeenth century with ideas of women toward it today.
   c. Property rights of women in seventeenth to eighteenth centuries and today.
   d. Susan B. Anthony and Women's Liberation Fighters of Today
   e. Man's world, Woman's place.

5. Prepare chart or graph:
   a. Steps in women's suffrage movement.
   b. Women's employment by major occupational groups.

6. Bulletin board (pictures, posters, cartoons, newspaper headlines, women's magazines):
   a. Women's rights 1607-1870.
   b. Women's liberation 1870-1973.
   c. Equal rights for women.

7. Interpretation of poetry:
   a. The following poem was written by Lady Winchelsea in the seventeenth century (*Atlantic Monthly,* March 1970, p. 83).

   > Debarred from all improvements of the mind,
   > And to be dull, expected and designed. . . .
   > Alas! a woman that attempts the pen,
   > Such a presumptuous creature is esteemed,
   > The fault can by no virtue be redeemed.
   > Good breeding, fashion, dancing, dressing, play,
   > Are the accomplishments we should desire;

To write, or read, or think, or to enquire,
Would cloud our beauty, and exhaust our time,
And interrupt the conquests of our prime,
Whilst the dull manage of a servile house
Is held by some our utmost art and use.

Questions for discussion: How does the poetry reflect the times? What might be the content of a similar poem of the 1970's?

b. The following is excerpted from Byron's *Don Juan.*

There is a tide in the affairs of women,
Which taken at the flood, leads
—God knows where.

Questions for discussion: What is Byron's attitude toward women? How does Byron reflect the attitudes of his times? What reaction might a woman have to this poem?

8. Quotations and statements for motivation, discussion, further inquiry and research:
   a. It's a man's world—woman's place is in the home.
   b. I don't think brains have any sex.
      —Margaret Mangam, New York State Supreme Court Justice
   c. Indeed it is difficult to imagine any creature more attractive than an American beauty between the ages of fifteen and eighteen. There is something in the bloom, delicacy and innocence of one of these young things that reminds you of the conceptions which poets and painters have taken of angels.
      —James Fenimore Cooper (1828)
   d. I ask no favor for my sex. All I ask of our brethren is that they take their feet off our necks.
      —Sarah Grimké (1837)
   e. We hold these truths to be self-evident: that men and women are created equal. . . .
      Seneca Falls Declaration of Sentiments and Resolutions (July 18, 1848)
   f. We will have every arbitrary barrier thrown down
      We would have every path laid open to women as freely as to men.
      —Margaret Fuller
   g. Pray to God—SHE will help you.
      —Susan B. Anthony, Elizabeth C. Stanton
   h. The rights of the citizen of these United States to vote shall not be denied or abridged by the United States or by any state on account of sex.
      —XIX Amendment to Constitution
   i. Equality of rights under the law shall not be denied or abridged by the United States or by any state on account of sex.
      —Proposed Equal Rights Amendment XXVII
   j. Man meekly submits to be the hewer of wood, the drawer of water, and the beast of burden for the superior sex.
      —James F. Muirhead, A Scots traveller (1898)
   k. In the 1970's women own about three-fourths of the stocks and bonds, seventy percent of the insurance policies and sixty-five percent of all savings accounts. They outnumber men by five million.

I. "He" turns up three times as often as "she." "Boy" occurs twice as often as "girl" in 1,045 of the most frequently used elementary school materials. "Wife" is mentioned three times as often as "husband"; males are mentioned more in all other family relationships except that of mother/father.

—American Heritage Word Frequency Book, John B. Carroll (Houghton-Mifflin, 1971)

II. Women's Struggle for Equality

A. How women fought for their rights
   1. Disabilities: political, social, economic, legal (See Theme I)
   2. Seneca Falls Convention, 1848
      a. List of grievances
      b. Comparison with Declaration of Independence
   3. Post-Civil War amendments: women denied the right to vote and equal rights
   4. Case studies: Emma Willard, Susan B. Anthony, Margaret Fuller, Elizabeth C. Stanton, Lucretia Mott

B. How women broke the education barriers
   1. Female Seminary, Troy, N. Y. 1821: refuted belief that mental exertion would damage woman's brain
   2. Establishment of private women's colleges: Mount Holyoke (1836); Vassar (1861); Wellesley (1870); Smith (1871); Bryn Mawr (1880)
   3. Coeducational public colleges in the West
   4. Public elementary schools for girls by latter part of nineteenth century
   5. Medical education for women: a curiosity before first half of nineteenth century. Case study: Elizabeth Blackwell

C. How women used organizations to advance their causes
   1. Alcohol: Women's Christian Temperance Union, Carrie Nation
   2. Suffrage: Campaign for "Anthony Amendment" (XIX Amendment); Susan B. Anthony, Elizabeth C. Stanton, Lucy Stone
   3. League of Women Voters: XXVI Amendment
   4. Population control: Margaret Sanger
   5. Aid to poor: Jane Addams, Lillian Wald, Emma Lazarus
   6. Religion: Women missionaries in West

D. How women moved into labor movement
   1. Employment of women and children in early factories
      a. Low wages, long hours, no advancement
      b. Discrimination in wage rates
      c. Sweatshops
   2. National Women's Trade Union League, 1905
   3. Trade union organizations: case study: Rose Schneiderman
   4. Women in unions today

E. How women served in World War I and II
   1. Wartime services
      a. Industry and armed services

b. Extension of rights and privileges

c. Flappers and fashions

d. Case studies: Alice L. Roosevelt, Eleanor Roosevelt, Frances Perkins

F. What were some careers women pursued?
1. Advertising, fashion, communication, interior decoration and cosmetics
2. Communications: editors, columnists, commentators
3. Entertainment: stage, radio, television
4. Government service: judges, senators, representatives, office holders and employees
5. Education
6. Sports and recreation
7. Case studies: Constance Motley, Margaret Chase Smith, Shirley Chisholm

G. Who were some creative women?
1. Art: painting, sculpture
2. Music
3. Literature
4. Performing arts
5. Films
6. Science
7. Case studies: select persons from each field

H. Why have women become more militant in the seventies?
1. Unfulfilled equality
2. Recommendations of President's Commission of the Status of Women
3. Equal Rights Amendment
4. War/Peace issue
5. Changing role in the family

I. How women have become more militant
1. Demands
2. Organizations: National Organization for Women
3. Case studies of selected leaders

Understandings and Related Concepts

Understandings

1. Women have overcome numerous forms of discrimination.

2. Women have achieved outstanding success in many fields.

3. Women had many leadership roles.

4. Women contributed to efforts for war, peace and human betterment

Concepts

1. Progress involves change toward a desired goal.

2. All persons have the right to an education that will insure maximum development and fulfillment.

3. The environment in which a person lives greatly affects opportunities for personal growth and development.

4. Cultural contributions are not the monopoly of any ethnic group.

5. Ethnic women have broken social, economic and political barriers.

5. No significant differences exist in the innate intelligence and capabilities of human beings from varying racial and ethnic backgrounds.

6. Battle for equality for women continues.

6. Change is constant in history.

Suggested Learning Activities

1. Ask students to:
   a. Bring into class one or two cartoons which depict the women's movement or liberated women. Have committee prepare bulletin board with selected cartoons or prepare overhead transparencies.
   Questions based on cartoons: How does the cartoon communicate its point of view? What is the message of the cartoon? Is the cartoon fair?
   b. Collect pictures of women who made outstanding contributions. Prepare brief essays or short biographical sketches. For discussion: Why should each be included among "Famous Americans."
   c. Prepare a cartoon or collage either attacking women's liberation or taking the opposite position.
   d. Analyze the coverage that women's liberation gets in the press.
   e. Prepare a tape or radio script to express a concept about women, e.g., "a woman's place is in the home"; "equal work, equal pay"; "man's world, woman's place."
   f. Maintain a diary or journal in which the main focus will be feelings, thoughts and events that pertain to sex roles, i.e., household chores, etc.
   g. Collect and analyze advertisements which create a "feminine mystique." Have students explain how the advertisements exploit or insult women.
   h. Look up reviews of books written by women. Questions for inquiry and discussion: Is there a difference in reviews by men and women? Are there extraneous comments? Give examples.

2. Committee or independent research projects:
   a. Examine: the various religions and their different attitudes toward the role of women; the developing sex roles in young children (e.g., girls play with dolls; boys with chemistry sets).
   b. Analyze women's magazines for differences in articles, advertisements, readership attitudes.
   c. Collect comic strips that have girls and/or women as characters in them. Choose one or two and explain the role of women in them.
   d. Review a few popular motion pictures. How do they depict women? Do popular films use women performers to promote the sale of tickets of admission?
   e. Choose a popular situation comedy on TV. Do the men seem as "silly as the women"? Explain.
   f. The Equal Rights Amendment would eliminate all legal distinctions between men and women. Find out some of the legal differences between men and women. How might the proposed amendment affect you?

g. Many professional and nonprofessional occupations are sex typed. Prepare a report including examples of such jobs, possibility of women entering such jobs, union attitude and policies. "Sexual Stereotypes": Do they exist? What is their meaning? What affirmative action can be taken to eliminate them?

3. For panel discussion of role-playing:
   a. Male versus female: a discussion on a controversial issue involving "Women's Rights."
   b. A woman applies for a job formerly held by a man.
   c. *Kinder, Kirche, Küche:* a mother ought not work.
   d. Should women be permitted to join all-male sports teams?
   e. Invite a leader of the women's liberation movement to speak to class. Follow up with class questions or interview panel or use "Meet the Press" format.

4. Surveys and research:
   a. Women public office holders in New York City, New York State, Federal Government; women ministers, rabbis, doctors and other professions in the United States with a comparison to men. Women teachers in a selected college, rank and salary as compared to men.
   b. Women leaders of countries of the world.
   c. Status of black and white women as well as other minorities in occupations, salaries received and compared with men in these occupations.

5. Interpretation of data (see tables on pages 15-17):
   a. What conclusions can you draw from the statistics?
   b. What changes, if any, have been noted in the last year?

6. Quotations, statements and data (adapted from *Time,* Special Issue, "The American Woman," March 20, 1972) for motivation, discussion, further inquiry and research:
   a. Black women are the lowest paid members of the work force; a black man with an eighth-grade education has a higher median income than a black woman with some college education.
   b. Spanish-speaking women are somewhat alienated from women's liberation.
   c. Los Angeles black activist Althea Scott says, "White women liberationists talk about the difficulties of getting into graduate or professional school. We talk about getting jobs in the five and ten. We're on the nitty-gritty level. Just let black women struggle at their own rate. They'll see they are women."
   d. Journalism:
   1971—44 percent of journalism students were women.
   1951—35 percent of journalism students were women.
   1971—35 percent of editorial personnel on American newspapers were women.
   1950—Approximately same as 1971.
   1971—45 percent of 5,941 "professional" employees on magazines were women.
   (Most of these women work for women's magazines.)
   Broadcasting women fare little better on TV and radio news; seen more as broadcast reporters on local programs.

(continued on page 17)

Profile of the Typical Woman Worker: 1920 and 1970

	1920	*1970*
Age	28 years old.	39 years old.
Marital Status	Single.	Married and living with her husband.
Occupation	Most likely to be a factory worker or other operative. Other large numbers of women in clerical, private household and farm work. Occupational choice extremely limited.	Most likely to be a clerical worker. Many other women in service work outside the home, factory or other operative work. About 500 individual occupations open to her.
Education	Only 1 out of 5 seventeen-year-olds in the population a high school graduate.	High school graduate with some college or post-secondary-school education.
Labor Force Participation	Less than one-fourth (23 percent) of all women 20 to 64 years of age in the labor force. Most apt to be working at age 20 to 24 (38 percent). Participation rate dropping at age 25, decreasing steadily, and only 18 percent at age 45 to 54. Less than 1 out of every 5 (18 percent) women 35 to 64 years of age in the labor force.	Almost half (49 percent) of all women 18 to 64 years of age in the labor force. Most apt to be working at age 20 to 24 (57 percent). Labor force participation rate dropping at age 25 and rising again at age 35 to a second peak of 54 percent at age 45 to 54. Can expect to work 24 to 31 more years at age 35.

Source: U. S. Department of Labor, Women's Bureau.

Statistics on the Economic Status of Women Workers

1. Wage or Salary Income of Full-Time Year-Round Workers, by Sex

Year	Median wage or salary income		Women's median wage or salary income as a percent of men's
	Women	*Men*	
1955	$2719	$4252	63.9
1960	3293	5417	60.8
1965	3823	6375	60.0
1968	4457	7664	58.2

Source: U. S. Department of Commerce, Bureau of Census, Current Population Reports.

2. Earnings of Full-Time Year-Round Workers, by Sex, 1968

Earnings	Percent of women workers	Percent of men workers
Less than $3,000	20.0	7.5
$3,000 to $4,999	40.0	12.6
$5,000 to $6,999	26.0	21.3
$7,000 to $9,999	10.9	30.9
$10,000 to $14,999	2.5	19.5
$15,000 and over	.4	8.2

Source: U. S. Department of Commerce, Bureau of Census, Current Population Reports.

3. Expected Salaries for June Graduates, by Sex and Selected Field, 1970

Field	Average monthly salary	
	Women	Men
Accounting	$746	$832
Chemistry	765	806
Economics, finance	700	718
Engineering	844	872
Liberal Arts	631	688
Mathematics, statistics	746	773

Source: Frank S. Endicott, *Trends in Employment of College and University Graduates in Business and Industry* (Northwestern University, 1970). Figures based on jobs and salaries offered by 206 companies during campus recruitment.

4. Median Wage or Salary Income of Full-Time Year-Round Workers, by Sex and Selected Major Occupational Group, 1968

Major occupation group	Median wage or salary income		Women's median wage or salary income as a percent of men's
	Women	Men	
Professional and technical workers	$6,691	$10,151	65.9
Nonfarm managers, officials and proprietors	5,635	10,340	54.5
Clerical workers	4,789	7,351	65.1
Sales workers	3,461	8,549	40.5
Operatives	3,991	6,738	59.2

Source: U. S. Department of Commerce, Bureau of Census, Current Population Reports.

5. Median Annual Salaries of Full-Time Employed Civilian Scientists, by Field, 1968.

Field	Median annual salary	
	Women	All workers
Chemistry	$ 9,000	$13,500
Earth and marine sciences	9,500	12,900
Atmospheric and space sciences	11,300	13,400
Physics	10,200	14,000
Mathematics	9,400	13,000
Computer sciences	11,800	14,100
Biological sciences	9,900	13,000
Psychology	11,500	13,200
Statistics	12,000	14,900
Economics	12,000	15,000
Sociology	10,000	12,000
Anthropology	11,000	12,700
Political science	9,700	12,000
Linguistics	9,600	11,500
All fields of science	10,000	13,200

Source: National Science Foundation, National Register of Scientific and Technical Personnel, 1968.

(continued from page 14)

    e. Courts:

        1972—No woman justice on the Supreme Court.

        1972—Among 97 federal appeal court judges, there was 1 woman.

        1972—Of 402 federal district court judges, 4 are women.

    f. Government:

        1972—Of 93 federal district attorneys, all are men.

    g. Law:

        1971—9.3 percent of total number of law students were women.

        1960—3.6 percent of total number of law students were women.

        1972—2.8 percent of lawyers are women; 9000 women lawyers out of total 325,000.

        1962—In West Germany, 33 percent of lawyers were women; in Russia, 36 percent of lawyers were women.

    h. Law enforcement:

        1972—1.5 percent of police forces in United States were women. In New York City, Gertrude Schimmel was first Police Captain and Deputy Inspector.

    i. Crime:

        Women commit far fewer serious crimes than men.

        1970—1,058,169 arrests of men; 215,614 arrests of women.

        1970—3 to 4 percent of prisoners in federal and state prisons are women.

j. Education:

1970—50.5 percent of those graduated from high school were girls.

1970—41 percent of college enrollment women; 59 percent of college enrollment men.

1971—Women received 40 percent of M.A.'s.

1971—Women received 43 percent of B.A.'s.

k. Teaching:

1971—85 percent of elementary teachers were women.

1971—21 percent of principals were women.

1970—20 percent of college and university faculties were women.

l. Salaries:

1970—Average annual income of college-educated woman over 25 is $5,125 *less* than a similarly-educated man.

1970—Average annual income of high school educated woman over 25 is $3,987 *less* than a man with the same diploma.

m. Medicine:

1971—7.6 percent of 345,000 doctors were women.

1961—6.0 percent of 260,000 doctors were women.

1971—1 percent of surgeons were women.

—20 percent of pediatricians were women.

—13.8 percent of anesthesiologists were women.

—12.9 percent of psychiatrists were women.

—6.8 percent of obstetricians were women.

—5.2 percent of internists were women.

1971—13.5 percent of incoming medical students were women.

1968—9 percent of incoming medical students were women.

1961—7 percent of incoming medical students were women.

n. Income:

1970—Average female employee earned 59 percent as much as similarly employed male.

1955—Average female employee earned 64 percent of wages paid to a similarly employed male.

1971—7 percent of women at work earned $10,000 or more per year.

40 percent of men at work earned $10,000 or more per year.

Marya Levenson
Social Studies
The Rogers Junior High School
Boston, Mass./1973-74

TEACHING ANCIENT HISTORY FROM A FEMINIST PERSPECTIVE

Assumptions

My teaching of history is based on the premise that the most important concept for students to learn is how people lived during each historical period. The questions— who had power? and what was life like for *most* people?—are more important than dates and leaders. Also the question—how did children live?—is an important focus since students identify most with other young people, even young people from ancient societies. Therefore, I emphasize role-playing and creative writing about the roles of working people, of ordinary women, men and children.

I do, however, work chronologically through the textbook, both because I don't know enough ancient history and because I feel the structure of the textbook is important for the students. Since the text is obviously sexist and racist, its bias becomes part of every lesson.

Sample Units and Lessons

1. Greece
Discuss Athens and Sparta, comparing child-rearing customs and the different treatment of male and female children. In Athenian democracy some people were slaves; only in noble families were girls taught to write and read; most women were kept at home, allowed out only to religious festivals, and were expected to be mothers. In the military oligarchy of Sparta, girls as well as boys received physical education; girls were expected to be good strong mothers of soldiers. Discuss similar modern-day sex-role "tracking": men's and women's roles in school, society and the family. Discuss these issues in the context of other ancient societies. Discuss Greece today, with its banning of miniskirts, etc.

Read the play *Antigone* aloud in class. Ask students to write "A Day in the Life of Antigone" and discuss Antigone as one model of women in Greece.

2. Rome
Discuss the textbook presentation of militarism, sophisticated bureaucracy, engineering and empire; and the parallels with the United States today. Discuss the bias of the text in light of slavery and the tyrannical aspects of Roman rule.

3. Egypt
Discuss Hatshepsut, the one female Pharoah. A quote from the text: "The people [read: men] were very angry that she was the Pharoah, and she allegedly dressed like a man and wore a man's beard to be able to fill the role. The line of descent was handed down through women and the society thought to be matriarchal at that time." Discuss. If the

above was true—that the society was matriarchal—why did the men have such an angry reaction to a woman as Pharoah? Was the society really matriarchal?

4. Babylonia: Hammurabi's Code
Many of the laws of this code are discriminatory against women. Item 143: "If she, a wife, has not been a careful mistress, has gadded about, has neglected her house and has belittled her husband, they shall throw that woman into the water."

Discuss what would happen to a man who did or did not do the above? Since another law of Hammurabi's Code says, "An eye for an eye," why is there no parallel law about what a woman can do if her husband does not carry out his role?

Other Ideas: Methods and Activities

1. Add a non-Western unit to the ancient history curriculum.
I chose India and China. For China, I read aloud from "Gold Flower's Story" (from *China Shakes the World* by Jack Belden and available from New England Free Press, 60 Union Square, Somerville, Mass. 02143). This is a tale of a young woman's experiences under the old sex-role codes of China before the revolution.

Discuss the treatment of Gold Flower at the hands of the men, the trial of the men and the concept of respect for old people in light of what the old man did to Gold Flower.

Students were horrified that in earlier times parents like Gold Flower's had been able to marry children off, that a young person had no choice about marrying, whether in India or China. Students were impressed by the new choices available to people in China under Chinese communism. I discussed the different forms communism takes in different places. I outlined the ways in which something called "communism" has been imposed on East Germany.

2. Use myths, stories, plays.
I used a) the young people's version of *Ulysses,* b) the Bible (discuss the story of Job along with the "Song of Job" by the modern rock group, Sea Train), c) Japanese haikus, d) Sappho's poems.

Discuss women's and men's roles and images as reflected in each of these pieces of literature. On the basis of Sappho's poems and students' previous work on Greece, discuss homosexuality and lesbianism among intellectuals in Greek society. Ask students to write haikus and poems after the patterns of poems they are reading. Duplicate these (unsigned or signed, with permission) and pass them around for further discussion.

The standard ancient history text I used is accompanied by a teacher's paperback with short supplementary readings. I often duplicated excerpts from these. For instance, I reproduced the Sumerian *Father's Lament,* a 3500-year-old complaint about a son for whom the father has worked and slaved to make a good life. Ask students to pretend to be their own fathers or mothers and to write a lament.

3. Bring in art books containing pictures of art of the period.
Ask students to examine these and to write down what they can tell from these pictures about how people lived. How did the farmers live? How did nobility live? How did women live? Have students make their own pictures of how people lived. Discuss the costumes and clothing represented.

4. Tools.

History and literature are usually taught through reading and writing. This verbal bias alienates some students from participating. Bring in and have students bring in a variety of present-day tools. Discuss the invention and evolution of tools, how they differed from society to society, how they changed over time. Discuss the importance of manual labor.

I brought in an Inkle loom, talked about weaving as a major human accomplishment and showed students how to make belts. I left the loom in the classroom during the year; both male and female students wove belts. Some students called the boys who did weaving sissies, and this provoked useful discussion.

5. Do a unit on immigration and prejudice.

My goal for this unit is to get students to evaluate whether these phenomena are part of *their* lives.

Class activity: Have students talk about the backgrounds of parents and grandparents. What countries did they come from, etc.? Discuss the impact of the Industrial Revolution and immigration on this country, in terms of who had money and power, in terms of economic class and tracking in students' own lives. I start a racism and prejudice unit with this kind of discussion in order to have students look at their own experiences, before asking them to identify with the discrimination of other groups.

I use parts of *The Color of Man,* a Random House unit based on a book by Robert Coles. It's accompanied by a teacher's manual with a complete but flexible plan. Some of it is abstract and intellectual—it begins with a discussion of natural selection and skin pigmentation. This information has little to do with the incidents of racism that students face each day—being shoved in the cafeteria or having a black person move into their neighborhood.

Ask students to write a list of all the slang words they know about race and ethnic groups (not to be passed in). Make a composite list on the board. Students might be shocked at this assignment, but they'll willingly participate. Discuss the fact that students know they are not supposed to think about these words. Discuss what this has to do with racism.

6. Hero/Heroine worksheet.
   a. Do you have a hero or heroine? Do you have people you admire?
   b. Do you admire the person(s) in every way, or just some of his/her personality traits?
   c. Would you want to be exactly like that person? Why or why not?
   d. Have you been influenced in any way by the person? In what way?
   e. Do you have any criticisms of your hero/heroine?
   f. Is your hero/heroine a leader of men and women? If not, how would you describe him/her?
   g. Do you agree that every young person needs someone to look up to? Why or why not?

h. Check the following characteristics which, in your opinion, are necessary for a hero or heroine. Explain each choice and add any not included.

1) athletic
2) honest
3) creative
4) good-looking
5) religious
6) a leader, able to exercise power
7) interested in helping people
8) scientific
9) dedicated to a cause
10) intelligent
11) political
12) member of youth culture
13) any others?

Merle Levine
Social Studies
The Wheatley School
East Williston, N. Y./1975-76

YE OLDE AMERICAN HISTORY

To Ye Student

The focus in this unit of study is not so much on "what happened" but on how it got recorded. Henry Ford said, "History is bunk." Carl Becker put it in a kinder way, "History is an act of faith." Whatever history is, it is a selection of events and individuals that reflects the values and expectations of the writer.

When someone asks you "How are things?" you probably only tell her/him about some "things." How do you choose the things to tell about? Do you choose different things to tell different people? How do you decide that? Are there some things you don't tell at all? How come? Of the things you say to everyone, do you say them the same way all the time? In fact, now that we're talking about it, how are things . . . ?

Historians are people, too. They select some events and not others, some individuals and not others. How historians make selections is what this unit is about. The information included has been taken from specialized research or from compilations of women's history.

Ye Learning Goals

To make ye aware of:
—how much is left out of history.
—what kinds of things are left out.
—how things are put into history.
—your own stereotypic attitudes.
—what stereotypes are.
—where your own attitudes come from.

Ye Evaluation

In which how much is learned and how well it is learned may be measured by:
—being able to identify stereotypic attitudes, values and reporting, in historical texts.
—courageously reevaluating your own attitudes, values and stereotypes.
—actively criticizing, researching or rewriting historical texts.

Ye Plan

In which are presented eight exercises containing diverse questions, projects and ideas for the reconsideration of American colonial history, the reevaluation of historical texts in general, and the development of both critical skills and personal values.

Ye Contents

Exercise I—Matching people to events.

Exercise II—Questions about colonial people.

Exercise III—Finding out about Martha Washington

Exercise IV—Two colonial views of women: Ben Franklin and Tom Paine.

Exercise V—Colonial occupations.

Exercise VI—Colonial education.

Exercise VII—Documents concerning: the Virginia Settlement, the Mayflower
Expedition, the Revolutionary Period.

Exercise VIII—Naming men and women in major movements or events.

Exercise the First

This is a matching exercise. Column A contains a description of an event in American colonial history. Column B contains the names of people connected with the events. Place the correct name next to the event.

Column A

1. One of the merchants who financed the Mayflower expedition.

2. Sued the House of Burgesses for the right to vote.

3. Made a daring, twenty-mile, midnight ride to rouse the colonial militia against the British.

4. Authorized by Congress to publish the official copy of the Declaration of Independence for distribution to the state legislatures in 1777.

5. Obtained the first patent in the American colonies.

Column B

Margaret Brent

Benjamin Franklin

Mary Katherine Goddard

Patrick Henry

Elizabeth Knight

Sybil Ludington

Sybille Masters

Sir Walter Raleigh

Paul Revere

Eli Whitney

How did you do? Did you get some of them right? Were you familiar with some of the names? Were all the names you were familiar with men's names? If you used any of the men's names in your answers, you are wrong.

Here are the answers:

1. Elizabeth Knight was one of a number of English merchant adventurers who financed the Mayflower expedition.
2. Mistress Margaret Brent, in the early days of the Maryland colony, sued the House of Burgesses for the right to vote. From 1642 to 1650, her name appears as attorney in the Maryland court records 134 times. She was relative, close friend, lover—nobody knows which—to Leonard Calvert, the first governor of Maryland, and acted as attorney also for his elder brother, Lord Baltimore. Governor Calvert died in 1647, making Mistress Brent his sole executor, and ordering her to "take all and pay all." She did. She possessed herself of his house and his property, assumed his position

as Lord Baltimore's attorney, and claimed the right to receive all rents and profits from his lordship's estate and to attend to all of the disbursements. Indignant questions were asked everywhere, attacking the legality of her actions, so she went to court. The court ruled in her favor. The first time the House of Burgesses met after Governor Calvert's death, she appeared before it and demanded the right to sit with them as a member and to cast two votes—one as executor to Leonard Calvert and the other as attorney to Lord Baltimore. She was so able, forceful and powerful that she might have succeeded so far as the Burgesses were concerned, but the new Governor, Green, on his own responsibility, resisted her demand. Failing to obtain the two votes, she demanded that all proceedings of that session of the Council be declared invalid. Her request was denied.

3. Sybil Ludington made the daring, twenty-mile, midnight ride. She was sent by her father, Colonel Henry Ludington, of the lower New York State area, to raise his militia and bring them back with her to report for duty. Word had been received that the British had burned a supply base in Danbury, Connecticut and the local militia was to start for Danbury at dawn to rout the British.

4. Mary Katherine Goddard was authorized by Congress on January 18, 1777 to print the official copy of the Declaration of Independence for distribution to the state legislatures. Her mother, Sarah Updike Goddard, publisher of the *Providence Gazette,* had taught her the printing and publishing business. Her brother, William Goddard, started the *Maryland Journal and Baltimore Advertiser,* and Mary Katherine made it famous through the years of the revolution. She was post-mistress of Baltimore until 1789, and also operated a thriving bookstore.

5. Sybille Masters of Pennsylvania was the first person in the American colonies to receive a patent. Interested in the grist mill process, she invented a machine for cleaning and curing corn and a method for making hominy (called "Tuscarora rice"). Her husband had to apply for the patent in her behalf, since, in accordance with English common law, as a married woman, she had forfeited all her civil rights.

The reason we don't know about the women in history is that:
—only the men did important things.
—mostly the women preferred to work in the home.
—women were not permitted to take part in colonial religious, economic or political life.
—men have written the history books.

Talk with your neighbor about which one of the above you chose. What were the reasons for your choice? Some people may be willing to share with the class. What do you think about these things today?

Your teacher will gather together all of the American history textbooks used in your school. Form small groups to work together on the same books. Divide the work among your group. Count the number of women listed in the index of your book. Make a tally of the class findings.

Reconsider your discussion of why women aren't in history books. Is there any statement you'd like to change? Is there any statement you'd like to make?

Exercise the Second

Some of our early history is very familiar to practically everybody, even if you spend most of your time sitting in the principal's office. However, some of that history nobody ever talked about. For instance, can you answer the following questions?

1. We all learned about William Penn and how wisely and tolerantly he governed the province of Pennsylvania. Who governed the province wisely and tolerantly after he died in 1718?
2. New York's John Peter Zenger was put into prison and prosecuted for "seditious libel" because he had published an article critical of the royal governor. Who printed the petitions that aroused public attention and support for his cause?
3. When Benjamin Franklin spent two long terms in England as agent of the Pennsylvania Assembly, who managed his business affairs back in Philadelphia?
4. When George Washington was trying to hold the cold and hungry Continental Army together through the grueling winter at Valley Forge, where was Martha Washington, and what was she doing?
5. Who was Betsy Ross?

Your teacher will take you to your school library to look up the answers. Did you have some success? If so, you are an excellent researcher—and you have an unusually good library. If not, perhaps you are discovering that the histories and reference books are apt not to be too helpful.

Here are the answers:
1. Hannah Callowhill Penn, second wife of William Penn, governed the province from the time of Penn's long illness until her own death in 1726. Under her leadership, the province enjoyed a comfortable prosperity.

2. (Anna) Catherine Zenger published the *New York Weekly Journal* while her husband was in jail, and worked on his behalf to win his acquittal.

3. Deborah Read Franklin had a good head for business, tended the book and stationery shop which was an adjunct of her husband's printing offices, and effectively managed his business affairs while he was away. She died before Independence, and Benjamin Franklin wrote that he missed his old companion, and also that they had never had the trouble they had feared. What he was referring to was the fact that they had had a common-law rather than a formalized, legal marriage. The old romantic story of Deborah seeing Benjamin coming into town, his moving into her father's house, and their becoming interested in each other, was true. But Benjamin later left town, and Deborah married a potter, John Rogers. She soon left him, however, and he went to the West Indies where, it was rumored, he already had another wife. It was thought that John Rogers had died in the West Indies, but there was no proof, so Deborah was not legally free to marry. It never caused them any difficulty, however, as Benjamin Franklin had commented.

4. Martha Washington was at Valley Forge in the terrible winter of 1777-78. Her calm and cheerful nature, her willingness to live in crude and uncomfortable quarters, her services to the poor and the suffering served as an inspiration, and were recorded in many of the military journals. She wintered with George Washington at various headquarters during the revolution and returned to Mount Vernon with the opening of

each campaign. Later, she said that she had heard the first cannon at the opening and the last at the closing of all the campaigns of the Revolutionary War.

5. Betsy Ross ran an upholstery business with her husband, John Ross, and continued to run the business after her husband's death while on militia duty. She supplemented her income by making flags for the state of Pennsylvania. She may have sewed the first American flag, but there is no historical evidence to support that story.

Had you assumed that William Penn, John Peter Zenger, George Washington, Benjamin Franklin, Betsy Ross:
—were married.
—were not married.
—or had you never given it a thought.

Had you assumed that in colonial days:
—the wives were busy having babies.
—the wives were not as capable as their famous husbands.
—woman's place was in the home; and work and home were separate.
—the wives were not trained in crafts.

Where did you get your ideas from?
—from what you were taught in school.
—from your books or textbooks.
—from ye olde movies or TV.
—from some other place.

Share your answers with your neighbor. Perhaps the whole class can arrive at some consensus: where do we get our ideas from?

Exercise the Third

Where do you find out, and what do you find out about—Martha Washington? Off to the school library for a day of research. List all of the books you use, and all the information you obtain. Copy exactly from the book: title, author, date of publication, information.

Your teacher will prepare a ditto sheet with all of the references that everybody in the class found. Compare the references. For each of the references, write a summary statement of what kind of person Martha Washington seemed to be.

Are there any differences among the references? If so, what are the main differences? List all of the reasons you can think of why the references might be different. Now, number each reason in your list, in accordance with how important that reason seems to you, number one being the most important reason, etc. If there aren't any differences, why not? List all of the reasons you can think of why the references might be similar. Now, number each reason in your list, in accordance with how important that reason seems to you, number one being the most important reason, etc.

Share your list with your neighbor. Have the whole class construct a collaborative list. Write the most important reasons on a big sheet of paper and keep it up in the classroom to check against as you do other work.

Here are our findings:

There were no references to Martha Washington in any of the following books:
1. *A History of the American People,* Woodrow Wilson (1918).
2. *The Colonial Period of American History,* Volumes I-IV, Charles M. Andrews (1934).
3. *Search for Freedom: America and Its People*, William Jacobs (1973).
4. *Seedtime of the Republic,* Clinton Rossiter (1953).
5. *The Growth of the American Republic,* Samuel Eliot Morison and Henry Steele Commager (1962).
6. *The Heritage of America,* Henry Steele Commager and Allan Nevins (1939).
7. *The Oxford History of the American Republic,* Samuel Eliot Morison (1965).
8. *The Rise of the American Civilization,* Charles A. and Mary R. Beard (1933).
9. *The United States of America: A History,* Volume I, Dexter Perkins and Glyndon G. Van Deusen (1968).
10. *A History of Colonial America,* Oliver Perry Chetwood (1931).

There was one reference to "Mrs. George Washington" in *The American Pageant,* Thomas Bailey (1961).

> Democracy had been something of a taint in the days of the Federalist aristocrats. Mrs. George Washington, after a presidential reception, was shocked to find a greasy mark on the wallpaper, left there, she was sure, by an uninvited 'filthy democrat.'

In *Notable American Women, 1607-1950: A Biographical Dictionary,* edited by Edward T. James, Janet Wilson James and Paul S. Boyer (1971), there is a lengthy essay on Martha Dandridge Custis Washington written by Mary Wells Ashworth.

> That December, making her first trip out of Virginia, Martha Washington joined her husband at his headquarters in Cambridge, Mass., and in subsequent years she made the difficult journey from Mount Vernon to his winter quarters in Morristown, N. J., Valley Forge, Pa., and Newburgh, N. Y., where her cheerful presence and the steadying sight of her constant sewing did much to encourage both the Commander and the troops.

> Mercy Warren, visiting her in Cambridge, found her complacent, affable, and unaffected, well suited "to soften the hours of private life, or to sweeten the cares of the Hero, and smooth the rugged paths of War."

> . . . she was . . . genuinely kind and sympathetic, and guests who found Washington somewhat aloof were grateful for her warmth and graciousness.

Now gather all of the American history textbooks again. Get back into the small groups you worked in before. Again, divide the work among the members of your group. This time, look up the women listed in the index. Write down all of the activities they were involved in and the adjectives used to describe them.

Can you draw any conclusions from your lists? What are they? Is there an "historical" view of women? Support your answer with information taken from your textbook search. Share your answer with your group. Then talk together with other groups. Is there a class consensus?

Exercise the Fourth

Benjamin Franklin, while he was away, wrote to his wife, Deborah, telling her what a good job she was doing, and how pleased he was with her handling of his business affairs. However, this is one of his public writings:

> Let us survey the morning dress of some women. Downstairs they come, pulling up their ungartered, dirty stockings; slipshod, with naked heels peeping out; not stays or other decent conveniency, but all flip-flop; a sort of clout thrown about the neck, without form or decency; a tumbled, discoloured mop or nightcap, half on and half off, with the frowzy hair hanging in sweaty ringlets, staring like a Medusa with her serpents; shrugging up her petticoats, that are sweeping the ground and scarse tied on; hands unwashed, teeth furred, and eyes crusted—but I beg your pardon, I'll go no farther with this sluttish picture, which I am afraid has already turned your stomach.
> —from *Benjamin Franklin,* Carl Van Doren (1938)

Another view was expressed by Thomas Paine, professional revolutionary, writer of the pamphlet, *Common Sense:*

> . . . who does not feel for the tender sex? Yet such I am sorry to say is the lot of woman over the whole earth. Man with regard to them, in all climates and in all ages, has been either an insensible husband or an oppressor; but they have sometimes experienced the cold and deliberate oppression of pride, and sometimes the violent and terrible tyranny of jealousy. When they are not beloved they are nothing; and when they are, they are tormented. They have almost equal cause to be afraid of indifference and love. Over three quarters of the globe Nature has placed them between contempt and misery. Even among people where beauty receives the highest homage we find men who would deprive the sex of every kind of reputation. "The most virtuous woman," says a celebrated Greek, "is she who is least talked of." That morose man, while he imposes duties on women, would deprive them of the sweets of public esteem, and in exacting virtues from them would make it a crime to aspire to honour.
> —from "An Occasional Letter on the Female Sex," *Pennsylvania Magazine* (August 1775)

Compare the two views of women:
—What are the main attributes?
—What are the good points?
—What are the bad points?
—What is their relation to men?
—What is their relation to society?
—Anything else you want to add.

What is the contemporary view of women? Look through your newspaper. Cut out all of the articles that have to do with women. (After everyone in your family has had a chance to read the paper, of course.)

1. List all of the kinds of things that are reported about women.
2. List all of the adjectives that are used in connection with the women.

Where the articles provide this kind of information:
—What are the main attributes of the women?
—What are the good points, as reported?
—What are the bad points, as reported?
—What is the relation of the women to men?
—What is the relation of the women to society?

Compare colonial and contemporary views of women: Have attitudes about women changed? If so, in what ways? Share your discoveries with your neighbor. Talk with the class about your findings.

Exercise the Fifth

Here is a list of colonial occupations. Check the ones you think women were engaged in:

Attorney	Chandler	Leather Worker	Sailor
Baker	Church Sexton	Manufacturer	Shipper
Barber	Confectioner	Mortician	Silversmith
Blacksmith	Doctor	Pewterer	Slave Owner
Bookbinder	Dressmaker	Pirate	Soldier
Bookseller	Explorer	Preacher	Tanner
Botanist	Ferry Boat Operator	Printer	Teacher
Brazier	Glazier	Publican	Whaler
Butcher	Iron Miner	Rope Maker	Wood-worker
Caterer	Landowner	Saddle Maker	Writer

Colonial records show that women were engaged in all of these occupations.
Attorney:
Rachel Miller had power of attorney for Jemima Wilkinson and handled the financial affairs of her church. Others: Elizabeth Haddon, New Jersey; Susanna Hartley, North Carolina; Elizabeth Smith, New York.
Barber:
Elizabeth Butler advertised herself as a capable barber in the local paper in Charleston, South Carolina (1765).
Blacksmith:
Heilke Pieterse of New York City, Jane Burgess of Maryland and Mary Salmon of Boston were blacksmiths. Anna Rutter Nutt of Pennsylvania, Mary Butler of Baltimore and Mrs. Erskine of New Jersey owned and operated iron mines, forges and furnaces.
Botanist:
Mrs. Carter was known for her productive orchards and for her successful grafting of fruit trees. Martha Logan raised seeds, plants and shrub-roots for sale. She also wrote a gardener's calendar to help her buyers.
Butcher:
Margaret Oliver and her mother of South Carolina were known as excellent butchers (1765).

Caterer:
Dutchess Quamino of Newport, Rhode Island, a manumetted Negro, ran a successful catering establishment.
Doctor:
Sarah Alock and her husband were doctors in Roxbury, Massachusetts. They collected a library of about 100 books, over half of which were in the field of medicine. When Sarah died in 1665, she was proclaimed a "virtuous woman of unstained life, very skillful in physick and chirurgery, exceeding active, yea, unwearied in ministering to ye necessities of others."
Explorer:
Mary Warenbuer Feree, a French Huguenot widow with six children, was personally helped by William Penn to acquire 2,000 acres of land from Queen Anne in 1711, and to organize a colonizing expedition of religious refugees who settled Lancaster County, Pennsylvania. Other: Lady Deborah Dunch Moody (see *Notable American Women,* Vol. II).
Ferry Boat Owner and Operator:
Abigail Smith Grimes operated a ferry boat between Rocky Hill Landing and South Glastonberry, that she had started in 1650. She was occasionally assisted by her daughter and granddaughter and at times by some of the men of the family. Others: Ruth Haskins, Massachusetts; Flora Dorsey, Maryland.
Fisher and Whaler:
Judith Barnard, in 1734, listed her estate as "a whole boat, oars, craft to boat, an outfit for shore whaling, one share in the old wharf, 5/12 share in the Sloop Ranger and 1/4 share in the mill." Other: Martha Turnstall Smith, Long Island.
Glazier:
Anne Vanderspiegel was a glazier and sold glass in New York City (1737).
Leather Worker:
Mary Cowley of Pennsylvania dressed buckskin and made breeches and other articles (1741). Martha Linton specialized in making harnesses, whips and other leather goods of calf and cowhide.
Manufacturer:
Anne Dickenson had a paper hanging manufactury in Philadelphia (1788).
Mortician:
Lydia Barrington (1729-1789) was a colonial nurse and midwife. She advertised in the Pennsylvania Gazette (December 4, 1766) her intention of opening a mortuary establishment and promised to "make Grave-Clothes and lay out the Dead in the Neatest Manner."
Preacher and Religious Leader:
Hannah Lloyd, a Quaker, was the daughter of William Penn's first magistrate. A well-known preacher, she traveled through New England and other sections of the new land. Others: Anne Hutchinson, Ann Austin, Katherine Scott, Mary Clark, Bilhah Abigail Frank, Barbara Ruckle Heck, Anne Lee Standerin. Anne Lee Standerin was born in Manchester, England, in 1738. Her father was a poor blacksmith. The second of eight children, she went to work in a cotton factory when she was a small child. Later, she worked at a hatter's and was cook in a public infirmary. She never went to school, but she learned whole books of the Bible by heart. She was said to have been a pious child and to have had heavenly visions frequently. When she was twenty-two, she joined a group of radicals known as "Shakers" because of their ritualistic shaking dance. In

1762 she married Abraham Standerin, a blacksmith, and had four children, all of whom died in infancy. Her grief at this loss added to her deep-seated belief in the depravity of man, and particularly, the depravity of sex. She preached against marriage and concupiscence as a deadly sin. She was imprisoned a number of times in Manchester, and once, she was stoned by a mob. In 1770, while in prison, she had a profoundly inspiring vision. In it, she found herself the "visible leader of the church of God on earth." God was revealed to her as a dual personality. Christ had been the masculine manifestation of God. She was the female manifestation, whose mission it was to establish the government of the "United Society of Believers in the Second Appearing of God." She was to usher in the millennium. In 1774, with eight followers, including her husband, brother and niece, she came to New York. She lived in New York City and did laundry work until her husband left her in 1775 for another woman. Then she joined the rest of her group at Watervliet, just north of Albany. She helped clear the land and build the houses. Between 1780 and 1784, she made a number of successful trips through New England to raise money and to recruit new members. She lived frugally, honestly and industriously, and died in 1784, utterly worn out. Followers carried on her church, and by a century later, there were twenty settlements in seven states and about 6000 members. There is a small group of Shakers still in existence.

Publican:

Elizabeth Marriott owned a famous tavern, The Sign of the Ship, in Annapolis, Maryland, where she is said to have amassed a fortune of £3000 by 1755. Her daughter, Anne Howard, inherited the tavern and entertained George Washington there in 1774. Others: Margaret Todd, Nancy Rumsey.

Revolutionary Soldier:

Margaret Cochran Corbin (1751-c.1800) was called "the first woman to take a soldier's part" in the Revolution. She fought and was wounded in the battle of Fort Washington. She was with her husband at Fort Washington on Manhattan Island when John Corbin, mortally wounded, fell by her side. With "distinguished bravery," she filled his battle station and was herself utterly disabled before the post was overcome. She suffered permanent disability through the loss of the use of one arm. She returned to Pennsylvania, where its Supreme Council on June 29, noting her heroism and helpless situation, allowed her $30 relief and recommended her for consideration by the Board of War of the Continental Congress because the rations issued to her were an insufficient provision. On July 6, Congress voted her, for life, or during her continued disability, half the pay of a soldier in service and a complete outfit of clothing or its value in money. Later, the Board of War provided for an annual clothing allowance. By 1780, she was formally enrolled in the Invalid Regiment, which was created in 1777 for those wounded in service. Others: Nancy Hart, "Molly Pitcher" (Mary Ludwig Hays McCauley), Deborah Sampson.

Sailor:

Louisa Baker was born in Plymouth County, Massachusetts, in 1792. When she was about twenty, she enlisted in the U. S. Navy. She served for three years on the frigate *Constitution,* took part in three military engagements, and was given her share of the prize money. When she returned to Boston she bought herself some beautiful dresses and wrote the story of her life, which was published in 1815.

Shipper:

Margaret Hardenbroeck de Vries Phillipse of New Amsterdam owned what was probably the first regularly maintained fleet of packet ships in the colonies. Although she married twice, she handled her own affairs, bought and traded in her own name, and frequently went to Holland as super cargo in her own ships. She is reported to have had unusually fine financial acumen and to have amassed a considerable fortune before she died in 1690. Other: Molly (Polly) Spratt Provoost Alexander.

Slave Owner:

Mrs. Stapleford offered Negroes for sale, along with groceries and gunpowder in Philadelphia, in 1742.

Wood-Worker:

Twenty-two Danish women were brought to Portsmouth settlement to saw lumber and make potash in 1731.

Beth Millstein
Adapted from a curriculum by June Chapin
Social Studies
Adlai Stevenson High School
Bronx, N.Y./1972-74

HISTORY OR HERSTORY: CHANGING ROLES OF THE AMERICAN WOMAN

Theme I—The Problem

1. Why a course on American women? Why status of women and children is important as a clue to understanding a culture?
2. Parallels to past coverage of blacks and other minority groups.
3. Stereotypes—or "Why Can't a Woman Be More like a Man?"
4. Definition of areas to be discussed, goals, techniques.

Theme II—School: A Case Study in Different Roles
(to be determined by students in committee and then used to create hypotheses)

1. Composition of school: professional staff (administration, chairmen, faculty by subject area), service personnel.
2. Curriculum: percent of boys, girls in given courses, i.e., advanced math, science, art, shops. Comparison of physical education programs.
3. Student activities: percent of boys, girls in clubs, nature of club leadership; percent of boys, girls in honors program, College Bound, Basic Skill classes.
4. Behavior: different expectations for boys and girls; privileges; types of referrals for boys, girls. Who has an easier time?
5. Hypotheses: does the school follow a typical pattern in role-playing and role expectation? Generalizations.

Theme III—How Did We Get Where We Are?
(overview of women in American life from 1607 to the present)

1. Earliest American women: Pueblos of southwest; women in nomadic tribes.
2. Role of women in Europe in 1500's and 1600's.
3. Status vs. realities of lives of colonial women.
4. Abigail Adams: "Remember the Ladies."
5. Effect of the frontier experience on women.
6. Slave women.
7. Women's education.
8. Women's Rights Convention, 1848: Case studies of Lucretia Mott, Elizabeth Cady Stanton, Sojourner Truth.
9. Effect of Industrial Revolution and urbanization on women's roles.
10. Contrast between women's tasks and Victorian idealization.
11. Diversity of opinions as to where and how women's reform should go: Addams, Anthony, Gilman, Woodhull.
12. Evaluation of above analyses.
13. Suffrage—the symbolic cause: why symbolic, how achieved, value?
14-15. The new woman of the twentieth century: war, automation.

16. The Pill and the sexual revolution.
17. The family and home—changing patterns.
18. Betty Friedan and *The Feminine Mystique.*
19-21. The birth of women's liberation—why? how? who? Greer, Millett, Steinem, Abzug, etc.
22. Evaluation: have you come a long way, baby?

Theme IV—The Socialization of Women

1. Are there physiological differences between men and women?
2. Are there psychological differences; male and female traits?
3. Attempt at definition—what is a woman? man?
4. How do women learn to play their roles?—fashion, manners, mother.
5. What do women learn from the media?—cartoons, Sesame Street, commercials, magazines, literature.
6. Should men and women be allowed more choice in roles?
7. Role-playing.

Theme V—The Role of Women in the 1970's

A. Family Patterns (Role-Playing)
   1. Effect of longevity.
   2. Marriage: why?—age, function.
   3. Children: why?—population explosion and its effect on women, the Pill.
   4. Divorce: why?—alimony.
   5. Interpersonal relationships: fostering of dependence, division of labor in the home, effect of outside employment—who has an easier life?
   6. Alternatives to present family life: effect on women, children, men.

B. Religion
   1. Role of women in various American religions.
   2. Effect of religion on women's role in American society.

C. Women in the Labor Force
   1. Working wives? who, why, how many?
   2. A man's world?—wage gaps, sex-typing, women in poverty, high cost of keeping women down.
   3. Advancement in protection: want ads, hours and conditions, unions, do women have to be "protected"?
   4. Do women want careers or jobs?
   5. Does education help or hurt?
   6. What should a high school girl train for?

D. Legal Equality
   1. What does "women's equality" mean?
   2. Current legislation.
   3. Legal restrictions on women: credit, business, property, juries.

Theme VI—Black Women—Case Study of a Special Problem

Based largely on *To Be a Black Woman: Portraits in Fact and Fiction,* Watkins and David, eds. (William Morrow & Co., 1970).

1. The burden of oppression.
2. Black on white; the black woman in the white world.
3. Black on black; the black woman in the black world.
4. A heritage rediscovered; the new black woman.

Theme VII—Toward the Future

1. Women's organizations—diversity in methods and goals.
2. Role of the moderate woman.
3. Will there be a new man?
4. Demands: child care, abortion, equality.
5. Methods: suits, confrontation.
6. How do other groups feel?—women, white and black men.
7. Where to and how?

June Namias
Social Studies
Newton North High School
Newton, Mass./1972-73

TOWARD TEACHING A FEMINIST UNITED STATES HISTORY

Introduction

Women's lives are not an aside to U. S. history. Except for the earliest years of the Republic, women and children constituted one-half to two-thirds of the population. This fact should be made evident in the histories of the United States and especially in the *teaching* of U. S. history. That men—white men, and in many cases, white men of a very particular class background—determined the lives of two-thirds of the population as well as of all the nonwhite and poor population, should be an explicit basis of, not just an aside in, U. S. history courses.

As a history teacher, this means reconstructing the past three-hundred-year history of people in the United States, especially women and children. Called "social" history or sometimes "cultural" history, this perspective has not been thought to be "real" history (maybe because it involved "herstory" or "kidstory"). What is necessary is not talk about great women, or even about the women's movement and the labor movement, but discussion of the question: What was existence like for most people—especially for women and children—in each period of U. S. history? (Just as Marx saw economics as an underlying reality, one can see existence as an underlying reality.) What were the power realities which necessitated a particular type of existence? Instead of examining only such factors as war, presidencies and economic depressions, to answer questions about daily life, one must look at the day-to-day substance of people's lives as they were affected by economic and political events.

Because the idea of "progress" has been important to the American consciousness, historians have stressed the new event, the "Big Change." Continuity appears in terms of the Puritan ethic or Social Darwinism. Overlooked in this scheme are the basics: the family as an institution is not examined and child-rearing is rarely dealt with, even though methods of child-rearing determine relations to authority, as well as attitudes towards tradition, violence, sex roles and dependence—all crucial in understanding national and political history. A more complete view of history than is now taught in high schools requires an investigation into the lives and activities of women as an historical force, into child-rearing and the lives and activities of children, and into the nature of the family as the focus of most women's lives and as the basic unit or institution in the society. Most high school U. S. history courses and most standard texts overlook half of the population as even a minor historical force, treat children (the historical counterparts of those we teach in schools) in an extremely cursory way and virtually ignore the nature and role of the family.

These issues alone are enough to call for a significant revision of the way history is taught. But there are a number of other issues which are also absent from standard history curricula. These include sex roles, communal living, economic communism, socio-economic class in America's past as it relates to race and sex, work and power, fashion and marketing and their relationship to consumption as well as style, the division of labor, and popular culture—what music, films, radio, T.V. and dance of a given period tell about society at that time.

In what follows, I describe some activities and materials used in my classes at Newton North High School in order to incorporate feminist issues into U. S. history courses. I use these materials and methods in order to satisfy my own curiosity; to include problems and issues that are not usually dealt with in traditional high school U. S. history courses; and to attempt a thorough understanding of U. S. life that includes the roles of women and the family. I focus on the period from 1830 to the present, in roughly chronological order.

Pre-Civil War Period

1. One way of understanding the role of women in nineteenth-century America is to look at the first feminist movement, its beginning and its growth.

Class activities:
Anne Firor Scott's *Women in American Life* (Houghton-Mifflin) is a useful beginning text for high school classes studying the feminist movement. Have students read aloud "The Declaration of Sentiments and Resolutions" from the first Women's Rights Convention at Seneca Falls, New York, July 19-20, 1848. Then break into small groups and discuss each complaint and issue of this document. Focus on such questions as: Are women making the same complaints/raising the same issues today? Are these complaints valid today? Have these issues been solved by the winning of certain legal rights by women?

2. The period just before the Civil War was one of great abolitionist, feminist and reform activity. There was also a constant voicing of vigorous opposition to these causes. Many such activities have been neglected in standard history texts. This exercise is designed to show that people who influenced the society of that time have been ignored by historians; that the "objectivity" of history is open to question; and that the infrequent appearance of information about women, the poor, blacks, dissenters and others in movements for social change, reflects a certain prejudice and a particular view of history.

Class activities:
a. Ask students to select an abolitionist, feminist or reformer, or a person who vocally or actively opposed one of these three movements. Have students use at least three sources (textbooks, *The Dictionary of American Biography,* encyclopedias, other biographical references) to find information about this person. Suggestions: Dorothea Dix, Sarah and Angelina Grimké, Frederick Douglass, Wendell Phillips, Harriet Tubman, Sojourner Truth, Lucretia Mott, William Garrison. Anti-feminist and pro-slavery people: Thomas Dew (see "Dissertation on Characteristic Differences Between the Sexes," *Up from the Pedestal,* Aileen S. Kraditor, ed., [Quadrangle, 1968], pp. 44-47) and William Fitzhugh.

b. After students have completed the assignment, discuss the following questions: What is the meaning of "objectivity" in the study of history? In your sources in particular? Why aren't certain people mentioned in many sources? What does this say about exclusion or inclusion of black people, the poor, women and movements for social change in history?

Post-Civil War Period

Following the Civil War, feminists were dealing with deep-rooted and radical issues, among them: the marital system, sex roles, the authority of the Bible, the structure of government.

Class activities:

a. Discuss the focus of the feminist movement on getting the vote. Duplicate or read aloud portions of the third section of Kraditor and discuss the idea of chivalry and its use in the arguments against enfranchising women. Emma Goldman's opposition to suffrage, outlined in her essay *Anarchism and Other Essays* (Dover), raises the question of the system vs. the vote and also the ways in which women buttress conventional morality.

b. Discuss the analogy of marriage to prostitution. The Victorian concept of good woman (girl), bad woman (girl) was central to nineteenth-century English and American life. Duplicate or read aloud the article in Kraditor; also see Dreiser's *Sister Carrie* (either film or selections of the novel) or *Maggie: A Girl of the Streets* by Stephen Crane. Discuss virginity, prostitution and marriage, and how sexual standards are related to life and power.

c. Throughout the nineteenth century, in different parts of the United States, a number of splinter religious groups and reform movements developed communal societies. These groups tried to come to terms with the issues of private versus community ownership of property; work defined in terms of sharing rather than in terms of isolated individual efforts; and desirable varieties of relationships and fidelity. A good resource is Nordoff, *Communistic Societies in America.* Duplicate and/or read in class "Oneida: An Early American Commune," *Family in Transition,* Skolnick and Skolnick, eds. (Little, Brown & Co.). This article raises issues of free love vs. fidelity; communal vs. family child-rearing; birth control and who should use it; private property vs. community ownership; group pressure vs. legal pressure. Have each student state which aspects of this commune he/she likes and dislikes and why. Break into small groups to talk about some of the above issues.

Turn of the Century to the Present

1. *Magazines.*

Magazines are useful sources for teaching history, especially if students are near large city libraries which have back periodical collections. (Back issues of magazines are also available on microfilm for purchase by school libraries.) At the turn of the century, many periodicals and some radical women's journals were published regularly. Victoria Woodhull and Tennessee Claflin edited *Woodhull and Claflin's Weekly* (selections available from Times Change Press, Penwell Rd., Washington, N.J. 07882), and Margaret Sanger edited *Woman Rebel.* (See also *Century of Struggle* by Eleanor Flexner [Harvard University Press] for still other publications.) Most libraries contain recent magazines that are good sources for information about life styles, fashions and political issues.

Class activities:

Ask each student to pick one or several magazines from the turn of the century (*Ladies' Home Journal, The Atlantic Monthly, The Nation, Arena, Harper's, Woman Rebel, The Masses*). The assignment: examine one magazine over a period of years or several magazines during one year for information on a specific topic of your choice—for example, women's manners, voting rights for women, women who work, fashions. Write a report of your findings.

2. *What did people look like?*
I was fortunate to have access to some excellent slides of working women in the latter part of the nineteenth century. I used them to begin a discussion of the pedestal image of women versus the reality of most women's lives. Slides are an excellent way of teaching about the issues of class, race and ethnicity. Find a variety of pictures or slides or make slides from pictures. Find pictures which depict immigrants; working women and children; wealthy families; black, Chinese and Indian people; women involved in social protest and on the frontier. Some useful resources for finding pictures of the nineteenth century are: *The Revolt of American Women,* Oliver Jensen; *Mill Child,* Ruth Holland.

Questions used on photographs:
a. Compare pictures of women from different classes. What can you tell about a woman's social class from her picture?

b. What was the ideal image of woman in the late nineteenth century?

c. What was life like for immigrant, black, working women? Which women were on which pedestal? (Compare a picture of Mrs. Belmont in her $500,000 pearls with a picture of a woman selling pretzels on the lower east side of New York.)

d. What do pictures of women and small children working in mills tell us? What do such pictures tell us about statements that refer to "the *men* who built this country"?

e. Look at pictures of women in corsets and in the bloomer costume. What was the fashion message of this period? Why was the bloomer movement so upsetting to people, especially to men?

f. Look at cartoons of women who were involved in social protest. What characteristics of these women do the cartoonists ridicule? Why were these women ridiculed? Is this ridicule of nineteenth-century activist women similar to the media's portrayal of activitist women today?

3. *Family and oral history.*
There is nothing better for learning history than actually to experience it. Living documentation, which gives students person-to-person contact and a sense that history is made up of real people's lives, is one of the best ways to teach history.

Class activities:
a. Have students ask their parents if there are items in their homes which belonged to relatives who lived in the nineteenth or early twentieth century. (Try the attic.) Perhaps they will find letters, diaries or pictures which parents would permit to be copied for sharing with the class.

b. Assign students to interview their parents and/or grandparents. In class, draw up a set of reasonable questions to ask about the period in which the people to be interviewed lived (e.g., the 20's, the Depression, World War II, the 50's, the 60's). Try to devise questions that will uncover political assumptions, the way people lived from day to day, life styles. Also devise questions of a more personal nature such as: What was high school like? Did people date? At what age? What was this like? What was child-rearing like in your family? In other families? Do you remember film or radio stars or the music of the time? Why were these important to people of your era? If tape recorders are available for use and those being interviewed don't mind, have students tape their interviews and play them for the class. It's important for students to hear the actual voices of people talking about their lives.

c. Students might interview older people around the school. This is good for public relations and a way for old and young people to realize they have similar experiences as well as different ones, based on the eras they have lived through.

d. If photographic equipment or family photographs are available, students interested in media could make a photo-collage or a slide show of the pictorial development of their family in the course of the last century. This could be accompanied by taped interviews with family members.

e. Find out if you have access to old school yearbooks and newspapers. These can be a gold mine of information about behavior, the issues of the day, social patterns and codes, the effects of economic class, and students' general attitudes.

f. It is going to be up to students to unearth historic materials about children and the history of children's lives. Ask your students to write their own biographies. Some of my students did oral histories of what they remember about John F. Kennedy's death and of other aspects of their lives in the late 60's and early 70's. A recently published book, *Children and Youth in America: A Documentary* by Robert H. Bremner et al, might serve as a useful resource.

4. *Autobiography, biography and fiction.*
For the twentieth century, autobiographies and biographies are especially useful. In addition to asking each student to read an entire biography of a woman who is known for something other than her marriage to a president, teachers can ditto paragraphs or sections from biographies of women about their girlhoods, family relationships, work and so on. Appropriate and readable biographies and autobiographies are available of Margaret Sanger, Elizabeth Gurley Flynn, Isadora Duncan, Jane Addams and others. Many history teachers assign short stories or novels as part of their history curriculum or urge students to read the literature of a period on their own. Especially useful are Kate Chopin's *The Awakening,* Willa Cather's *My Antonia,* Edith Wharton's *The House of Mirth* and Theodore Dreiser's *Sister Carrie.*

5. *Media resources.*
Films: "The Inheritance" (available from B'nai B'rith), deals with the activity of men and women in the American labor movement. "Dorothea Lange: The Closer for Me" and "Dorothea Lange: Under the Trees" (available from Film Library, Boston University, 765 Commonwealth Ave., Boston, Mass. 02215), a moving two-part documentary of the artist's life and work, also includes Lange's powerful photographs of the 1930's.
Record: "Hard Times," taped interviews made by Studs Terkel of women and men, recalls the depression days of the 1930's.
Slide show: "Women in History" includes material on medieval England, seventeenth-century England, nineteenth-century England, and women in revolt (available from Pat Arnold, Cambridge-Goddard Graduate School, 2 Upland Road, Cambridge, Mass. 02140).

6. *Speakers.*

Make use of local and school resources by inviting speakers to visit your classes, especially people who can talk about earlier times. Also invite women who have expertise in fields such as economics and law, and in what are known as "women's issues," such as day care, divorce and child custody. Members of the Women's Law Collective in Boston gave talks to my classes that enlivened traditional units on the U. S. Constitution, communal systems, and working women in the nineteenth century. For the 1960's and 1970's, ask people who were involved in the civil rights movement to talk about their activities, about the kinds of actions they have taken, and the work they are presently involved in. Young women especially are inspired by hearing women just a bit older talk about their lives and work.

7. *Black women.*

In dealing with the black struggle in the nineteenth and twentieth centuries, I think it is very important to talk about the critical role of black women. Readings are a useful way to start such discussions, and magazines such as *Ebony* and *Essence* are good sources for articles about black women, both past and present. Anne Moody's *Coming of Age in Mississippi* includes a beautiful chapter about the author sitting-in at a lunchroom counter during the civil rights movement of the 1960's.

Conclusion

It is imperative that we make sure that what has happened to the study of black people's history not happen to the study of women's history. That is, that regular textbooks merely add one chapter to their grossly racist content and then consider complete the task of presenting black history. Our real task as teachers is to incorporate women, and black and working people into our *entire* curriculum. All courses should deal with child care, the family, child-rearing, the marriage system and sex roles. And most of all in order to teach about women, courses should not only deal with *famous* women.

Eleanor Newirth
Social Studies
John F. Kennedy High School
Plainview/Bethpage, N. Y./1972-73

WOMEN IN SOCIETY

Readings:
Century of Struggle, Eleanor Flexner (Atheneum, 1968).
Sisterhood Is Powerful, Robin Morgan, ed. (Vintage, 1970).
The American Woman: Who Was She? Ann Firor Scott, ed. (Prentice-Hall, 1971).
Up from the Pedestal, Aileen Kraditor, ed. (Quadrangle, 1968).
Women in American Life: Selected Readings, Ann Firor Scott, ed. (Houghton
    Mifflin, 1970).
Selections from newspapers and magazines.

Films & Tapes:
Billie Jean King
Betty Tells Her Story (New Day Films)
Anything You Want to Be (New Day Films)
The Woman's Film (Newsreel)
The Silenced Majority (Media Plus)

Women in Society, an elective semester course offered by the social studies department
to 11th and 12th graders, met four times a week for forty-five minute periods. I approached the course both as a study of the history of women in the United States and
as a means through which students could explore their own experiences and feelings
about the issues related to this history. I tried throughout to relate historical issues to
current ones and to students' own lives. I did little formal lecturing and for most of the
course I saw my role as facilitator. Several speakers were invited to talk about specific
issues: i.e., abortion (representatives from the Right to Life and from the American Civil
Liberties Union); homosexuality (from the Gay Activist Alliance); legal discrimination
(from the National Organization for Women—NOW); and consciousness-raising (members
of local C-R groups).

What follows is an outline of the course as taught, with notes about questions used to
spark discussions and descriptions of assignments.

I. Introduction

A. Activity: Ask students to create two collages entitled "Man" and "Woman."
    Be clear about whether you are asking students to think about how *society* perceives
    males and females or how the students themselves do. Questions for discussion—after
    qualities illustrated by the collages for each sex have been put on the board:
    Which qualities do you view as positive? negative?
    How did these differences come to be?
    How do these differences affect us?

B. Men and women in other societies.

Assignment: readings on the Zuni and the Sioux from *Women in American Life,* henceforth called WAL, pp. 4-8. Students were asked to choose one of the following questions to answer:

1. Is woman's and man's place in society determined by biology? by environment? Develop your argument by citing at least three examples from the reading and your experience.

2. Describe the process of socialization for Sioux women as they grow from childhood to womanhood. Compare it to your own experiences.

3. Compare the rights held by Zuni women with those held today by women in the United States. Draw some tentative conclusions about attitudes of Zuni society towards women. Based on your experiences and the collages, draw tentative conclusions about U. S. society's attitudes toward women.

C. Biology vs. environment.

Assignment: Read "Biological Imperative," *Time,* January 8, 1973. This article reports the findings of Dr. John Money, a Johns Hopkins University psychologist, who has been studying physiological sources of and changes in the conventional patterns of masculine and feminine behavior. The article refers specifically to instances of individuals who, although born biologically "male" or "female," have been reared successfully as members of the opposite sex. This assignment generated startling and difficult discussion for the class, since it raised issues most of us take for granted: questions about the long-term emotional effect of changes in masculine and feminine behavior and about the influence of environment on the development of the sex roles of individuals.

II. Women in Colonial America: Early Nineteenth Century United States

A. The position of married women.

Using Flexner (p. 7), we discussed the following quotation from the 1632 *The Lawes Resolutions of Women's Rights (sic)* and its relevance for the position of married women today:

> Man and wife are one person, but understand in what manner. When a small brooke or little river incorporateth with Rhodanus, Humber or the Thames, the poor rivulet looseth its name, it is carried and recarried with the new associate, it beareth no sway, it possesseth nothing during coverture. A woman as soon as she is married, is called *covert* in Latin, *nupta,* that is, *veiled,* as it were, clouded and overshadowed, she hath lost her streame. . . .
> To a married woman, her new self is her superior, her companion, her master.

B. Women who tried to enter the public sphere, rather than remain in the private or domestic one.

Assignment: Read the following documents and answer the following questions about them.

1. Governor John Winthrop's description of his friend's wife—from his diary (WAL, p. 12). What is Winthrop's view of women? What biological assumptions are made about women when compared with men? How is the Bible used to justify the position of women in society?

2. Anne Bradstreet's poetry (WAL, p. 16). How did Bradstreet expect her poem to be received? What is her plea in the last stanza?

3. "The Trial of Anne Hutchinson" (WAL, pp. 13-15) and "Remember the Ladies" by Abigail Adams (WAL, pp. 2-24). Students chose one of the following activities:
   a. Write a dialogue between Abigail Adams and Anne Hutchinson, in which they discuss women's oppression and rebellion as they knew it.
   b. Both the church and the government in these documents could have been accused of hypocrisy. Write the dialogue in which both John Adams and Rev. John Cotton are tried in a "court" of law for hypocrisy.

C. Black women.
   Assignment: Read "Slave and Master" by Linda Brent (WAL, pp. 24-26). Answer question number one and any one of the other three:
   1. What similarities existed between the conditions faced by both black and white women in American society during the nineteenth century?
   2. What special difficulties did the black slave woman face?
   3. What can help explain the lack of solidarity between white and black women when women were as oppressed as Linda Brent was?
   4. Does the black woman in society today continue to face difficulties because she is both black and a woman?

III. Women as Abolitionists

A. The clerical view of the rightful domestic place of women.
   Read Chapter 2 of Kraditor's *Up from the Pedestal.* Discuss especially the "Pastoral Letter of the Massachusetts Congregationalist Clergy" (1837), which specifically criticized the Grimké sisters:

   We cannot, therefore, but regret the mistaken conduct of those who encourage females to bear an obtruse and ostentatious part in measures of reform, and countenance any of that sex who so far forget themselves as to itinerate in the character of public lecturers and teachers. (Kraditor, p. 50)

B. Assignment: Read "The Beginning of Agitation" (Kraditor, pp. 53-66). Answer question number one and one of the others:
   1. What relationship existed in the mid-1800's between the anti-slavery movement and the equal rights movement for women?
   2. How does Sarah Grimké interpret what the Bible has to say about women's role in society?
   3. Do you think Angelina Grimké viewed liberation for women as meaning to want to become like a man?
   4. Both writers recognize that women's loss of rights has been accomplished by society's keeping women as "trinkets and playthings and appendages." Explain.
   5. Why were the Grimké sisters considered "radical" in 1837? Would their ideas be considered so today? Explain.

IV. Education for American Women

A. Nineteenth-century feminist educators.
   Assignment: Read in *The American Woman—Who Was She?* (henceforth, TAW—WWS) pp. 62-64. Also WAL, "A Case for Female Education" by Emma Willard (pp. 46-47),

and "Training Women to Be Teachers" by Catharine Beecher (pp. 49-51). Compare the goals of education for women as viewed by both feminists.

B. Education as a major instrument in changing the status of women.
   Questions for discussion with the class—all with the idea of then and now in mind:
   1. Education for what purpose?
   2. Are women better suited for certain professions—teaching, nursing, for example?
   3. Should women be encouraged to fulfill their own talents and interests—even if these bring women into areas not associated with "feminine" qualities?
   4. Would education make women better wives and mothers?
   5. Does going to college mean, for women, getting an "MRS" degree?
   6. If so, where does this belief come from? What effect does it have on women students?
   7. Do colleges have the right to refuse admission to women because men would allegedly make better "use" of their education?

C. Education as a major instrument, continued.
   Assignment: Read "Progress by 1900" by Carrie Chapman Catt (TAW—WWS p. 46). Discussion of goals expressed and conditions for women then and today. Teacher contributes contemporary statistics on women in various professions today (engineering, veterinary medicine, dentistry, etc.), including religion. Discussion of whether Catt's expectations for women have been fulfilled.

D. One theory that attempts to explain one part of the problem: Matina Horner's studies.
   Assignment: Read "Why Women Fear Success" by Vivian Gornick, *Ms.* (Spring 1972), p. 50. Discussion also of a film that focuses on socialization: "Anything You Want to Be."

V. Women as Workers

A. Working class women in the nineteenth century.
   Assignment: Read "A Week in the Mills" by E. D. Perver and "A Critic of the Lowell System" by Catharine Beecher (WAL pp. 27-32). Questions for discussion:
   1. Where do these writers disagree? What accounts for their differences?
   2. What conclusions can you draw about conditions in the Lowell factories?

B. Working women in the nineteenth century.
   Read "An Overview, 1800-1900" (TAW—WWS, pp. 15-19). Questions or topics for discussion:
   1. The relationship between working women and unions.
   2. Was it better or worse for women to work in conditions as arduous as the Lowell factories?

C. Women in the work force today.
   Assignment: Read the "Major Occupation Groups and Selected Occupations of Employed Women April 1968," a table from the *Handbook on Women Workers* (Women's Bureau, Department of Labor, Washington, D. C.). Also, a document packet prepared from U. S. Labor Department statistics on women workers. Questions for discussion:
   1. What factors influence a woman to join the work force?
   2. Is there a relationship between these statistics about women in the work force and social attitudes toward women and work?

3. What reasons can be given to help explain the differences in earnings for women and for men? Why do some women with three years of college earn less than some men with eighth-grade educations?
4. What conclusions can reasonably be drawn about women and work? In what way might such conclusions affect your attitudes toward work and careers?
5. What redress is open to women who have been discriminated against?
6. What do you think of men who hold traditionally female jobs?
7. What other information would be helpful for a better understanding of women and work?

D. A case study of a working wife and mother.
Mrs. Zager wants to work outside the home and her husband feels differently. The teacher presents two brief arguments, one stressing the advantages of women who work and the other the disadvantages. Problems for discussion:
1. Do you agree with Mr. Zager that there would be a decrease in the family's "division of labor" and a resulting increase in "shared work"? Why or why not?
2. Do you agree with Mr. Zager that an increase in shared work would be less efficient and less economical than having Mrs. Zager stay at home? Why or why not?
3. What would be the effects on her children, if Mrs. Zager went to work outside the home? Why would you predict these effects on the children? Which would be harmful, which beneficial? Why?
4. What additional information would you like to have in order to decide whether Mrs. Zager should go to work? What part of this information do you consider to be important in determining whether a wife or mother should take employment outside the home? Why do you think these factors are most important?
5. It is often said that the two roles of modern American women—as wives and mothers, on the one hand, as workers on the other—are in direct conflict with each other. Do you agree with this statement?

VI. The Women's Suffrage Movement

A. The Seneca Falls Convention of 1848.
Assignment: Read "The Declaration of Sentiments" (WAL, pp. 64-67; *Up from the Pedestal,* pp. 183-188). Questions:
1. What did feminists hope to accomplish by their declaration of 1848?
2. What do the demands and grievances expressed by feminists reveal about the position of women in that society? Cite examples.
3. The double standard of morality—what is it? Does it still exist—and in what ways?
4. How can you explain the reluctance of some feminists to demand the vote?
5. In what areas of life today would the demands of Seneca Falls still be relevant?

B. The struggle for suffrage.
1. Assignment: Read *Sisterhood Is Powerful,* pp. 15-20. Questions:
   a. What changes occurred within nineteenth-century society that affected the role of women and made the idea of suffrage for women more acceptable?
   b. Of those arguments in favor of granting suffrage to women, which surprised you and why?
2. Assignment: Read document summarizing "Arguments Opposing Women's Suffrage," (excerpted from *Up from the Pedestal,* pp. 189-203). Questions:
   a. What assumptions about women underly many of these arguments?

    b. Which arguments help to explain logically why the vote would be a dangerous step for women and society? Why?

    c. Can a woman be president?

3. Assignment: Read TAW—WWS, pp. 102-105. Questions:

    a. What accounts for the final success of the suffrage movement in 1920?

    b. How would you explain the length of time and the variety of tactics needed in order to pass the nineteenth amendment?

VII. Women Involved in Other Social Reform Movements

Assignment: Read handouts containing brief descriptions of reformers Dorothea Dix, Jane Addams, Anna Julia Cooper and Margaret Sanger. Read also "The Cause of the Exploited Worker" (TAW—WWS, pp. 107-109); "The Woman's Bible" by Elizabeth Cady Stanton (*Up from the Pedestal,* pp. 113-114, 118-119); "On the Bloomer Costume" by Elizabeth Smith Miller (*Up from the Pedestal,* pp. 123-124); "Marriage Documents" (*Up from the Pedestal,* pp. 148-150).

VIII. The Modern U. S. Feminist Movement

A. After the nineteenth amendment—the twenties.

1. Assignment: Read *Sisterhood Is Powerful,* pp. 26-28; WAL, pp. 118-128. Questions:

    a. What positive and negative effects on the status of women in U. S. society followed from the passage of the nineteenth amendment?

    b. Many of today's feminists criticize the first women's movement because it failed to confront issues about marriage, family, sexual preference and sharing of household responsibilities. Do you agree with these criticisms?

2. Assignment: Compare the so-called "new woman" of the twenties as portrayed by F. Scott Fitzgerald in "The Jelly Bean" (WAL, pp. 124-128) to the feminists of the nineteenth century.

3. Assignment: Read "The Economic Base of the New Morality" by Suzanne LaFollette (WAL, pp. 129-132). Questions:

    a. What similarities are there between the emancipation of women in the twenties and today?

    b. If women are "liberated," does this mean that they will dominate men?

    c. Is the domination of men the goal of today's movement?

    d. Are women today accepting marriage as only one of many options open to them?

    e. What place does virginity have in today's world? Does it have any "market value"?

B. The thirties.

Assignment: Read "Women Workers through the Depression" by Lorine Pruett (TAW—WWS, pp. 27-28). Questions:

1. What was the effect of the depression on the movement for women's equality and on the possible new life styles for women?

2. Compare Ms. Pruett and the suffragists on the question of the vote's significance for changing the role of women.

3. Compare the views of Ms. Pruett and the Fitzgerald flapper regarding the responsibilities of the "emancipated woman."

C. The forties.
Assignment: Read "The Postwar Years" (WAL, pp. 154-158); and "The American Family—1947" (TAW—WWS, pp. 168-170). Discussion of the dramatic change in women's roles between 1940 and 1947.

D. The fifties.
Assignment: Read "The Rise of the Feminine Mystique" (TAW—WWS, pp. 170-174). Discussion of the "feminine mystique" today. Visit from a local consciousness-raising group.

IX. The Current Feminist Movement

Note: All of the following filmstrips are part of the series called *The Silenced Majority,* available from Media Plus.

A. "Liberation Now," a filmstrip survey of the past and present feminist movements in the United States. Discussion of similarities and differences.

B. "Women, Jobs and the Law," a filmstrip presenting the problems of economic and legal discrimination experienced by U. S. women. Questions:
   1. What are the legal implications for women who marry—with special regard to the use of their husband's name, question of property rights and place of residence?
   2. Should the law restrict women's rights after marriage? Discuss.
   3. Are such laws necessary to protect women and to strengthen the institution of marriage?

C. Assignment: Read "The Equal Rights Amendment: What's In It for You?" by Ann Scott, *Ms.* (July 1972). Questions:
   1. Are you in favor of or opposed to this amendment; Why?
   2. What psychological and moral effects might the passage of this amendment have on men and women?

D. "Women and Education," a filmstrip on the subject of sex-role stereotypes as a barrier to equality of education for women. Questions:
   1. What experiences have you had that verify the filmstrip's portrait?
   2. How might men benefit from equality between the sexes in jobs, education and interpersonal relations?
   3. What might society be like if children were taught that there are no intellectual and emotional differences between men and women? What would "feminine" and "masculine" mean in such a society? How would we dress, speak, walk, work and think about ourselves?

E. "This Ad Insults Women," a filmstrip on sexist advertising. Questions:
   1. How important is the media's construction of images in our society?
   2. Assuming that feminists are successful, how might companies change their advertising for such commodities as detergents, deodorants, airline travel?
   3. Assignment: Choose three ads and decide whether they are insulting toward women. Bring them to class and prepare to explain your point of view.

F. "Rapping with the Feminists," a filmstrip interview with Kate Millett, Megan Terry, Florynce Kennedy and Jacqueline Ceballos. Questions:
   1. What interested you most about the views of these feminists?

2. Does language oppress women? Explain your views?

3. How does Florynce Kennedy feel about being both black and female? Do you think her view is a reasonable one?

X. Marriage and Motherhood

Note: The class chose to pursue these two topics as a culminating experience of the course.

A. Marriage.

Assignment: Read "The Dynamics of Marriage and Motherhood" (*Sisterhood Is Powerful*, pp. 46-52); "The Case Against Marriage" by Caroline Bird, *New Woman* (September 1971), p. 30; "Marriage Documents" (*Up from the Pedestal*, pp. 148-150); "I Want a Wife" by Judy Syfers, *Ms.* (December 1971); "How to Write Your Own Marriage Contract" by Susan Edmiston, *Ms.* (December 1971). Exercises:

1. Write your own marriage contract which contains: principles upon which the marriage is to be based; individual responsibilities; methods for changing the contract; time limit. Try to make certain that your contract meets your needs and overcomes the weaknesses pointed out in the readings above.

2. Using two well-thought out arguments, either defend or reject the idea of the marriage contract as a new, effective force for making marriage meet the changing roles of women and men.

B. Housework.

Assignment: Read "I Want a Wife" by Judy Syfer (see above); "Women Are Household Slaves" (*Up from the Pedestal*, pp. 346-353); "The Value of Housework" by Ann Scott, *Ms.* (July 1972); "Confessions of a Househusband" by Joel Roache, *Ms.* (November 1972). Questions:

1. What is your view of housework? Who does the housework in your home?

2. How might attitudes toward housework be changed if Ms. Scott's ideas were carried out?

3. In what ways were Mr. Roache's experiences similar to and/or different from the experiences of the women who analyzed housework?

4. How would you deal with housework if you subscribed to the criticisms of its present traditional arrangement in most homes?

C. Motherhood.

Assignment: Read "Dynamics of Motherhood" (*Sisterhood*, pp. 52ff.); "Childless by Choice" by Susan B. Wright, *New Woman* (September 1971). Questions:

1. What factors would you weigh in making a decision about whether to have children? about when to have them?

2. What would having children bring to your life?

3. What sort of a life might you expect were you to have no children?

4. What difficulties might having or not having children bring to your life?

XI. Final Reaction Paper

Describe how you have been affected by the readings and discussions, films, speakers and your own projects. Comment on your attitudes about such areas as: parents; marriage; equal rights; social change; other males/females; love, dating, sex; housework; feminists; children; your future.

Lois F. Yatzeck
Social Studies
Kaukauna High School
Kaukauna, Wisc./1970-73

WOMEN IN HISTORY

Course History

I have been teaching a nine-week unit on "Women in History" in the Social Studies Department at Kaukauna High School since the fall of 1970. The initial enrollment was predominantly female, with two entirely female classes, but by the spring of 1973 the ratio was four to three, female to male students. Fifteen students seems to be an optimal class size. I initiated the course because I was asked to teach what I wanted to. Students chose to take the course, among seven or eight others offered during each class hour, for the usual reasons students choose courses: it looked easy, I was a new teacher and they had some interest in the subject.

Purpose

As a teacher, I hoped:
—to explore what women's role has been in history.
—to explore why it has been that way; what have been the factors in changing it.
—to encourage the women and men in my classes to look critically at their behavior and life expectations, to see if they wouldn't want to do things differently.
—to encourage dialogue and meaningful interaction between the females and males in the class.
I was also pursuing my own questions about woman's role.

I. Introduction—Warm-up

1. Organize class into couples and groups (*Herstory,* a game described in Resources below).
2. Get acquainted by nicknaming each other.
3. Interview each other (in couples) about Equal Rights Amendment.
4. Male-Female survey *(Herstory).*
5. Essay on an ordinary day in one's life ten years from now: include encounter with most important male and female in one's life at that time.
6. Draw stick images of one's relation to the opposite sex; one's relation to the ideal of one's own sex.
7. Write: What does it mean to be a woman? What does it mean to be a man? Discuss in groups/ come up with group statement.

II. Images of Women

1. Reading assignment on "Images of Women" (in ancient religion and mythology: my own essays—see description in Classwork and Assignments below).
2. Answer question: What positive and negative (constructive and destructive) characteristics do women have—according to the articles?

3. Read and discuss image of women (and men) in biblical account of Adam and Eve.
4. Role-play: Single girls ask boys for date (in groups); boy's steady confronts boy for going out with another woman; interview POW wife who has been waiting for husband to come back for six years (has own job and possibility for advancement); POW, returned, wants to move to new job for self.
5. Discuss in class: cultural patterns, basic nature of men and women.

III. Women in Primitive Society

1. Discuss why people marry.
2. Assign reading: "Women in Primitive Societies" (my essay).
3. Answer question: What is the relationship of men and women in primitive society? Why? Why do people marry in primitive society?
4. Have students work on worksheet and do research on different tribal patterns in polygamous groups (two or three girls to a boy or vice-versa). Evaluate advantages and disadvantages of experience.
5. Discuss hypothesis: Men and women were treated as equally important in primitive societies, although they had definite assigned roles.
6. Film on Stone Age Cave Men (TV).

IV. Women and Ancient Civilizations

1. Assign reading: "Women in Ancient Civilizations" (my essay).
2. Answer question: What were main reasons for marriage in Greece and Rome? Compare roles of women in Greece and Rome.
3. Discuss: Is our own society patriarchal? Why? How did it come about?
4. Read a Christian marriage ceremony (role-play).
5. Discuss why have a ceremony; what's involved in marriage commitment; at what point would you divorce?

V. Changing Status of American Women

1. Have all students change partners: Divorce; note how they feel about "divorce." Write new "marriage" agreement; discuss.
2. Read: "Changing Status of American Women" (my essay).
3. Answer question: How has her role changed in history? What are the reasons?
4. List famous non-American women and what they have done.
5. List famous American women and what they have done.

VI. Independent Research Projects on American Women

VII. Small Group Discussions
(on questions that students wanted to ask each other)

VIII. Women in American History/Boy vs. Girl Contest
(at this point we used Seneca Falls Convention material most effectively)

IX. Final Exam

Classwork and Assignments

The first time I taught the course, I had students write papers on women from different eras in history; had the rest of the students read them; supplemented this with lectures based on my own reading. The papers were remarkably good and the students enjoyed the course. By the second time I taught the unit, in the spring of 1970, I had prepared four eight-page papers on women from different eras in history. They were titled "Images of Women," "Women in Primitive Societies," "Women in Ancient Civilizations" and "The Changing Status of American Women." In the first paper, I emphasized early beliefs about woman's sexual nature and "magical" fertility, her role as "Mother Earth," her various aspects as creator, craftswoman, warrior, source of wisdom and the Great Mother. The second paper argues basically that women were treated reasonably well in primitive societies because their labor was valuable to the survival of the family unit. The third paper explores the rise of patriarchy and suggests that changing from an agricultural society in which women provided the necessities of life produced a change in the status of women. The fourth paper traces the changing role of women in America, with major increases in opportunity coming as the result of the wars. I also used a student paper on women's liberation.

Students were responsible for understanding the ideas in the papers as well as for an independent research project. I broke the class into two or three groups for weekly discussions. In-class activity also included role-playing.

During the second year, I used the papers again, assigned an independent research project, but also asked the students to choose any topic related to sexual roles that interested them and to lead a group discussion on that topic. I also tried to include more discussion on male roles and images, since the number of males in the class had increased. The group discussions during this second year of the course were its most exciting aspect: women and men hammering at each other about abortion or behavior in the back seats of cars. Some surprising reversals in attitudes were expressed. Some boys were far more ready to have girls get involved in politics than the girls were. I also experienced a strong challenge from one fellow who felt that my emphasis on having women have equal opportunities in jobs was taking away from the value and dignity that women already possess in the home. I had to acknowledge that women's liberation was not simply about women having jobs, but that they should experience worth and dignity in whatever they choose to do.

Resources

Resources used by students for independent research included: *Ms.; Masculine/Feminine: Readings in Sexual Mythology and the Liberation of Women,* Betty and Theodore Roszak, eds. (Harper and Row, 1969); *Up from the Pedestal,* Aileen S. Kraditor, ed. (Quadrangle, 1968); *Up Against the Wall, Mother,* Elsie Adams and Mary Louise Briscoe, eds. (Glencoe Press, 1971); *The Feminine Mystique,* Betty Friedan (Dell, 1963, 1970); and various editions of *American Heritage.* Materials used in class included: Helen Reddy's record, "I Am Woman"; "It Happened," a film about an unexpected pregnancy; and a film about abortion. We also discussed the television program, "Stone Age Cave Men," and the results of attitude surveys devised by some of the students.

The last time I taught the course I also used *Herstory,* a simulation game prepared by Interact ($10.00 from Box 262, Lakeside, Calif. 92040). While I was not always in tune with these materials, I was often instructed by the techniques of *Herstory* and used many of the materials and suggestions to good advantage.

We had a problem with one book, *Our Bodies, Ourselves,* by the Boston Women's Health Collective (Simon and Schuster, 1973), a handbook on women's sexuality and health. In 1971-72 when it provoked extremely negative community reaction, the Social Studies Department concluded that the book challenged the mores of the community so strongly that it was not worth the struggle to insist upon using it. I haven't used it since, though I consider the book a valuable resource.

Evaluation

The first time I taught the course, the papers were remarkably good and the students seemed to enjoy the course. Three students definitely changed their ideas about babies, careers and life styles. I felt also that one girl's relationships with others definitely improved. What I did not expect (or hope for) was that hostilities between the sexes would become more evident, as they did. So for some students, participation and interest were different from that in other classes, while for others it was just another course. Role-playing, some class discussions and the small group discussions led by students were the most effective activities. And finally, while I didn't intend the course to be "feminist," it inevitably was: I feel strongly that women have an independent role to play and the students picked up my attitude pretty quickly.

My department (Social Studies) was all male before I was hired, so that reaction to the course was, at least in part, also reaction to me. I experienced both interest and amusement. From the first, some male teachers have come into the class on various occasions. Since the issue we face is not only how women see and experience their roles, but how men see and experience theirs, I have become convinced of the need to deal as fully with the male role as with the female one. Only I can't do it. Thus I see the importance of having male perspective presented. Four of us are now working on an umbrella course called "Search for Identity" which will provide the structure for examining both female and male roles.

Courses dealing directly with sex-role development are badly needed and would probably be more crucial even than women in history. I plan to revise my course considerably before teaching it again. I think I can get at the issues better by looking at actual accounts of how women live in different cultures. Now I think the course needs to rest; it needs a new emphasis and better material.

I want to say an additional word about why I have taught this course. Being a woman has always been a problem to me. There was even a time when I felt I was the embodiment of the suffering of women during our time. Trained to achieve like a man, I was not accepted into a man's profession (the Christian ministry). Called to become an individual, I failed as a wife. I feel I spent most of my married life absolutely torn in two between my desires to be a good wife (and always failing) and my search for personal fulfillment in a profession (never achieving it). Now, two years after a divorce that I was reluctant to seek, I have a sense of personal peace and perspective that would make it possible to be a wife again, if that should ever come about, though it is not necessary.

I don't blame my former husband nor my parents nor "society" for my past unhappiness. I was simply unable to define myself, make a harmony within myself. Now I can; and I feel I have much to give to my world, perhaps especially to other women.

Final Exam

Part I Your Life (30 minutes, 5 points for each answer):
1. Review your description of a day in your life ten years from now. How would you live it differently if I were to ask you to describe that day again?
2. Think of a possible situation ten years from now in which you would meet the most important male in your life. What would you do and say?
3. Think of a possible situation ten years from now in which you would meet the most important female in your life. What would you do and say?
4. In what ways do you imagine you will be dependent upon this important male?
5. In what ways do you imagine you will be dependent upon this important female?
6. In what ways will the above-described important people be dependent upon you?
7. Review the conversations you had with them. Do they (the conversations) in any way reflect their need of you or your need of them? Should they?

Part II Woman (10 minutes, 5 points for each answer):
8. Read "I Am Woman." Comment on how you feel about the ideas of this song by Helen Redding.
9. Is your reaction to the song consistent with or contradictory to the ideas you expressed in questions 4, 5 and 6 above? Explain your answer.

Part III Women Today (20 minutes, 1 point for each idea expressed):
10. Women, because of their ability to give birth, have been powerful sex symbols through the ages.
    a. Give examples of ways women can use their life-giving capabilities constructively besides bearing and raising their own children.
    b. Give examples of ways women can use their life or sexual power destructively.
11. In some primitive societies, women are treated well. In others, they are treated badly. Yet in all primitive societies they play an important role in keeping their families fed and clothed. Consider the American woman today.
    a. Does she play an important role in our society? Explain your answer.
    b. Is she treated well or badly? Explain your answer.
12. The bearing and raising of children has been a constant responsibility of women from ancient to modern times. Yet women have been able to do other things as well. Some have ruled countries.
    a. What qualities do women have which make them as capable as men of being political leaders?
    b. What qualities of women would make you hesitate to vote them into political office?
13. American women have achieved in many areas of life outside of the home, yet many still feel their place is in the home. Presuming that this attitude won't change a great deal in the next twenty years,
    a. What kind of education do you think you want your daughters to have?
    b. What kind of education do you think would best prepare you for your role in life?

2
Literature

Dorothy Burman
English
Stuyvesant High School
New York, N. Y./1975-76

THE FEMININE IMAGE IN LITERATURE

Readings:
Woman in Sexist Society, Vivian Gornick and Barbara K. Moran, eds. (Basic Books, 1971).
The Feminine Image in Literature, Barbara Warren, ed. (Hayden Book Co., 1973).
A Doll's House, Henrik Ibsen.
Ethan Frome, Edith Wharton.
Plays by and about Women, Victoria Sullivan and James Hatch, eds. (Vintage Books,
    1974). Includes *The Children's Hour,* Lillian Hellman; *The Women,* Claire Boothe;
    Wine in the Wilderness, Alice Childress.
Women and Literature, an annotated bibliography of women writers (available from
    Sense and Sensibility, 57 Ellery St., Cambridge, Mass.).

Audio-Visual:
Man and Woman: Myths and Stereotypes in Literature and the Arts, a sound-slide set
    (available from The Center for Humanities, Inc., 2 Holland Ave., White Plains, N.Y.).

This is a fifteen-week course offered as an elective in the senior year. The students take
an exam in English and math to enter this specialized public science high school. Thus,
the class consists of average to very bright youngsters. The course, with suitable varia-
tions would also be appropriate for juniors in high school or students in college. Both
young men and young women have been in the class.

Objectives

The course was instituted two years ago because of the teacher's growing awareness of
the lack of female authors represented in the standard high school (and college) curriculum, as well as the unrealistic portrayals of women in many of the books the students
read ("perfect" Lucy in *A Tale of Two Cities;* "patient" Penelope in *The Odyssey,* etc.).

There were also many student protests about boys having better gym facilities than girls
in the school; a group called "Students against Sexism" was formed. Stuyvesant itself
had been an all male school until a few years ago when one assertive young woman brought
a legal suit that made the school coeducational. Thus, the major objective of the course
included an attempt to raise students' awareness of female (and also male) stereotypes,
primarily as seen in literature, but also as experienced in the world in which we are living.

Course Sequence

1. Introductory consciousness-raising including a personal survey with such questions as,
"Where did you get your last name? Why wasn't it from your mother? What books by
female authors have you read as required works in school? What women writers can you
name before the eighteenth century?"

2. Definitions of key words to be used during the term such as sexism, stereotypes, male chauvinism, feminism, etc. Statistics about the good and bad news about women in different careers.

3. How do you see yourself? An analysis of so-called male and female traits taken from "Clinical Judgments of Mental Health," Broverman, Broverman, Vogel, et al.

4. Alternatives to sexist language. Do we talk about a lady lawyer? An old maid? Do we say everyone should bring his book? (What about *her?*)

5. Discussion of statements often heard that "Women are naturally this or that . . ." Excerpts (mainly taken from *Woman in Sexist Society*) are read and discussed to refute or support these statements. For example: "Men and women are naturally biologically different" ("Psychology Constructs the Female," Naomi Weisstein); "Patriarchies are the natural form of society" ("Women in Other Cultures," Ruby Leavitt); "The natural role for a woman is to be a wife and mother" (*The Feminine Mystique,* Betty Friedan); "Men are naturally greater artists, and anyway there are no great women artists" ("Why Are There No Great Women Artists?" Linda Nochlin).

6. Students start to compile a journal to be handed in at the end of the term stressing the image of women and men in popular culture (the media, etc.). It includes examples of sexism or the lack of it in cartoons, ads, greeting cards, songs, TV programs, movies and live theatre. Students are asked to rewrite or compose their own nursery rhymes, fairy tales or song lyrics that are nonsexist.

7. Each student writes a letter to *Ms.* or some other magazine telling about his or her own experiences with sexism in school, with finding their lives limited because they are male or female, or on similar topics.

8. Each student chooses a full-length work of nonfiction or a collection of essays for a book review and possible oral report. (Source of bibliography: *Sexism in Education,* Emma Willard Task Force on Education, P.O. Box 14229, Minneapolis, Minn.).

9. The class is divided into coed groups of five or six which meet about once every two weeks during class time for discussion of consciousness-raising questions. (Source of topics: "Consciousness-Raising for Young Women Ages 14-19"—also fine for young men with some changes—Greater Champaign Area Chapter, National Organization for Women, 809 S. Fifth, Champaign, Ill. Topics for mature students at a college level available also.)

10. Background material and brief survey on the actual position of women in history starting with biblical times. (Source: *Women out of History: A Herstory Anthology; Emerging Woman.)* Discussion includes revolts against sexism starting in ancient Greece and Rome; matriarchies; the feminist movement in America, its early roots and modern rebirth; women in math and science.

11. Chronological overview of the feminine image in literature. (Major source: *The Troublesome Helpmate: A History of Misogyny in Literature,* plus teacher's own choices of literature, mimeographed for class use.) Reading and discussion of the following: the two possible versions of the creation of man and woman from Genesis in the Old Testament; proverbs from the Book of Proverbs showing how women were mainly either put on a pedestal or feared as a temptress; excerpt from St. Paul; excerpts from

The Odyssey and Greek myths showing the double standard for Odysseus and Penelope, the reasons for Hera's jealousy; Pandora's being given responsibility for evil coming into the world; from Chaucer, a comparison of the patient, submissive Griselda in "The Clerk's Tale" with the assertive, worldly Wife of Bath; examples of either the idealization of women or the extreme opposite in writers such as Donne, Herrick and Shakespeare; the old maid stereotype from characters in Gilbert and Sullivan operettas (Katisha in *The Mikado,* Ruth in *Pirates of Penzance*); quotes from Freud and Philip Wylie (*Generation of Vipers* and "mommism"). Wherever possible, both positive and negative portrayals of women are noted such as the mainly positive views of strong women like Ruth and Judith in the Old Testament and the strong women in many Greek plays such as *Electra, Medea* and *Antigone.*

12. Discussion of works of literature from the anthology, *The Feminine Image in Literature.* The editor has chosen works of poetry, short stories and essays (mainly by male writers reflecting that until the nineteenth century there were few recognized women who were published, with the exception of Jane Austen). The book begins with women portrayed as almost totally unreal and idealized ("La Belle Dame Sans Merci" by Keats; "Lygeia" by Poe) until the last section of the anthology where women are portrayed as androgenous human beings. Some works included: "Miss Temptation," Kurt Vonnegut; "The Strength of God," Sherwood Anderson; "Lappin and Lapinova," Virginia Woolf; "The Birthmark," Nathaniel Hawthorne.

13. Reading and discussion of several full-length works: *Ethan Frome,* Edith Wharton; *A Doll's House,* Henrik Ibsen; *The Children's Hour,* Lillian Hellman; *The Women,* Claire Boothe; *Wine in the Wilderness,* Alice Childress.

14. Each student chooses one full-length work (novel or play) by a man or a woman, for a term paper which includes such topics as: actual historical position of women at the time the work portrays; events in the life of the author that might have influenced his or her attitudes towards women; how the major female character sees herself; how the major male character sees her; is each one a stereotype of a well-rounded character? Does either one have a traditional male or female role? Does either one revolt against this role? How? (Sources of reading suggested for students: *Women and Literature; Images of Women in Literature,* pp. 428-432; *Sexism in Education,* pp. 54-55.)

Further Reading for Students and Teachers

Anthologies:

Adams, Elsie, and Briscoe, Mary Louise, eds. *Up Against the Wall Mother.* New York: Glencoe Press, 1971.

Berg, Stephen, and Marks, S. J., eds. *About Women: An Anthology of Contemporary Fiction, Poetry and Essays.* New York: Fawcett, 1973.

Cade, Toni, ed. *The Black Woman.* New York: Mentor, 1970.

Cahill, Susan, ed. *Women and Fiction: Short Stories by and about Women.* New York: Mentor Books, 1975.

Euripides. *Four Plays about Women.* New York: Washington Square Press, 1973. Includes *Medea, Helen, Trojan Women, Electra.*

Ferguson, Mary Anne, ed. *Images of Women in Literature.* Boston: Houghton Mifflin, 1973.

Kirschner, Linda, and Folsom, Marcia, eds. *By Women: An Anthology of Literature.* Boston: Houghton Mifflin, 1976.

Kriegel, Harriet, ed. *Women in Drama.* New York: Mentor, 1975.

Nonfiction:

Dore, Anita Wilkes,*The Emerging Woman.* New York: Mentor, 1970.

Forfreedom, Ann, ed. *Women out of History: A Herstory Anthology.* Los Angeles, Calif., P. O. Box 25514.

Rogers, Katherine. *The Troublesome Helpmate: A History of Misogyny in Literature.* Seattle: University of Washington Press, 1966.

Stanford, Barbara. *On Being Female.* New York: Washington Square Press, 1974.

Other sources:

The Feminist Press, SUNY/College at Old Westbury, Box 334, Old Westbury, N. Y. 11568. Send for complete catalogue.

National Organization for Women, National Public Information Office, 47 E. 19 St., New York, N. Y. 10003. Send for list of slide shows and films from NOW chapters.

Women's Action Alliance, 370 Lexington Ave., New York, N. Y. 10017. Send for list of publications.

Women's Bureau Employment Standards Administration, U. S. Department of Labor, Washington, D. C. 20210. Send for list of publications.

Mary Fontaine
English
Milford High School
Milford, Ohio/1973-74

WOMEN IN LITERATURE

Texts:
Lysistrata
The Stepford Wives
The Taming of the Shrew
The Feminine Mystique
A Doll's House
Tess of the D'Urbervilles
Selected short stories and poems

Films and Tapes:
In addition, I showed the film version of *A Doll's House;* the recent television production of the same play; a video tape of a discussion on feminism called "A Woman's Place" (an ABC television special); and a short but excellent film called "Anything You Want to Be" (New Day Films).

As co-coordinator of the Cincinnati NOW Education Committee, and "resident feminist" at the Milford High School, I decided in the winter of 1973 to organize and propose a women's studies course. Getting permission from the administration to offer such a course proved difficult but not impossible.

Thirty female students, eleventh- and twelfth-graders, elected to take the proposed course. (The school's total student population is 1,020—ninety percent white.)

Objectives

The stated objectives and description of the course: Students will have the opportunity to examine the portrayal of women in literature of the past and present. A minimum of four compositions will be required. This course will be aimed at analyzing the portrayal of women as characters in literature. Their strengths, weaknesses and abilities will be examined as well as the extent to which this portrayal is influenced by, reflects and influences the woman's role and status in society. The study will proceed chronologically from a play by Aristophanes (*Lysistrata*), through Victorian literature (*Tess of the D'Urbervilles*), to modern fiction and nonfiction.

The real purpose of my course, however, was consciousness-raising, particularly concerning the misrepresentation of women in literature and the stereotyped portrayal of women characters. It was, therefore, a feminist course designed to create an awareness of sexism and even misogyny in literature. If biased, it was so intentionally, in an attempt to counteract years of traditional teaching in which women are either ignored or misrepresented in literature. (One project which worked well was aimed at illustrating that women are usually expected to identify with and see themselves portrayed through male protagonists in literature. When women are the protagonists, males rarely take the work seriously or identify with the female protagonists. We used a story in which all the protagonists were male, and as a class project, rewrote it so that all were female, and then tried the work on male students in other classes.)

I honestly attempted to be objective: I allowed my students to learn from the literature rather than from me. This approach seemed to be a good one, since it relieved the defensiveness of the students. I encouraged class discussion and questions about "women's lib." Because there were no male students in the class, the women seemed to feel less inhibited and were eager to relate characters and situations from various works to their own lives. I used this approach, therefore, whenever possible.

Results

Most of the students who elected to take the course were either unaware of or uninformed about feminism; many were mildly curious; and some were openly hostile. But by the end of the quarter, only one remained opposed to the idea of equality between the sexes. Others were either sympathetic to the women's movement or interested in becoming actively involved in feminist causes and activities.

I encouraged my students to participate in discussions and projects and to become more aware of attitudes towards women as they exist in school and the wider society outside. Attitudes and behaviors did change as students consciously observed sexism in action: they became aware of discrimination and they learned about the meaning and goals of feminism.

Several of the other teachers have reported noting an increased participation in class activities among the students who took my course. They are less likely to overlook or accept the slighting of women either by classmates, teachers, administrators or textbooks. The number of research papers and independent study projects related to feminism has increased significantly as well; and a group of women students asked the men's health class to permit a panel of women to observe and participate in their discussion of females, sex and related topics.

Most of what I attempted to do was successful. The only significant change I will make for next year's class will be to encourage some males to elect the course. Perhaps the female students will be able to convince them better than I.

My main advice to teachers attempting to initiate such courses into their school systems is to be persistent. The administration was reluctant and assumed that there would be little student interest. The community reaction to my course was mild surprise—neither negative nor positive reactions have been brought to my attention, and this is a conservative community.

My main advice about teaching the course is to allow the literature to work for you. When students discover the poor portrayal of women in literature, they will not need to be told about it by you. The discovery is a meaningful one for them, and you can help them to relate the female characters' lives to real-life situations.

Suggestions for Quarter Projects

Each student will be required to prepare a quarter project to be shared with the rest of the class. You are not limited to the suggestions below; however, each student must hand in a description of her project by November 19. Once you have declared your choice, you may not change it. Contrary to popular belief, women *can* make up their minds!

All projects will be presented in written and in oral form and may be visual if desired. Projects are due two weeks before the end of the quarter. You will be given time in class to work on them, and you will be expected to turn in a progress schedule each week explaining in detail what you have accomplished during that week.

1. Read one of the following books and prepare a written report on it:
   Beauvoir, Simone de. *The Second Sex.* New York: Bantam, 1970. Includes a section on "The Myth of Women in Five Authors"—Montherlant, D. H. Lawrence, Claudel, Breton and Stendhal.
   Fiedler, Leslie A. *Love and Death in the American Novel.* New York: Dell, 1960. Important criticism of American male novelists. The book deals with their immaturity—that is, their inability to deal with their sexuality, their relationships with women and their obsession with death.
   Gagen, Jean Elizabeth. *The New Woman: Her Emergence in English Drama 1600-1730.* New York: Twayne, 1954. A study of female characters in English plays and their relationship to real women.
   Hinkley, Laura L. *Ladies of Literature.* New York: Hastings House, 1946. Information about Fanny Burney, Jane Austen, Charlotte and Emily Brontë, Elizabeth Barrett Browning and George Eliot. The book is not as bad as the title.
   Howe, Florence, and Bass, Ellen, eds. *No More Masks: An Anthology of Poems by Women.* New York: Anchor Press/Doubleday, 1973. Eighty-seven twentieth-century American poets and an introduction about the evolving poetic consciousness of American women poets.
   Klein, Viola. *The Feminine Character: History of an Ideology.* New York: International University, 1948. "The hypothesis of this study has been the view that the social and cultural situation at any given time is expressed in ideologies and reflected in all products of the human mind: in art, in science, in literature." Extremely interesting.
   Martin, Wendy, ed. *The American Sisterhood: Writings of the Feminist Movement from Colonial Times to the Present.* New York: Harper and Row, 1972. Selection of materials on the intellectual, political and social questions raised by both feminist movements.
   McCarthy, Briget G. *Women Writers: Their Contribution to the English Novel.* Cork: Cork University Press, 1948. Volume I or Volume II.
   McCarthy, Mary. *On the Contrary: Articles of Belief.* New York: Noonday, 1962. A collection of critical essays on "Politics and the Social Scene," women's magazines, women's colleges and "Literature and the Arts."
   Millett, Kate. *Sexual Politics.* New York: Doubleday, 1970. An explanation of male-female power-structured relationships, with examples from literature.
   Papishvily, Helen Waite. *All the Happy Endings.* Port Washington: Kinnikat Press, 1956. A study of the popular novels women wrote in the nineteenth century and

how these books helped women at home develop "survival techniques" that are still considered part of female culture.

Rogers, Katherine. *The Troublesome Helpmate.* Seattle: University of Washington Press, 1966. A survey of both direct and indirect manifestations in literature of hatred, fear or contempt for women from Biblical and classical times to the twentieth century.

Schneiderman, Beth Kline, ed. *By and about Women: An Anthology of Short Fiction.* New York: Harcourt Brace Jovanovich, 1973. Nineteen modern short stories.

Violette, Augusta Genevieve. *Economic Feminism in American Literature Prior to 1848.* New York: B. Franklin, 1971. Feminism in the writings of Thomas Paine, Sarah Grimké, Margaret Fuller, Emerson and others.

2. Analyze the portrayal of females in a significant number of children's books. Your report may take the form of a research paper or a visual project with a written and oral explanation.

3. Conduct a well-researched, documented study of sexism as it may or may not exist in the high school. This study must be conducted intelligently, maturely and objectively. Your report may take the form of a research paper or a visual project with a written and oral explanation.

4. Conduct an in-depth study of women as portrayed in some aspect of the media. Your report may take the form of a research paper or a visual project with a written and oral explanation.

5. An original writing (short story, poems or play) which reflects a positive image of a woman protagonist. *Careful:* Do not attempt this unless you have a background in creative writing or experience in writing original works.

6. A research paper which makes an in-depth study of the portrayal of women in a particular author's works.

7. An in-depth study of the mythological origins of sexism.

8. A research paper examining the role of women in a particular period of history.

9. An in-depth study of the role of women in a culture other than our own, for example "Women in China."

10. An in-depth study of the Women's Movement—this can be either an historical study of a study of the present-day movement and should include such things as objectives, methods and degree of success.

11. Take an existing work of literature which you feel portrays women poorly and re-write it so that this portrayal is positive. *Careful:* This requires much more than a simple role reversal!

12. An in-depth study of the role, purpose and value of women as viewed by religion.

Study Questions on *A Doll's House*

1. Explain the "lark and squirrel" theme.
2. Discuss the relationship between Helmer and Nora.

3. "Poor Christine, you are a widow." "Poor thing . . . and he left you nothing." How does this exchange between Nora and Mrs. Linde explain the degree of attachment of Nora to those she loves, upon which the force of the resolution depends?

4. Discuss Helmer's character. Why is it important that he not be portrayed as a complete fool and villain?

5. "Christine! It's good to be alive and happy!" Why does Nora's joy of living become important in the play? What illustrations of this joy can you find?

6. "Whatever is dictated by love is right." Discuss this as the basis for Nora's logic throughout the play.

7. Nora will tell Helmer about the money "Someday . . . when I am no longer as nice-looking as I am now."

8. How does Nora's conversation with Mrs. Linde about her "secret" reveal the main theme of the play?

9. Discuss the idea of "moral disease" in the play.

10. Discuss Nora's relationship with her children.

11. When does the climax of the play occur?

12. What is the contrast between what Nora believes she has done for Helmer and what he believes she has done?

13. "Nora! —No, I must read it once again—Yes, it is true! I am saved! Nora, I am saved!" "And I?" "You too, of course . . ."

14. When does Helmer *really* love Nora? Why does he love her *then?*

15. "Nora's deserting her family was an irresponsible act of a giddy, immature female." Defend or reject.

16. Helmer asks Nora, at one point, where Nora would be financially if he were not there. What is her reply and how does that idea contribute to her leaving?

17. Up to the time of the conflict, what did Nora see her role as being in the family? Does she later see that role as being unworthy of her?

18. What is the "miracle of miracles" to which Torvald refers at the end of the play?

19. Why does Nora eagerly anticipate the "miracle" to which she refers in the play? What would that miracle do for her? What is the basis for it?

20. What is Ibsen criticizing in the play? What is the main theme?

21. In what ways did Nora sacrifice her honor for Torvald?

22. What is the purpose of introducing Dr. Rank to the play?

23. Speculate as to what happens after Nora leaves.

24. Do you think Nora was right and justified in leaving? Explain your answer thoroughly.

25. If Nora had not left, what do you think she should have done? Would anything have changed?

26. Do you think Torvald was sincere in his sorrow and promises at the end of the play? Why or why not?

27. What similarities can you see between the play and real life today?

Renee Hausmann
English
The Madeira School
Greenway, Va./1973-74

WOMEN IN THE NOVEL OF CHARACTER

Texts:

Austen, Jane. *Emma.* Boston: Houghton Mifflin (Riverside edition), 1957.

Hurston, Zora Neale. *Their Eyes Were Watching God.* New York: Fawcett World Library, 1965.

Schneiderman, Beth Kline, ed. *By and about Women: An Anthology of Short Fiction.* New York: Harcourt Brace Jovanovich, 1973.

Spark, Muriel. *The Prime of Miss Jean Brodie.* New York: Dell, 1961.

Wharton, Edith. *The House of Mirth.* New York: New American Library (Signet Edition), 1964.

Woolf, Virginia. *Mrs. Dalloway.* New York: Harcourt, Brace & World, 1953.

Introduction

The Madeira School is a private girls' preparatory school in Virginia, with an enrollment of more than 300. The students are largely from upper-middle socio-economic backgrounds, and there is a small minority of black students. The school and the students themselves feel that they must acquire a relatively classical background to insure entrance into the highly competitive Ivy League colleges. Under this pressure, students frequently prefer that their courses familiarize them with the past, "their heritage," rather than confront contemporary issues. For example, although the history department includes courses in political science and economics, the school offers no sociology courses. The English curriculum as a whole is a very conventional one. Freshmen and sophomores study mythology (primarily Greek), *The Odyssey,* Shakespeare, and some novels and plays of accepted stature (e.g., *The Scarlet Letter, The Glass Menagerie, Hard Times*). During their junior and senior years, these young women enjoy an elective system for their English courses. The first half of the junior year is devoted to American literature and the second half to courses such as the nineteenth-century novel.

During my first year at Madeira, in contrast to this pattern of the curriculum, I suggested a semester course entitled "Women in the Novel of Character." Other offerings for seniors that year (1973-74) included "American Writers in Exile," a seminar on James Joyce, "Modern Drama," and a seminar on nonfictional prose. The students' motivations behind enrolling in my course were by no means entirely feminist. A few students actually wanted a feminist approach to literary topics; several others were interested in women writers, although timidly rather than stridently. Many students, however, simply wanted to read fiction, and others were even opposed to a "women's liberation" focus. Working within this framework of skepticism and/or little interest, I structured the course as an investigation of the fictional portrayal of women by women in a traditionally academic way (tehnique, style, structure), while stimulating discussion of the possibilities for women presented in Western literature. Respecting the students' preferences and refusing to propagandize, I correctly assumed that the literature itself would raise essential issues in a nonrhetorical way. Feminist ends could be achieved without polemic. Students examined respected novels from a different perspective, forgetting the questions traditionally asked and asking their own.

The novels' central characters—Lily Bart, Emma Woodhouse, Janie Starks, Jean Brodie and Clarissa Dalloway—each search for a position in society that answers individual needs, allows personal integrity and stimulates creative self-expression. Each is thwarted; each comes to terms with this frustration in her highly individual way. Despite the different periods the novels represent, students were able to see similarities in the treatment of women as saleable commodities, as creatures whose most valuable asset is their appearance, and as persons who experience tremendous hardship if their self-expectations do not match the limited expectations of their society. Why, for example, students began to ask, about *The House of Mirth* (1905) and *Emma* (1816), do the male characters have such freedom to be nonconformist, impetuous, even irascible? Why are the repercussions for these men so slight? Lawrence Seldon, in *The House of Mirth*, need not feel compromised when Lily Bart is seen leaving his apartment; Frank Churchill, in *Emma,* is described as having a character marked by "vanity, extravagance, love of change, restlessness of temper..." (p. 157), but these defects are easily forgiven, even overlooked, in light of his charm. Yet Emma and Lily must content themselves with playing society's superficial games and are reproached, in Lily's case destroyed, when they tire of or transgress the rules. The society of Austen's Highbury is microcosmic, but its pettiness is magnified in Edith Wharton's New York.

Janie Starks, in *Their Eyes Were Watching God* (1937), like Lily Bart, is immediately established as an unusually vibrant, feeling woman. Nevertheless, for both of these characters, we are led to ask: What is the product of their creativity? What affirmation is there? Is it not possible to define oneself in any way but through or with a man? Jean Brodie in *The Prime of Miss Jean Brodie* (1961) represents a formidable woman who reverses society's standards and often takes the "male perspective." Poor Mr. Lowery, for example, after they have slept together, wants to marry her, to salvage his honor; Miss Brodie, however, refuses such preposterous behavior. She certainly approaches sex with a casualness and a calculation traditionally reserved for men. But Jean Brodie fails: her strong spirit distorts and destroys others and herself. Again, we ask why there is no affirmation. Is it because she ignores rather than transgresses society's standards that Miss Brodie is punished? Clarissa Dalloway in *Mrs. Dalloway* (1925), was perhaps the most complex character we studied, since Virginia Woolf does show Clarissa affirming and expressing her creative self through her party, the moments of recaptured time, a personal sense of time. Yet, one may see Clarissa as a dismal failure as a mother and her marriage as a hollow compromise of her own best self. We cannot help but wonder regretfully what Clarissa might have done or been had she had the strength not to marry. The young vital woman Clarissa recalls in her memories of the past has become a hostess, an incomplete person: "Every time she gave a party, she had this feeling of being something not herself." (p. 259).

Clarissa and Janie represent married women; Clarissa is the only character with children; Emma and Lily are constantly involved in schemes of marriage, their own and others; Jean Brodie is the only one who disdains the idea and institution. Yet, these characters have a frightening similarity in their mutual inability to attain any type of lasting self image; to achieve any personal integrity within society's boundaries; or to exert their imaginative natures in any but trivial, powerless ways. As the course progressed, students explored these similarities, critically questioned their origin (many wanted to conclude the frustration was due to personal weaknesses of the characters), and asked why women held no substantive power in the society. Obviously, discussions had to move between consideration of highly private problems and motivation of the characters and the public world of society's standards: we asked how the two interrelate.

Method and Purpose

Although we read a common body of works in "Women and the Novel of Character" for obvious reasons of discussion and analysis, students were encouraged to follow their own inclinations in written work, not limited to novels but extending to poetry and autobiography. I chose the five novels forming the nucleus of the course, and countless times I defended this choice to students and faculty alike. My colleagues challenged the quality of the writers themselves. Woolf and Austen, of course, posed no problems, but Wharton, Hurston and Sparks were accused of being "second rate." I pointed out that male writers whose position is clearly not among the great—Sinclair Lewis, for example—abound in various courses. Colleagues also disapproved of the "distorted perspective" and "imbalance" created by a course using women writers exclusively; here I pointed out that the curriculum at large is based on an imbalance of a male majority or totality. Students occasionally wondered about the validity of the course, since they were not familiar with all of the writers on the reading list; again, they were fearful that they were not sufficiently acquainted with the acknowledged "masters." Although I was able to answer these questions and doubts, I realize, especially among my colleagues, that I was not always able to quell them. The point to be made is that students can be taught to write coherently, to think critically and imaginatively, and to master skills of vocabulary, grammar, etc., using a reading list of writers other than Milton and Shakespeare. Furthermore I had to explain repeatedly that I was not opposed to or questioning the worth of traditional writers; I simply felt there was a significant aspect of experience being ignored by exclusive concentration on these men.

I wanted novels both by and about women for two distinct reasons. First, I realize that most curricula on both the high school and college level include few women writers, thus implying that the tradition of Western literature in which these students have grown up is a male tradition, the conclusion being that literary excellence is male. Although this educational imbalance is changing rapidly, the students at Madeira had, until this course, read only the Brontës, My Antonia and perhaps some poetry by Emily Dickinson. Most had never heard of Wharton, Hurston, Spark or the majority of writers on the attached bibliography. I feel that, as part of their education, students need to see the experience of women not only through male writers' interpretations, but from the perspective of women themselves, if only to have a basis for comparison. My second reason concerns a writer's identity: if students are to see their own work as serious, they benefit from studying the work of other women authors in terms of technique and style as well as in more psychological terms of confidence-building. The few who were writing poetry and fiction when they entered the course were stimulated to probe more deeply and develop a more distinctly individual style; the others were encouraged to begin writing. The results in both cases were not just heartening but exciting. (See the poetry at end of syllabus.) The students began to feel participants rather than spectators in the making of literature.

The discussions and essay topics in the course always centered on subjective interpretation of the novels, encouraging the students to consider the works in light of their own lives. To strengthen the students' analytical thinking and to sharpen their handling of traditional literary techniques, we considered formal matters of structure, style, narrative. Moreover, those students who were uncomfortable with an overtly feminist approach were assured that they were receiving the desired skills of literary analysis. Students wrote on a weekly basis: no exams were given. Interpretative essays included such topics as:

1. "There were moments when she [Lily Bart] was conscious of having to pay her way." *The House of Mirth.* Discuss the ways in which the novel is concerned with paying one's way.
2. A good deal of the moral passion of *Emma* arises from Austen's understanding of and feelings about the problems of women in her society. Explain.
3. Discuss why you feel Janie in *Their Eyes Were Watching God* is or is not a model for women. Is she an admirable character?
4. In *Mrs. Dalloway,* discuss the images of women. What options does Woolf see for women? What roles do they play? Consider other characters besides Clarissa and draw comparisons.

A second type of assignment encouraged freer, more imaginative writing but with a definite goal: students were asked to emulate the style or technique of the writer being studied. After reading *The House of Mirth,* students wrote a description demonstrating the interplay between mood and perception of setting. While studying *Emma,* students constructed their own dialogues somehow related to the novel. When they read *Mrs. Dalloway,* they experimented with the stream of consciousness. Such assignments provided a complementary approach to the critical expository essay, enabling the student both to understand the relationship of the writer to her material and to grapple with the literary techniques first hand.

A third part of my approach in this course involved a question-centered discussion. At the beginning, I provided general discussion and study question; by the end, students assumed the responsibility of writing their own. This method reinforced my contention that the literature should be approached through questions, that the literature is valuable when seen not simply answering but raising questions. The questioning approach is essential in any women's studies course where the literature often must be re-evaluated, where frequently the whole purpose is to reassess conventional, established views of the author's meaning. Again, discomfort was felt by some students who were accustomed to the security of preconceived discussion where the teacher asked set questions designed to establish a particular interpretation. Furthermore, the question approach was necessary in this course where each novel was examined from both the various characters' perspectives as well as the author's. What was Jane Austen saying about women and their role in society? Our interpretation of Emma herself is significant—what kind of a person is she, what are her motivations? But this interpretation pivots on Austen's attitude toward herself and women in her society. The dual perspective of women writers and women characters stimulated students to ask probing questions about the function of literature, to challenge the accepted critical views, to inquire into the authors' lives.

Individual Author Project

This questioning approach and the creative analytical balance culminated in an outside project in which each student chose one writer, read several of her works, inquired into her life, and wrote (1) a critical paper of five to seven pages, using no secondary sources; (2) an emulation of some aspect of her style; and (3) a creative response to the writer (see description and bibliography at end of syllabus). This project was assigned approximately six weeks before it was due; weekly writing assignments were suspended during the final few weeks. Nearly every student became deeply involved with her writer, and my primary function became to focus the work, to limit the reading possible during this time. Several students chose poets. Many ideas were initiated by stories in *By and about Women.* The efforts to emulate style were excellent: for example, a delightful short story caught the humor and characterization of Eudora Welty; another student captured Dorothy Parker's combination of pathos and cynicism through dialogue. One of the most sophisticated examples of student work I have ever encountered attempted Virginia Woolf's stream-of-consciousness technique, shattering time. I say "sophisticated" because this student, using personal material, demonstrated her growing ability to sublimate the personal into metaphor and simile—to create art. Very fine poetry resulted, and several students wrote elaborate diaries. Several students responded through painting and photography, one through an interpretive dance, another through a dramatic monologue.

This project contributed more than any other element to the students' interest in women writers and in their own writing. For most, the independence given them generated enthusiasm. After the projects were finished, each student reported her work to the class, very much in the fashion of a seminar group. She discussed the works she read, reported on whatever she felt was interesting or useful about the writer's life, discussed the focus of her critical paper, and shared, if she wished, her efforts to emulate a writer's style and/or her creative response with the class. Students left these classes with an excellent annotated bibliography as well as a heightened sensitivity to their peers' ideas and expression. Moreover, many of the students most skeptical of a reading list which seemed "women's lib," found themselves drawn to women writers through a common sensibility: they were experiencing the excitement of discovering one's own feelings, thoughts, fears mirrored in literature.

Approach

1. *The House of Mirth*
When *The House of Mirth* opens with Lawrence Selden being "refreshed by the sight of Miss Lily Bart" (p. 5), Edith Wharton plunges the reader into the superficiality of turn-of-the-century New York society, where a woman is defined by her beauty and her ability to use that fleeting appearance to marry "well." The sad fact of Lily's fading beauty at age thirty pervades the novel. *The House of Mirth* was an excellent beginning for this course because students were fascinated by its plot and characterization, and because Lily offers a devastating case of woman confined. The fact is that Lily *is* lovely, but her loveliness is not superficial as her charm is not solely manipulative, but based in an intelligent, imaginative sensibility. However, Lily's attempts to maintain her integrity are challenged by society's standards and expectations. As Lily makes her way through the cloying world of the Dorsets, Trenors and von Osburgs, she is unable to develop the

sensitivity we see in her conversations with Selden. The conflict between Lily's desire for comfort (wealth) and her personal morality invites various interpretations from the class. Is Lily herself unquestionably weak? For what does U. S. society prepare women except to marry? Is independence possible for Lily? Many students argued that Lily is not a character worthy of sympathy because throughout the novel she never even tries to define herself except through a man. Is, then, the only power available to a woman the status and position of her husband? Are her only sources of power her appearance and ability to manipulate the men who wield power? Regardless of the interpretation the student chose, because Lily "was so evidently the victim of the civilization which had produced her that the links of her bracelet seemed like manacles chaining her to her fate" (p. 9), this novel raises significant questions about the possible roles for women.

2. Emma

At first Emma seems a simplistic character, concerned with the superficialities of arranging marriages, being a proper hostess for her beloved Hartfield, and appearing her best at various parties and social occasions in provincial Highbury. The idea of a hint of protest in this novel was outrageous to students who were acquaintances of Jane Austen from very traditional readings of *Pride and Prejudice.* We began by probing into the attitude of an author who refers to her heroine as "the fair mistress of the mansion" (p. 15) and by other such ironic hyperbole. We examined this young woman who, we are told, "had always wanted to do everything" (p. 32), but who found it "much easier to chat than to study, much pleasanter to let her imagination range and work at Harriet's fortune than to be labouring to enlarge her comprehension" (p. 52), a young woman characterized by an acute sense of "the inferiority of her own playing and singing." See D. W. Harding, "Regulated Hatred: An Aspect of the Work of Jane Austen," *Jane Austen: A Collection of Critical Essays,* ed. Ian Watt. (Englewood Cliffs: Prentice-Hall, 1963). We see this same Emma, however, playing parlor games with sparkling cleverness and manipulating others masterfully. We conclude, therefore, that Austen's ironic tone toward Emma indicates an anger toward waste. Emma's self-expression, her creativity, are limited to domestic affairs. Her intellectual powers, evident throughout the novel, have never been cultivated; they are not qualities society finds valuable, or necessary, for a woman. And Austen clearly finds this attitude reprehensible.

With the exception of Mrs. Elton, the other women characters also demonstrate basically admirable qualities which have been stunted or distorted by society's limitations. Well-meaning Miss Bates prattles and is consumed by trivia. Harriet Smith, basically a well-intentioned young woman, is led to believe her life depends upon a "good" marriage. Lovely and talented Jane Fairfax is attached to the selfish, vain Frank Churchill. What we as modern readers begin to see is that all of these women's machinations to marry well and all of their absorption by domestic details is not petty—it is most decidedly not evidence of their superficiality. Rather, Austen is protesting society's confining roles prescribed for women. The achievement of domestic felicity becomes their self-definition, their creative outlet, their only source of power and pride.

In this course students began to reappraise Austen and her concerns. Two superb essays helped to diffuse the traditional views: "Regulated Hatred: An Aspect of the Work of Jane Austen" by D. W. Harding and Virginia Woolf's lively portrait of "Jane Austen" in *The Common Reader* (Harcourt, Brace & World 1953). As we discussed and analyzed

Emma, we appreciated an author whose Mr. Knightley advises Emma to consult her friend Harriet who "will give you all the minute particulars which only woman's language can make interesting. In our [men's] own communications we deal only in the great" (p. 371). Ironically, the language of Jane Austen and her thoughts about human nature defy the simplification of gender.

3. *Their Eyes Were Watching God*

"Ah done growed ten feet higher from jus' listen' tuh youn, Janie. Ah ain't satisfied wid mah self no mo'" (p. 158), declares Phoeby at the end of Janie's tale of self-discovery through, or at least with, the help of men in *Their Eyes Were Watching God.* Janie, the main character and narrator of the novel, is an imaginative young woman whose life is a series of marriages: two disappointments and an ultimate, though tragic, fulfillment. The The students enjoyed the novel since they felt Janie's excitement and sense of possibility. Moreover, the narrative frame of Janie relating the saga to her friend Phoeby creates a friendly, inviting tone—one more experienced woman passing on her thoughts and emotions to another less experienced friend.

Janie, reared by the myth of marriage as the only route of expression and satisfaction for a woman, wonders, "Did marriage compel love like the sun the day?" (p. 21), and finds in the youth of her first marriage that certainly it does not. Feeling, however, that the myth is true even if her specific case has not worked out, she marries again, this time smothered by Joe Starks' possessiveness. Realizing that Joe and the marriage were "building a high chair for her to sit in and overlook the world" (p. 55), Janie begins to understand herself and her own needs for an active participating life. Furthermore, she realizes that Starks crushes any possibility of self-development: "You done lived wid me for twenty years and you don't know me at all. . . . Mah own mind had tub be squeezed and crowded out tuh make room for yours in me" (p. 74). After Jody's felicitous death, Janie meets, loves, and marries Tea Cake, a playful and passionate man who helps Janie's "great tree" (p. 11) of life to bloom. His untimely and tragic death leaves her content with the memory of a life fully lived: "Ah done been tuh de horizon and back and now Ah kin set heah in mah house and live by comparisons" (p. 158).

Although some of the students felt that Janie had never asserted herself but rather depended always on men, others felt that she simply found her best self through association with a truly extraordinary human being: Tea Cake. Everyone was struck by the sense of life Janie generated, and they sympathized with her search for individual expression. Also, they sympathized with her faith in, as well as disillusionment with, marriage. The students felt that despite whatever cultural differences there might be, Hurston presents a revealing sense of what it is to be a woman searching for herself. The opening lines of the novel exemplify this consciousness which is sustained throughout:

> Ships at a distance have every man's wish on board. For some they come in with the tide. For others they sail forever on the horizon, never out of sight, never landing until the Watcher turns his eyes away in resignation, his dreams mocked to death by Time. That is the life of men.

> Now, women forget all those things they don't want to remember, and remember everything they don't want to forget. The dream is the truth. Then they act and do things accordingly. (p. 5)

4. *The Prime of Miss Jean Brodie*

The Prime of Miss Jean Brodie presented more problems than any reading in the course, perhaps because the basic situation of Jean Brodie and "her girls" was too close to the students' own situation. Telling students that I wanted the course to include at least one book that did not center on marriage, I defended the choice and do feel that the book ultimately precipitated thought about another aspect of women's experience: the intelligent, independent, single woman. Why, we asked, was Jean Brodie so possessive of her students? Whe need she live her life through others? Was her case merely another example of a woman deriving power from sources other than herself? Despite her fiercely independent veneer, was she actually too uncertain of herself to act alone?

Jean Brodie clearly is superior to the persons surrounding her. She is first of all described as being physically larger than others in the novel, her size symbolizing her strength and emphasizing her overwhelming presence. "Give me a girl at an impressionable age, and she is mine for life" (p. 12), she warns and promises, thus predicting her own downfall. But as we see her nurturing "the Brodie set," we are envious of the attention these girls receive. Jean Brodie is an intellectual of the first order, obviously better educated and more capable than any of her colleagues. Intimidated by no one, she jousts and wins in logical fencing with the headmistress: "like most feminists, she talked to men as man-to-man" (p. 53). Moreover, her moral code is an individual independent one, heedless of society's rules of male or female behavior. Nonetheless, Jean Brodie is not finally admirable. She is a parasite on her students, manipulating them to participate in activities—including careers and sexual liaisons—in which she herself does not. They "betray" and destroy her, leaving us to ask again if women who refuse society's traditional plans for them are destined to unhappiness.

We approached the analogy of Miss Brodie to fascism and discussed the novel's religious implications, especially the importance of Calvinism. The students, however, were not fond of the book, even if it did stimulate their thinking, and I feel that the struggle to prove its merit and relevance may be too great, at least at this school.

5. *Mrs. Dalloway*

Although the most complex of the novels studied during the course, *Mrs. Dalloway,* as well as its celebrated author Virginia Woolf, fascinated the students. They were by this point in the course quite prepared to study the stream-of-consciousness and the more problematic novel. In addition, they found Woolf's sensibilities to bespeak a more clearly female viewpoint than any writer we had read. Woolf's concept of time intrigued them. Mrs. Dalloway's morning walk down Bond Street in which past, present, and future blend into her reality drew students into Clarissa's lively but doubt-torn mind: "She felt very young; at the same time unspeakably aged" (p. 11); she fears her lack of knowledge and accomplishment, "yet to her it [life] was absolutely absorbing" (p. 11). During this simultaneously mundane and momentous walk, Clarissa's planned party, her past love affairs, and her omnipresent fears all become apparent. Mrs. Dalloway's is a life of feeling, which in her constant self-analysis becomes the substance of the novel:

> It rasped her, though, to have stirring about in her this brutal monster!
> to hear twigs cracking and feel hooves planted down in the depths of
> that leaf-encumbered forest, the soul; never to be content quite, or
> quite secure, for at any moment the brute would be stirring, this hatred,

which, especially since her illness, had power to make her feel scraped, hurt in her spine; gave her physical pain, and made all pleasure in beauty, in friendship, in being well, in being loved and making her home delightful rock, quiver, and bend as if indeed there were a monster grubbing at the roots, as if the whole panoply of content were nothing but self-love! this hatred! (p. 17)

Through *Mrs. Dalloway* we discussed a middle-aged woman—a woman once beautiful, a woman who has lived through her husband, a woman whose sole child is grown. Clarissa, as we know her, has lived her life for other people, helping them, listening to them, making them comfortable: the result is a hollow sense of self, a fear and desperate need of approval. She thinks of herself "being laid out like a mist between the people she knew best" (p. 12). Clarissa's vanity, her self-absorption, her suspicion are paramount as we meet her at this time of decision in her life. She does not know what direction her life will take because her previous life has prepared her for nothing: "She had the oddest sense of being herself invisible; unseen; unknown; there being no more marrying, no more having of children but only this astonishing and rather solemn progress with the rest of them; up Bond Street, this being Mrs. Dalloway; not even Clarissa anymore; this being Mrs. Richard Dalloway" (p. 14). Why, we ask, does woman's "usefulness" cease at middle age? Moreover, the students felt that this dilemma is not unique to the privileged and wealthy woman Clarissa represents but is perhaps even more terrifying to the less affluent. Clarissa's situation is a painfully common one: rather than developing herself, she devotes herself to the nurturing of others. *Mrs. Dalloway* is concerned with the consequences of this design of living.

The question of creativity is basic to a discussion of *Mrs. Dalloway* because Clarissa does express herself, she does use her imagination, during the parties. Are they enough, we ask, and find that, again, Clarissa must reach out, living through other people, bargaining for her fulfillment through their approval. Clarissa enters the party "at her worst— effusive, insincere" (p. 254), but we know that this behavior is necessary because of "how much she wanted it—that people should look pleased as she came in. . ." (p. 13). Clarissa recognizes her many critics and knows that she is often accused of giving parties because she enjoys having famous people about her. Nevertheless, we see that the parties are prompted by her urgent need to be a part of the excitement, the adventure, the artistry: "What she liked was simply life" (p. 183). The final party, that concludes the novel, however, "was too much of an effort. She was not enjoying it. . ." (p. 259). What, though, is Clarissa's alternative? The probing, sensitive Clarissa longs to participate in life, yet we see her even in the midst of the party standing outside, unhappily observing herself: "She had schemed; she had pilfered. She was never wholly admirable" (p. 282). As the novel ends, the probing seems to continue, and Clarissa herself is not able to change or give direction to her life.

To understand the novel in depth, we examined other aspects, although always in light of this approach. The perspectives of Clarissa's counterpoint, Septimus Warren Smith, and of her former lover, Peter Walsh, were discussed at length. The effect of Septimus' suicide on Clarissa, as well as of the passages on "Proportion" and "Conversion," is essential. Peter is especially important to an analysis of Clarissa, since she feels she has salvaged her individual self by marrying Richard and refusing Peter. Likewise, Woolf's minor women characters (Sally Seton, Lady Bruton, Miss Kilman, Elizabeth Dalloway) are excellent points of discussion in terms of women's options as Woolf sees them. Reading *Mrs. Dalloway* is, of course, difficult for most high school students, but a close and guided reading of the novel is rewarding. In this particular course, the novel allowed us to discuss not only the middle-aged woman but artistry itself, the art of living one's life.

Evaluation and Effects

The suspicion with which many of the students initially viewed women writers eventually gave way to enthusiasm. As the students discussed the writers with whom they were newly acquainted through the course's reading or the outside project they were continually surprised to find that the authors are neither unknown nor disreputable. One student returned from a college interview asking if she could write a paper on Sarah Orne Jewett, a writer suggested by the interviewer when the student described the project for this course. Often a student would bring to me a book by one of the authors on the bibliography—a copy found on the bookshelves in her home. Another student recounted to me with amazement that one evening when she had been describing to her family a short story read for this class, her father said it sounded like Dorothy Parker; he was right, and he himself had read this woman. As students realized that many of these writers are persons of recognized literary merit, they began to question the reason for the relative obscurity of many women writers. If they are writers of excellence, the students asked, why have they been excluded from courses, bookstores, anthologies?

The Madeira School has a "Mother's Day" in late fall when the students' mothers are invited to participate in classes. After having studied *Emma* and *The House of Mirth,* in the class in which mothers were present we discussed the problems these women encountered, and the roles to which society has relegated women. We gave the discussion a more contemporary focus by asking also to what extent society can determine women's options and expectations. Many of the mothers were anxious to discuss these questions and talked with me afterward about their interest in the writers. Likewise, when the students began work on their projects, frequently they were pleased to find their mothers had suggestions. One student asked me if I had ever heard of "Eudora Welty," a writer suggested to her during a family dinner. Another student was delighted to find that her mother had read Iris Murdoch and had suggestions for her critical paper in the project. The very nature of the material in this course opened a dialogue between students and their families and acquaintances.

Even if some students left the course remaining largely uninterested in feminism, they had been introduced to several women writers and to questions being asked in contemporary society. Simply generating this interest is reason enough to repeat the course. Furthermore, nearly every student had begun her own "creative" writing of one sort or another, writing which has continued during this second half of the year. Several students requested a history course, centering on the accomplishments of women. Many students have approached me about offering a similar literature course in women poets. Although such a course has not yet been instituted, I have used contemporary women poets in my senior writing seminar this term with great success. Students marvel that they had never heard of these poets, even though many of them have received such formal recognition as the Pulitzer Prize and the National Book Award.

In fact, the inclusion of women writers in the English curriculum as a whole seems to me one of the most felicitous effects of the course "Women in the Novel of Character." Because of the enthusiasm of the students for such writers as Edith Wharton, Katherine Anne Porter, Willa Cather and Virginia Woolf, other instructors are using women writers as part of the regular curriculum on all levels, certainly not yet in equal proportion to the male writers, but more frequently than before. Often during the year and again this spring, as we planned electives for next year, I defended a course on women writers when my colleagues suggested instead that I treat modern poetry, for example, using both men and women writers. I explained that hopefully the equal study of male and female writers will soon be a norm; but at the present, since our students are unaware of all but a very few women writers, I feel a course in which we study women writers alone is both necessary and desirable to develop students as critics and writers of literature.

Students' Poetry

"Reflections on Another Writer" by Karen Haney

Tattered clothes of evenings
Spent reading your books.
Those words worn on my thoughts,
Pages marked in indecision.
What right
To set the sun above your head
And ask for many colors
In each line.
I was careful when you wrote
What no one understood.
Forgetting their questions,
I asked my own—
Sometimes the edges of your portraits crumbled away.

"Untitled" by Leslie Hyde

they forgot when it happened:
His friends
became their friends,
as did Hers;
they saw less of them
(they had each other).
there was no separating where
His eyes broke off and
Her eyes began.

people often remark
How well they complement each other
like the colors in the study:
he picked out the drapes;
she chose the lamp shades.

their laughter:
like the clink of glasses when they celebrated
their victory over Time.

but the years laughed back;
they saw themselves in pieces:
a mirror shattered.
She warned
don't cut your
Self—
the glass is sharp.

He didn't know

but She had left
a long time
gone.

He wasn't sure
where to look;
He shook his head and
slept late that Christmas.

Individual Author Project

The purpose of this project is to encourage each of you to read and find out about one
particular author in some depth. Read the author's writings and some other person's
criticism and/or comments (if you wish) about her and her work. Investigate biographical
information; examine her techniques of writing—her style. In other words, get to know
the writer and her work. Then, respond to your writer in several different ways, each of
which should demonstrate a sensitive acquaintance with her.

1. *A five- to seven-page critical essay.* This analytical writing, though it may consider
biographical information, need not consult critical sources. You are the critic here. Your
paper may be an analysis of any aspect of the writer's work.

2. *Some example of emulation of the writer.* Select a technique or an element of your
author's style and emulate it—see what you can learn from her. For example, your paper
on Edith Wharton this week is emulating a technique; if you work on a poet, you may
write a poem using similar image patterns, verse patterns, etc.

3. *"A creative focus."* Respond in some imaginative, creative way to your writer's work
and her person. You may respond in some piece of your own writing, or you may respond in another medium: photography, painting, dance, music. (If you select a medium
that involves performance, we'll arrange an audience.)

Schedule:

1. (Date)—*A prospectus.* In about one page, explain to me who you have chosen and
what you plan to read. The amount of reading will vary according to the author. Several
short novels, one or two novels, plus short stories, one or two novels plus an autobiography
or biography, poetry. The amount and type of work will be discussed with me.

2. (Date)—*An outline.* I want a clear plan of the critical paper you are writing, plus a complete bibliography of your work thus far; in addition, I want some idea of the technique or stylistic element you are planning to emulate and some idea of the "creative response" (I choke on this term) you are planning.

3. (Date)—*Entire project due.* Bind all of your work into a folder with a complete bibliography of the sources you have consulted and books, articles, etc., that may be consulted for further study.

Suggestions for collateral reading and individual author project:
1. Jane Austen—*Pride and Prejudice; Sense and Sensibility; Persuasion; Northager Abbey*
2. Elizabeth Bowen—*The Death of the Heart;* short stories
3. Charlotte Brontë—*Jane Eyre; Villette*
4. Emily Brontë—*Wuthering Heights*
5. Willa Cather—*My Antonia; Death Comes for the Archbishop; A Lost Lady; The Song of the Lark; The Professor's House*
6. George Eliot—*Middlemarch; The Mill on the Floss; Adam Bede*
7. Ellen Glasgow—*Barren Bround; Vein of Iron; The Woman Within*
8. Zora Neale Hurston—*Dust Tracks on the Road; Jonah's Gourd Vine*
9. Shirley Jackson—*We Have Always Lived in the Castle; The Haunting of Hill House; Life Among the Savages;* short stories
10. Sarah Orne Jewett—*The Country of the Pointed Firs*
11. Doris Lessing—*The Golden Notebook; The Summer before the Dark; Martha Quest;* short stories
12. Carson McCullers—*The Member of the Wedding; Reflections in a Golden Eye; The Heart is a Lonely Hunter*
13. Iris Murdoch—*Flight from the Enchanter; A Severed Head; The Sandcastle*
14. Flannery O'Connor—*Wise Blood;* short stories
15. Joyce Carol Oates—*The Wheel of Love; Them; Wonderland; Expensive People*
16. Dorothy Parker—short stories; poetry
17. Ann Petry—*The Street;* short stories
18. Katherine Anne Porter—*Flowering Judas; Pale Horse, Pale Rider; Ship of Fools*
19. Muriel Spark—*Memento Mori; The Girls of Slender Means*
20. Gertrude Stein—*The Life of Alice B. Toklas; Ida; Three Lives*
21. Eudora Welty—*Golden Apples; The Optimist's Daughter; Losing Battles*
22. Edith Wharton—*Ethan Frome; The Age of Innocence; A Backward Glance*
23. Virginia Woolf—*To the Lighthouse; A Writer's Diary;* essays; *A Room of One's Own; Virginia Woolf,* a biography by Quentin Bell
24. Poetry by—Sylvia Plath; Anne Sexton; Denise Levertov; Diane Wakoski; Amy Lowell; Emily Dickinson; Elizabeth Bishop; Louise Bogan; Marianne Moore; Muriel Rukeyser; Adrienne Rich; Nikki Giovanni; Gwendolyn Brooks

Renee Kasper
English
John F. Kennedy High School
Bellmore, N. Y. /1975-76

IMAGES OF WOMEN IN LITERATURE

The expressed goal of the twelfth grade mini-course, "Images of Women in Literature," is consciousness-raising through reading, writing and dialogue. The scope of the course may be apprehended through the materials included but what must be stated is that the course, given twice a year, is under constant revision, gaining in strength, hopefully, from suggestions made by the students. I must say frankly that, in creating the course, I stole from everybody and anybody I could, but I owe a special debt to *Images of Women in Fiction,* Susan K. Cornillon, ed. (Bowling Green Press, 1972), and to several articles in various editions of *English Journal.*

Course Outline

Week 1   Introduction to course and requirements designed to give the class and teacher a chance to get to know each other
Stranger from a planet
Consciousness-raising
Reaction paper to *Women Pro & Con*—homework
Distribution and explanation of bibliography for outside reading assignment—due week 8

Weeks 2-3   Background of Greek theatre
Women's role in society (use some of Medea's speeches)
Antigone
Writing assignment on *Antigone*—homework

Weeks 3-4   Contemporary readings from *About Women,* Stephen Berg and S. J. Marks, eds. (Fawcett World, 1974).
Bettelheim's "Growing Up Female" (essay)
Gilman's "The Fem Lib Case Against Sigmund Freud" (essay)
Kempton's "Cutting Loose" (essay)
Jong's "The Prisoner," "Penis Envy" (poems)

Week 5   Old Testament—Creation/Proverbs
New Testament—St. Paul/Corintheans/Ephesians (excerpts)
Mythology—Lilith

Weeks 6-7   Middle Ages—*Ancrene Riule* (excerpts)
Medieval poetry—growth of courtly love
Greer's "The Stereotype" (*The Female Eunuch, About Women*)
One contemporary story on theme—woman as sex object
Two poems on same theme
Chaucer's *Wife of Bath*
Shaw's *Saint Joan*
Writing assignment on *Saint Joan*—homework

Week 8　Class discussion of outside reading

Week 9　Sixteenth-seventeenth centuries
　　　　Shakespeare—excerpts from plays
　　　　Milton—those portions of *Paradise Lost* that correspond to parts of
　　　　　　of Genesis read in class

Weeks 10-11　Introduction to comedy of manners
　　　　School for Scandal
　　　　Writing assignment—comparison of another comedy with
　　　　　　School for Scandal

Week 12　Nineteenth century
　　　　Dark Lady archetype—witches
　　　　"La Belle Dame Sans Merci"/"Lygeia"/"Christabel"
　　　　Contemporary poetry about witches

Week 13　The experience of black women
　　　　Walker's *Jubilee* (excerpt)
　　　　Baldwin's "Exodus" (excerpt from *Go Tell It on the Mountain*)
　　　　Poetry about Harriet Tubman
　　　　Wright's "Bright and Morning Star"
　　　　Bontemps' "Summer Tragedy"
　　　　Hansberry's *Raisin in the Sun*
　　　　Cleaver's "To All Black Women from All Black Men" *(About Women)*
　　　　Giovanni—poetry
　　　　Distribute assignment sheet for final projects—due week 20

Weeks 14-15　Realism
　　　　Howell's "Editha"
　　　　Cather's *My Antonia*
　　　　James' *Daisy Miller*
　　　　Writing on *Daisy Miller*

Weeks 16-17　Naturalism
　　　　Chopin—"Story of an Hour"/*The Awakening*
　　　　Paper on *The Awakening*
　　　　Alternatives—*Sister Carrie, Maggie, Girl of the Streets*

Weeks 18-19　Twentieth century
　　　　Women and madness
　　　　Gilman's "The Yellow Wallpaper" (read in class)
　　　　Short story from anthology
　　　　Poetry—Frost's "Servant to Servants," Morgan's "Invisible Woman,"
　　　　　　Plath
　　　　Spinsters and old maids—poems and a story
　　　　Katherine Ann Porter—"Old Mortality," "Noon Wine"
　　　　Hellman/Thompson/Parker—all good

Week 20　Final projects
　　　　Last day—evaluation of course by students

We also use films when they apply, records of songs and plays, and we talk a lot about what is going on in the newspapers and on television.

There is too much—much too much. Obviously, all of this cannot be covered, especially if the classes contain interesting people. It's very frustrating.

First Exercise

Visitors from a strange planet of androgynous beings land in the United States. After hearing about the movement for women's liberation, they demand that you explain what it means to be a woman in the United States. You draw on all of your experiences and your knowledge of anthropology, biology, history, sociology, economics, art, music and literature to tell them the following five things.

First Homework Assignment

Please write responses to the following. You may omit any question which you would prefer not answering.

1. Why did you select this course and what do you expect from it?
2. What is femininity/masculinity to you?
3. Are you happy each morning. Why or why not?
4. When did you first become aware of your role as a woman/man (girls do this, boys do that)?
5. Were you treated differently from your brothers/sisters?
6. Are you proud to be a woman/man? Why or why not?
7. What do you envision as your future family situation? Who will you live with? How will the family support itself? What will be your role within the family? If there are children who will take care of them? Where will you live?

Write a Reaction Paper to the following (From *Women Pro & Con*).

1. I have never met a chaste woman who did not become the better for being seduced. Married women are, instance by instance, better-natured than unmarried ones. Though for really good women there is only one place to look: the cemetary. —Brisson
2. A woman employs sincerity only when every other form of deception has failed. —Scott
3. Once a woman has given you her heart you can never get rid of the rest of her. —Vanbrugh
4. A woman who is guided by the head and not by the heart is a social pestilence; she has all the defects of the passionate and affectionate woman, with none of her compensations; she is without pity, without love, without virtue, without sex.—Balzac
5. A man is in general better pleased when he has a good dinner than when his wife talks Greek.—Johnson
6. Woman is generally so bad that the difference between a good and a bad woman scarcely exists.—Tolstoy
7. The normal woman is well aware that marriage is far better for her than spinsterhood even when it falls a good deal short of her hopes.—Dampless

8. The man-hating woman, like the cold woman, is largely imaginary. She is simply a woman who has done her best to snare a man and has failed.—Norton
9. To be beautiful is enough! If a woman can do that well who shall demand more from her? You don't want a rose to sing.—Thackeray
10. Women are made to be loved, not to be understood.—Wilde
11. Earth's noblest thing, a Woman perfected.—Lowell
12. Women of genius commonly have masculine faces, figures and manners. In transplanting brains to an alien soil God leaves a little of the original earth clinging to the roots.—Bierce
13. A woman's preaching is like a dog's walking on his hind legs. It is not done well: but you are surprised to find it done at all.—Johnson
14. A woman with a masculine mind is not a being of superior efficiency; she is simply a phenomenon of imperfect differentiation—interestingly barren and without importance.—Conrad
15. I will not say that women have no character; rather, they have a new one every day.—Heine
16. The tongue of women is their sword; they take care not to let it rust.—Chinese Proverb
17. Women better understand spending a fortune than making one.—Balzac
18. To endow a woman with reason, thought, wit, is to put a knife into the hands of a child.—Taine

Additional Assignments

In order to complete the requirements for English 175, it will be necessary for you to carry out two of the following related activities:

A. One additional reading assignment will be required during the first quarter. Choose from the following bibliography or see me if you have a personal choice. You will be asked to commit yourself in writing to your selection within one week.

Women Writers before the Twentieth Century
Austen, Jane. *Pride and Prejudice.* 1813. *Emma.* 1816.
Brontë, Charlotte. *Jane Eyre.* 1847.
Brontë, Emily. *Wuthering Heights.* 1847.
Eliot, George (Mary Ann Evans). *The Mill on the Floss.* 1860. *Middlemarch.* 1872

Twentieth-Century Women Writers
Angelou, Maya. *I Know Why the Caged Bird Sings.* 1970.
Brooks, Gwendolyn. *Maud Martha.* 1953.
Canfield, Dorothy. *The Homemaker.* 1924.
Cather, Willa. *My Antonia.* 1918.
Didion, Joan. *Play It as It Lays.* 1970.
Fitzgerald, Zelda. *Save Me the Waltz.* 1932.
Glasgow, Ellen. *The Battleground.* 1902. *Barren Ground.* 1925. *They Stooped to Folly.* 1929.
Hurst, Fanny. *Lummox.* 1923.
Hurston, Zora Neale. *Their Eyes Were Watching God.* 1937.
Hellman, Lillian. *An Unfinished Woman.* 1970.

Laurence, Margaret. *The Diviners.* 1974. *The Stone Angel.* 1964. *The Jest of God.* 1966.

Lessing, Doris. *Martha Quest.* 1952. *The Golden Notebook.* 1962. *Summer before the Dark.* 1973. *Memoirs of a Survivor.* 1975.

McCarthy, Mary. *The Group.* 1963.

McCullers, Carson. *Reflection in a Golden Eye.* 1941. *Member of the Wedding.* 1949.

Oates, Joyce Carol. *Them.* 1963.

Plath, Sylvia. *The Bell Jar.* 1970.

Schulman, Alix Kates. *Memoirs of an Ex-Prom Queen.* 1972.

Smedley, Agnes. *Daughter of Earth.* 1929.

Walker, Margaret. *Jubilee.* 1968.

Wharton, Edith. *The House of Mirth.* 1905.

Woolf, Virginia. *To the Lighthouse.* 1927. *Mrs. Dalloway.* 1925. *Orlando.* 1928.

B. Choose one of the following activities. You may work alone or with one or more students, depending upon the project chosen.

1. From current newspapers and news magazines, compile a list of female "firsts," giving the source. For example, explore the areas of space travel, athletics, politics, art, etc. Do not use a resource book.

2. Study some of the women's magazines like *Cosmopolitan* and *Ms.,* or *Redbook, House Beautiful, Bride, Seventeen.* Examine carefully both the content and the advertising. Then present an oral report of your findings to the class as you display the magazines.

3. Find at least one example of sexist stereotyping in each of the following: a novel, a motion picture, a television show, a comic book. Prepare for class discussion.

4. Locate in the library four magazine articles on some aspect of art created by women. On separate cards give full information concerning the location of the articles together with an abstract of not more than one hundred words for each article.

5. Prepare a good panel discussion on "How rigid are the views toward sex roles in my school/community?" Perform in class.

6. Prepare for class presentation a critical analysis of sexism in three fairy tales.

7. Arrange a "Biography Bee" for the class. From your biographical reading or from library research, compile accounts of twenty-five women, outstanding in any field. On separate cards record three sentences about each one. Divide the class into two teams. A contestant who correctly identifies the subject on the first sentence gains three points for his/her team; on the second sentence, two; on the third sentence, one. Here is an example.
   a. Born a slave, I escaped from slavery on a Maryland farm, where the overseer had dented my skull with a two-pound weight.
   b. For ten years I kept returning to the South to aid escaping slaves, using one branch of the Underground Railroad.
   c. At one time rewards as high as $12,000 were posted for my capture because I had helped more than 300 slaves to escape. (Answer: Harriet Tubman)

8. Prepare your own marriage contract. Compare it to a traditional marriage contract. Read them to the class.

9. Write a speech for a woman announcing her candidacy for the Presidency of the United States. Include a description of her qualifications, the specific locale of the announcement, and her reasons for running for office.

10. Select a one-act play by a woman which you consider suitable for oral reading. Appoint a director; cast, rehearse the reading of the play; present it to the class.

11. Read and analyze as to content and form ten poems by contemporary feminist poets.

12. Write a research paper on the connections between language, semantics and self-concept.

13. Group write and perform a skit on one of the following topics:
    a. A man speaking to a group of women on the topic, "Woman Means Submission."
    b. An automobile salesman delivering a sales pitch on a particular model to a man and then to a woman.
    c. The only female executive working in an office.

14. Some literature reflects women's revolt from home and hearth. Read: Henrik Ibsen's *A Doll's House;* George Bernard Shaw's *Mrs. Warren's Profession.* Write a paper about the strengths and weaknesses of these women as well as the conditions of their lives.

15. Read three science fiction novels which depict women and their lives. Prepare a panel discussion of the roles of men and women in the future.

16. Read at least three novels by one of the following writers (prepare for class presentation an analysis of the kind of women depicted, the lives they lead and the ends they meet): James Fenimore Cooper (*Leatherstocking Tales* only), Nathaniel Hawthorne, Ernest Hemingway.

17. Your own thing.

Final Evaluation

1. How would you rate each of the following works as to enjoyment derived from your reading (use 1 for the lowest and 5 for the highest)?

   Antigone   *School for Scandal*   *The Awakening*
   St. Joan   *Daisy Miller*

2. How would you rate each of the following as to the fruitfulness of class discussions (use 1 for the lowest and 5 for the highest)?

   Antigone   *School for Scandal*   *The Awakening*
   St. Joan   *Daisy Miller*

3. Comment please on the method of testing or the writing assignment. Have you any suggestions for other ways of evaluating student progress?

4. Basically, the course is arranged chronologically, with occasional contemporary readings from *About Women* when appropriate. Would you prefer a different sequence? What?

5. Was the initial consciousness-raising assignment and discussion of value? Why or why not?

6. Please comment on the usefulness or enjoyment of:
   Bible/Genesis/St. Paul/Proverbs
   Folklore/Lilith
   Middle Ages/Medieval Poetry

Chaucer and the *Wife of Bath*
Shakespeare/Milton
Witches
Experience of Black Women
Madness

7. The free reading for the first marking period was designed to introduce you to some good women writers. There were some weaknesses in the assignment. How may we improve it?

8. Was the final project of value to you, either your own or as an observer of other projects?

9. Obviously, one of the goals of the course is an attitude change. How successful do you think we were?

10. Any suggestions for improvement? (Constructive criticism, please.)

Carol Lindsay
English
New Canaan High School
New Canaan, Conn./1972-73

WOMAN AND MAN IN LITERATURE

Readings:
Edith Hamilton, *Mythology*
Sylvia Plath, *The Bell Jar*
Edith Wharton, *Ethan Frome*
J. D. Salinger, *Nine Stories*
Henrik Ibsen, *A Doll's House*
William Golding, *The Lord of the Flies*
William Faulkner, "Barn Burning"
Doris Lessing, "To Room Nineteen"
John Knowles, *A Separate Peace*
Hemingway novels (one read by each student)
Poetry by Shakespeare, Donne, Robert Browning,
  Elizabeth Barrett Browning and others

Other resources:
I used a tape I made at the second annual NOW conference in New London,
Connecticut. I invited a group of faculty members and their spouses for a
panel discussion on marriage. Also, I used several films.

Course Outline

Unit I: Women and men in childhood and adolescence.
Unit II: Courtship and marriage.
Unit III: Later on: what happens when the children leave home? when one asks
          what have I done with my life?

Projects

1. Papers on most of the assigned reading.
2. Paper on one book from a list I prepared. My idea here was to give students a chance
   to read a classic and to explore it from the point of view of sex roles. This assignment
   might have worked better, had I assigned a contemporary book.
3. Final project: a study of sex roles through magazines, interviews, questionnaires,
   music, etc. Good results from this project.

Goals

1. To deepen the students' ability to read, understand and appreciate literature.
2. To make students aware of the roles they play as men and women so that they can
   evaluate these and deal with them.

There were other goals but these were the principal ones. I feel they worked well together. Books became more fascinating to students who had some stake, direct and personal, in what the literature had to say. Students also had to read carefully and perceptively to get what was there. In short, the course provided a good reason to read. As far as the second goal is concerned, I can only point to a senior who told me she found the course too painful. Her sister had just divorced and her mother spent most of her free time at a bridge table. What, she asked, would become of her?

I taught the course to make the above happen, to make students look at themselves in a special way, to give them the chance to know a little more before they make unhappy mistakes. Lest that sound depressing, I don't mean it to. It just seems to me that students are bombarded with too many lies and that somewhere they need the chance to look at what is being done to them.

Because my bias is frankly feminist, I asked a sympathetic male teacher to be a resource person for the male point of view. He attended many classes and was invaluable in revealing or urging the males to reveal those aspects of adolescent manhood which women often never learn about.

Teaching Methods

My teaching methods depend a good deal on the class and on the material. I find my job is much easier if I provide the class with good, exciting, controversial reading. I want them to come to class trying to "figure it out" or wanting to talk about what they've just read. That's what we do on an average day. I begin by offering an opinion or, more likely, by asking a question which allows for gut level responses by anybody, not only the verbal students. From there we move to "why" questions: Why does Esther in *The Bell Jar* act so funny? If these questions are difficult to answer, we try to find parallel situations in our own lives and look for clues there. On a good day, the students may get into arguments among themselves: the people who like Esther versus those who don't.

Interest in the women's liberation movement was different here from that in any other class I've taught. Students more often looked to each other for insights, worked better with each other, felt more deeply, worried more (in a healthy way—not about grades), cared more about the people in their reading than in any class I've taught. The reason: the subject matter on which the literature was hung meant more to students than *The Scarlet Letter* taught in a traditional way. In short, the course called attention to who students were, what would be expected of them, what options for a good life they had, what would be the nature of that good life. Students suffered and enjoyed in ways I never thought possible in a high school classroom.

Karen Sagstetter
English
H. W. Schroeder High School
Webster, N. Y./1973-74

MALE AND FEMALE ROLES IN LITERATURE

This is a ten-week elective course offered by the English Department. All classes are mixed-ability and mixed-grade levels (10-12). The community is middle class (not upper or lower) and contains a mixture of professional people, farmers and blue collar workers. This is not only a literature course, but also a course on sex roles in society, culture and media.

I. Introduction

I asked students to complete the following statement: "After first term finals, Anne (John) finds herself (himself) at the top of her (his) medical school class." In a later session, I had students compare their answers to these statements with the results of Matina Horner's study on the fear of success ("Fail, Bright Women," *Psychology Today*, November 1969).

II. Perception and Misperception

We spent a day discussing perception and I used transparencies of pictures that can be interpreted in several different ways. (I made transparencies from "Perception and Misperception," available from the Center for Teaching International Relations, Graduate School of International Studies, University of Denver, Denver, Colorado 80210.) My goal was to get students thinking about how we allow into our heads information that fits our preconceptions, while we filter out the rest.

III. Images of Women and Men in Advertising

I asked students to bring in advertisements (two with female emphasis, two with male) that they felt represented images of men and women. We discussed: the product being sold; the method used to sell the product; the effect on readers of such ads; the stereotypes portrayed.

As we defined and located stereotypes, we developed descriptions for each one. Our list included: housewife, mother, liberated woman, temptress, tomboy, prostitute, bitch, dumb jock, working man (blue collar), businessman, father, son, playboy, henpecked husband.

I showed the class some ads that used two people, usually a man and a woman, and I asked about their *relationship*. For example, in an ad for diamonds, the woman and man look very sexy and appealing; he is placed above her in the picture. She looks up at him gratefully.

IV. Sex-Segregated Small Group Discussions

I divided the class by sex. My department head (male) worked with the male students and I worked with the female students. We asked the following questions to get each group talking:

a. If you could make three changes in the personality of the man (woman) currently closest to you, what would they be?
b. What do men (women) want me to be like?
c. What do I want the opposite sex to be like?

These questions opened up a number of topics for discussion: the master/slave relationship and its dehumanizing effects on both parties; whom teen agers confide in (men? women? mothers? fathers?); how parents treat high school students; what high school students expect of themselves.

Many students said they were expected to be independent and were expected not to conform to a social role, but during the discussions it became clear that all are affected by social expectations. The men felt a lot of pressure from their mothers to be strong, independent and financially solvent; the women were expected to be dependent, good housekeepers and not competitive with men. One man said: "I don't really care to have more responsibility than I have now, but I don't have much choice. . . ."

It was hard to get students to talk freely in these discussion groups, perhaps because they only met twice and students didn't get to know each other. In order to get discussion going, I often read, anonymously, responses to questions I had asked the class to write about.

Assignment: Write a short paper evaluating your own expectations of the opposite sex. Are they stereotyped expectations? Do you feel you are being fair? How would you feel if someone expected the same behavior from you? In class I summarized the papers and distributed them (with students' permission) for each sex to see what the other had written.

V. The Fear of Success

We analyzed the class stories on the fear of success which students had written the first day of class. We then read and discussed the Horner article, though many students found it difficult. I had students pair off and do the following physical exercise in order to bring home the point about expectations and their effect on one's will: Two people face each other (sex doesn't matter) and grasp hands. Then push as hard as you can. Continue this until you know how you feel about this contest. Do you want to win? Do you want to lose? Do you feel indifferent?

VI. Women and Men in Literature

Discussion of characterization in literature: how does an author delineate a character? We began with a showing of *Goldfinger,* the James Bond movie; the students loved this.

Assignment: Write a characterization of James Bond and also one of Pussy Galore.

Class activity: Role-play the characters in *Goldfinger* but in a situation you create. The only rule: men have to play women characters and women have to play men characters. (This activity was a howling success in some groups and a failure in others. I then thought it might be better to role-play familiar situations.)

Class activity: Role-play a familiar situation (a date, family dinner, etc.). Again men must play women, and women, men.

All through these class sessions, we discussed students' perceptions: women are physically weaker than men so they shouldn't do construction work; any woman that wants a job doing anything these days can get it and that's not fair; alimony exploits men; "what do you care if I don't shave my legs?" etc.

VII. Short Stories and Poetry

During the rest of the course, we read short stories and poetry. Interspersed were discussions about social and biological aspects of sex roles. Also, a couple of classes about images of men and women in painting, a student-made tape on images of men/women in music, etc.

VIII. The Initiation Story

I wanted to find some fables that portrayed a young person proving himself or herself. I had trouble finding one that featured a female that actually demonstrated courage or strength, rather than obedience and beauty. By searching in anthologies I found:
> "Mustmag," an Appalachian folk tale, in *A World Remade: Comedy,* Northrop Frye and W. T. Jewkes, eds., (Harcourt, Brace, Jovanovich, 1973).
> "The Man Who Killed the Sea Monster," an Eskimo legend, in *A World Elsewhere: Romance,* Frye and Jewkes, eds., (Harcourt, Brace, Jovanovich, 1973).

Similar in focus, but more complex as literature:
> "Jade Snow Wong," a tale about a Chinese girl and her struggle to become independent from her traditional family, in *Asian-American Authors,* Kai-yu Hsu and Helen Palubinskas, eds., (Houghton Mifflin, 1972).
> "The Bear," a story by William Faulkner, in *Stories from Six Authors,* William Buckler and Arnold Sklare, eds., (McGraw-Hill, 1960).

The class discussion centered on initiation rites in general; what it means to grow into a woman or man. I explained some of the research on sex differences, aggression in men and women, how society interprets the same behavior differently for women and men.

Additional materials;
> "The Development of Sex Differences," a short article by Eleanor Maccoby, in *Mademoiselle* (February 1970).
> "The Young Aggressors," an article by Seymour and Norma Feshbach, in *Psychology Today* (April 1973).

IX. Love/Romance

We used some of the materials listed below: I usually used pieces where analysis of both male and female roles was possible. The students loved the old pulp fiction; they laughed at the obvious stereotypes.

Erich Neumann, *Amor and Psyche: The Psychic Development of the Feminine*
    (Pantheon, 1956).
P. G. Wodehouse, "Goodbye to All Cats," in *A World Remade: Comedy.*
James Joyce, "Araby" and "Eveline," in *The Dubliners.*
F. Scott Fitzgerald, "The Last of the Belles," in *Taps at Reveille.*
Sam Walker, "The Purple Heart of Erlik," Clement Wood, "Enter the Vampire," in
    The Pulps ed. Tony Goodstone (Chelsea House Publishers, 1970).

X. Mothers/Fathers

The poetry listed below is excellent to use for this topic. (There's a wealth of material about mothers and fathers, you just have to uncover it.) A friend who's studying classics taught one class on Xenophon: What makes a good wife? What are good manners? Anything on men's liberation is pertinent and interesting. NOW has a task force on men that can provide resources.

Fathers/poetry:
    Robert Hayden, "Those Winter Sundays," in *Wish and Nightmare,* ed. Frye and
        Jewkes (Harcourt, Brace, Jovanovich, 1973).
    Anne Sexton, "Begat," in *The Book of Folly.*
    Phyllis McGinley, "First Lesson" in *Times Three.*

Mothers/poetry:
    Anne Sexton, "Mother and Daughter," in *The Book of Folly.*
    Eve Merriam, *Family Circle.*
    Robert Duncan, "My Mother Would Be a Falconress," in *Bending the Bow.*

Prose:
    Sally Benson, "Profession: Housewife," in *Fictional Biography: 2,* ed. Roberta Koch
        Suid (Houghton Mifflin, 1973).
    Xenophon, "Oeconomicus."
    William Faulkner, "A Rose for Emily," in *Stories from Six Authors.*
    Ernest Hemingway, "The Short Happy Life of Francis Macomber," in *The Short
        Stories of Ernest Hemingway.*

Men's Liberation:
    Robert Gould, "Measuring Masculinity by Paycheck," *Ms.* (June 1973).
    Teresa Levitin et al., "Seven Deadly Half Truths," and "A Woman Is 58% of a Man,"
        Psychology Today (March 1973).
    Jim Schoettler, "Male, Damn It," *Saturday Review* (March 10, 1973).
    "Now, Men's Liberation," *Time* (May 10, 1971).

Evaluation

I asked for one 1,000 word paper or equivalent project of the student's choice. Projects could be stories, slide-tape shows, analyses of books, trends, fairy tales, comic books, novels, movements. If students didn't want to design their own project, they had the option of doing a take-home exam. The exams asked students to read a story and analyze the characters in terms of sex roles. Students were also asked to write an essay about one of the articles we had read during the course.

Most of the short written assignments were not graded (exception: characterization of James Bond and Pussy Galore). The project or exam was 25 percent of the final grade and the shorter assignments counted 75 percent (pass/fail).

In the future this course will probably be team-taught by myself and a male social studies teacher for credit in both the English and social studies departments.

Patricia Winks
English
George Washington High School
San Francisco, Calif./1972-73

WOMEN IN LITERATURE

Course History and Purpose

I initiated this course out of wanting to teach something I was excited about. I am still idealistic enough to believe that if I am excited about the material, my students will be too. I also think that this course is terribly important. I want to warn, encourage, make aware, raise questions, turn our accepted ideas about women upside down and see what is still important. Most of all, I want the women in the course to feel a tremendous sense of possibilities, choices. As for the men, I want them to realize that giving women a wider range of experiences in no way diminishes their own.

I teach this course because I asked for it and because I feel I am qualified. I am a woman. I also happen to be married, with four children, stayed home for fifteen years (except for working for my M.A. and later my teaching credential, but you know what I mean, I didn't receive a paycheck), went to work. When I look at my arbitrary course divisions—woman as virgin, witch, housewife, psychotic, mother—I've been there.

First semester I began with eighteen students (sixteen female, two male) and second semester, fifteen (fourteen female, one male). I would prefer about twenty, either all women or more evenly divided.

Course Outline

I. Woman as Sex Object

Aristophanes, *Lysistrata.* We use a modern translation, very explicit (but I understand more double meanings each time I read it). The modern translation gets us off to a good start because it is funny and we are made aware of the different kinds of female stereotypes. I tell the students about the place of women in Athenian society (the lady, the slave, the different levels of prostitute) and we find that history doesn't quite jibe with literature. The sad thing about *Lysistrata* is that women do not seek to change their roles in society.

Dana Densmore, "On Celibacy," in *Liberation Now!* ed. Babcox and Belkin (Dell, 1971). Densmore goes well beyond suggesting a sex strike. This essay shows *Lysistrata's* tactics, but with a different motivation. Densmore is logical enough and radical enough to generate excited reaction.

Irwin Shaw, "The Girls in Their Summer Dresses," in *Selected Short Stories of Irwin Shaw.* A modern story that shows (as if we didn't know) that we're still sex objects—and that we go along with this.

II. Virgin or Witch

Selections from Old Testament (New English Bible version used for greater clarity):

Adam and Eve. Note the two creation stories: first time "male and female," second time the rib version. Why do so many more of us know only the rib version?

Rules on menstruation from Leviticus. This leads to good discussion of the whole menstrual taboo and the old myths that are still with us.

Story of Samson and Delilah. If you really read it you see what Samson was. A real sadist: whether the women liked him or not never occurred to him. Delilah was the patriot.

David and Bathsheba. Again, Bathsheba's feelings are ignored.

Proverbs: A Capable Woman (not a housewife, but a business).

Ecclesiastes. Here are included warnings about women. Notice the change in tone, which is getting more and more misogynist.

Susanna and the Elders. Lends itself to discussion of rape and how a woman proves it.

Selections from New Testament:

Jesus on divorce. He didn't approve of divorce and by doing so claimed he was protecting women.

Jesus on adulterous women. Look for paragraphs which illustrate that women were part of the ministry.

Selections from Paul which illustrate the direction Christianity was to take on the subject of women's role.

The medieval lyrics, found in standard texts, include anonymous poems to the Virgin Mary; a brief section from Dante's *Paradiso* extolling Beatrice as she introduced him to God (more or less); then two ballads: Thomas Rymer (the fairy queen took him away) and Lord Randall (girl friend poisoned him). What do these lyrics say about strong or idealized women? About men's images of women?

Nathaniel Hawthorne, *The Scarlet Letter.*

III. Romantics and Realists

Malory, "Lancelot and Elaine," Le Morte d'Arthur. I use this story to illustrate the split in the knight's attitude: Elaine was like a wife to Lancelot, so how could he love her? Guinevere was the forbidden, the dangerous—and in fact the person in control of the relationship. Since many of the medieval ideas of love (even the idea, which many think is terribly modern, that marriage will spoil a beautiful relationship) are very much alive today, it's interesting to note the source of these ideas.

Other readings:

Elizabethan lyrics.

D. H. Lawrence, "The Horse-Dealer's Daughter."

F. Scott Fitzgerald, "Winter Dreams."

Nursery rhymes.

IV. Mother

Edith Wharton, *The Old Maid.*

Betty Rollin, "The Motherhood Myth."

Poems by Gwendolyn Brooks, Anne Sexton, Adrienne Rich.

V. Housewife

Doris Lessing, "To Room 19," in *A Man and Two Women.*

Susan Griffin, "The Sink."

Pat Mainardi, "The Politics of Housework."

Poems by Sylvia Plath and Anne Sexton.

VI. Men versus Women: Misunderstandings

Ernest Hemingway, "The Short Happy Life of Francis Macomber."

Dorothy Parker, "Mr. Durant."

Katherine Mansfield, "Bliss."
Susan Glaspell, "A Jury of Her Peers."

VII. The New Woman
Henrik Ibsen, *A Doll's House.*
Sylvia Plath, *The Bell Jar.*
Essays from *Liberation Now!*

Assignments

I. Outside readings for three papers, due March 5, April 9 and May 7
  A. Two book reports, preferably one novel and one biography of a woman. For your report, do *not* summarize the story, or the woman's life. Try to incorporate answers to the following questions in essay form. Give examples to justify your answers.
    1. What is the role of women in the culture described?
    2. Is the heroine adjusted to her social role or does she feel alienated?
    3. How does she feel about men in general? in particular? about other women?
    4. How does the heroine get what she wants? If she doesn't get what she wants, why not?
    5. Does the heroine seem real to you? Have you ever had any feelings like hers?
    6. How does the author seem to feel about the heroine? about men?
    7. (Novel) If the author is a man, does he treat women realistically? If a woman, does she treat men realistically?
    8. (Biography) Do you feel that the woman you read about was successful according to *your* standards? according to her own standards? according to the standards of her society?

  B. One of the following:
    1. Analysis of a play (read or seen) with a woman as central character.
    2. Analysis of a film which has a woman as central character.
    In your report, you may use the questions given in I. A.
    3. Review of magazine article or essay about women. Summarize briefly the facts you have learned, the author's interpretation of these facts, and your agreement or disagreement with the author's findings. If the article deals with the author's opinions rather than with facts, challenge these opinions— don't simply report them.

II. Project, due June 4
This may be a creative or a research project: If you decide to do a creative work, it should represent a comparable amount of effort.
Possible topics might be:
—study of different types of women's magazines
—women as portrayed in popular songs
—women in commercials
—women in films or TV today
—women's changing role reflected in films of the last forty years
—sexism in textbooks
—women and girls in children's literature
—women in religion

—the working woman
—the single woman
—women and the language
—women in a particular culture
—women of a particular age group (adolescent, young married, middle age, old age)
—female archetypes (see reading list)
—study of work of one woman writer
—sociological study (interviews, questionnaires) on women as they see themselves, as they are seen by men, what their roles should be
—women in art
—changing attitudes toward marriage and the family

III. Tests

At the conclusion of each unit, you will be given essay topics based on our readings. Sometimes the tests will be take-home essays. Be prepared to get writer's cramp!

IV. Class participation: essential!

Examinations: Examples

The Bible and Medieval Woman (answer any four of the following questions)
1. Let us assume that men are the menstruating sex. Write five new laws of Leviticus.
2. Write a dramatic monologue from the point of view of one of the following:
   a. Eve—what goes on in her mind before, during, and after the Fall?
   b. Delilah—how she really felt about Samson, why she betrayed him, and how she felt afterwards
   c. Bathsheba—how she really felt about David, Uriah, the quickie wedding, the lost baby
   Provide motivations for a character's actions, or, if she is acted upon rather than acting, provide her reactions to what others do to her.
3. Depending upon your own disposition, write at least fifteen lines of:
   a. Proverbs—A Capable Husband
                    —or—
   b. Ecclesiastes—a woman writes about husbands to beware of
4. Assume it is 1495 and a woman is accused of witchcraft in a small town in Germany. Christ returns to earth, to the very town. On the basis of his pronouncements in the New Testament, how do you think he would view the proceedings, and what recommendations would he make? Would his recommendations be taken? Now assume that Paul returns to earth, to the same town. How would *he* view the proceedings, and what recommendations would he make? Would his recommendations be taken?
5. Find five contemporary illustrations (in current film, popular song, advertising, TV, best-seller book, comic strip) of the virgin-or-witch attitude toward women. Please be specific and explain. (Don't simply write, for example, "the Brand X commercial," because chances are strong that I haven't seen the commercial.)

Wuthering Heights (take-home essays)
1. Is Heathcliff a believable character? Explain. Are you sympathetic to Heathcliff? Trace your reaction to Heathcliff through the course of the novel.

2. Compare the trio of Catherine, Heathcliff and Hindley with the later trio of Cathy, Linton and Hareton. In what ways are they similar? In what ways are they different?
3. Answer a. or b.
   a. Catherine Earnshaw: alive or dead, she is the center of the story.
      Agree or disagree? Discuss.
               —or—
   b. Why is the second half of the novel needed?
4. What is the role of a woman at Wuthering Heights and at Thrushcross Grange? How did Catherine Earnshaw, Cathy Linton and Nelly Dean adapt to their roles at both places?
   From your conclusions, and from your reading of the book, what do you think Brontë herself thought the woman's role should be?
5. We are never told certain parts of the characters' history or mental attitudes. Try to fill in one of the following gaps in such a way that subsequent events are illuminated. You might wish to narrate in the first person.
   a. Heathcliff's life before he came to the Earnshaws
   b. Heathcliff's life during the three years he was away from the Heights and Catherine married Edgar
   c. What Catherine thought of married life before Heathcliff returned
   d. How Edgar felt about his wife after Heathcliff returned
   e. What Heathcliff actually did to Linton

Lyric Poetry: Coy and Not-So-Coy Mistresses
1. "To a Coy Mistress" offers the poet's arguments against playing hard-to-get. How would you turn down Andrew Marvell? (You must address yourself to his argument.)
2. List at least three repulsive conversational tactics of a would-be seducer (male). 3. Of a would-be seducer (female).
4. List at least three effective conversational tactics of a would-be seducer (male). 5. Of a would-be seducer (female).
6. There have actually been complaints that in this liberated age women aren't coy enough. How would you turn down a forward mistress?
7. Would a contemporary poet write something like "To a Coy Mistress"? Why or Why not?
8. Do you think good love poetry is still being written? Why or why not?
9. If you were to write a contemporary romantic poem, what would be its subject and the situation?

Evaluation

Class activity was primarily discussion of the assigned reading, interspersed with background material on such topics as the role of women in ancient Greece, peculiar customs regarding menstruation, and the lives of the authors whose work we studied. The class was most successful when we made connections between the literature and our own experience. For example, the Bible story of Susanna and the Elders leads logically to a discussion of rape: how do we prove it? Poems on abortion by Anne Sexton and Gwendolyn Brooks got us started on this topic.

As for participation, the first semester was marvelous. I always looked forward to the class because I never had to worry about what we would do. The second semester was different. I had a much quieter group with much more traditional attitudes. They looked to me to juggle and to keep all the dishes in the air. I tried everything to get them talking—and with success—such things as goofy questionnaires and situations to analyze (see previous examples).

I had to scrap some of the readings we did the first semester because the new group couldn't handle them. In fact, I cannot imagine sticking to my course outline each semester: so much depends on the students and their interest. For instance, when I gave the second semester group a choice of selections to read next, they chose *The Scarlet Letter* which I hadn't expected at all.

We had a few speakers during the course—from NOW and the Women's Studies Program at Sonoma State College. And once I used a slide presentation on the images of girls in elementary readers and books. Films were another question because of their prohibitive cost. We did have two from the Canadian Film Board.

One problem—I had to be careful not to be condescending while at the same time being honest. I found it difficult to deal with high school age groups on the sex-role issues. I couldn't say, "Drop that sex role," just after they've learned it.

I would like to see the course as part of the curriculum as long as there is a need. I wish we had a comparable Women in History course, but I'm trying to fill in the gap here, too, as I'm learning. I wish there wasn't a need for separate courses. And I wish more teachers taught about women as an integral part of their courses. I have tried to explain to several (female) teachers about the gaps in the school history textbooks, but beyond saying politely, "Maybe you could come talk to my class sometime," they obviously felt that women's invisibility in history wasn't really important.

3

Inter-
disciplinary

Martha Barrett
Social Studies
Charles E. Ellis School
Newton Square, Pa./1971-72

FEMALE-MALE ROLES: INTERDISCIPLINARY SOCIAL STUDIES COURSE

Course History

Ellis is a small private girls' school of students from widely differing economic, academic and social backgrounds. Under the new social studies program, eight nine-week courses are offered and the most popular are given to any interested tenth- to twelfth-graders. The cut-off point is fifteen students; each student decides whether to receive a percentage or pass-fail grade.

During Independent Study Week of 1970-71 when seniors were away from campus, the "Problems of Democracy" course held a week of discussions about women's rights. It was then that I discovered how ignorant I and other teachers and students were about this subject. This was the time when the idea for the course was born. Interestingly, in the spring of 1971, there was little interest on campus in women's liberation as compared with the following year. By 1972, the publicity of the women's movement had hit Ellis: fifteen students in grades ten to twelve signed up for the course.

Purpose

The course aimed to examine the variety of female-male role concepts held by other cultures and the history of the feminist movement in the United States; to allow students to evaluate their present and future attitudes and actions as women; to eradicate the misconceptions held about women's liberation; and to support the students' sometimes vague, sometimes guilt-ridden desires to "be somebody," "do something."

Classwork

1. With the aid of the biology teacher, we began the course by attempting to separate which female-male roles are strictly biologically determined, partially biologically determined, and strictly culturally determined. This took a few days—and what a way to start a class! Quite a bit of yelling went on. Some contended that everything was cultural and others thought everything was biological. Who knows?—this is what we eventually concluded. This topic brought out in the open all the questions to be explored and certainly got everyone involved immediately.

2. Each student prepared a fifteen-minute oral report on female-male roles in another culture. The reports were effective: the students listened attentively. The test I gave at the end of this section was an open-notebook one. The week before the reports, we defined a list of anthropological terms that they would come across in their reading. They were eventually tested on these. The bibliography used in the reports included the following. (I didn't assign these books; these are the sources the students found and the parts they chose to read.)

Kiowa Indians—Alice Marriott, *Kiowa Years,* ch. 2-5, 10 and 13.
Sirrono—Allen R. Holmburg, *Nomads of the Long Bow,* pp. 91-335.
Samoans—Margaret Mead, *Coming of Age in Samoa,* pp. 20-85.
Indians—Paul Thomas Welty, *The Asians,* ch. 12-13.
Eskimos—Peter Freuchen, *The Eskimos,* Part I, ch. 2-4, Part II, ch. 3, 7.
Bushmen—Elizabeth Marshall Thomas, *The Harmless People,* entire book.
Pygmies—Colin M. Turnbull, *The Forest People,* entire book.
Mexicans—Oscar Lewis, *Five Families,* ch. 1.
Egyptians—Henry Hobbett Ayrout, *The Egyptian Peasant,* pp. 118-128.
Africans—Paul Bohannan, *Africa and the Africans,* pp. 158-173.
Todas—S. Queen and R. Haberstein, *The Family in Various Cultures,* pp. 18-43.
Hopi—Ibid., pp. 45-65.

There were also reports given on the Amish and the family structure in pre-revolutionary China.

3. At this point we were about three weeks into the nine-week course. The second major project was discussion of Miriam Schneir's book, *Feminism: The Essential Writings,* a chronological anthology of the best speeches and writings concerning women's rights—from Abigail Adams through Virginia Woolf, excluding material on the suffrage movement. In the discussions, in spite of the fact that we were studying the *history* of female-male roles, almost every topic was still relevant to our lives today. The book also gives brief biographical sketches of many women. From this, the students gained factual knowledge of the women's movement from the 1700's to the 1930's, and also learned the fundamental grievances that have made women question the roles allotted them in our society.

4. During the last week and a half we held three classes to which we invited adult guests, selected by the students, to be part of a panel discussion. We opened these classes to any students and teachers who wanted to attend. The classes were held in the student lounge to avoid lining up people in front of the class: we wanted a discussion rather than a confrontation. Most students and teachers from other classes attended. Each panel consisted of people of various ages, marital status, philosophies. The students did an excellent job choosing people with divergent views.

Some of the longest discussions centered around the division of labor within the home, homosexuality, the need for a career. I had assured the adults involved that they didn't have to answer personal questions. Of course some of the adults were up-tight about attending, but we made sure that those invited, including two housewives, would not be offended. The students were considerate. When the issue of homosexuality came up, the principal of the school (a male) took the traditional side of this issue, a new male chemistry teacher, who's a feminist, was on the other side, and the three young husbands on the panel took a middle position. It was the first time at this school that homosexuality had ever been publicly discussed. As a result of this course, and particularly because of open discussion on these panels, the students gained confidence in discussing sex-role issues.

Assignments

1. A collection of cartoons, advertisements, articles from newspapers and notes on TV

programs and commercials. Students were encouraged to look for news of the women's movement; issues involving women's rights, i.e., the abortion hearings, constitutional amendments, handling of local rape cases; sexist attitudes expressed in any form. They were to make a folder of these; occasionally we discussed and analyzed their findings. At the end of the course, we put these materials in the library clippings file for use by other students.

2. A three- to six-page paper investigating in depth an aspect of female-male roles. Some of the topics chosen were: contraceptive techniques, homosexuality, Old Testament views of women, job discrimination, sexist child-rearing, abortion laws.

Out-of-Class Activities

Attendance at a NOW meeting in Philadelphia by part of the class. This was a highly educational experience because of the content of the discussion, the people present and the current business of the organization. Almost every student signed up to be a member of the organization.

Evaluation of the Course

The course was an unqualified success, not only for the students in it, but for the rest of the school. The subject of feminism became a topic of conversation within the faculty itself and between faculty and students in other classes; the course brought a sense of awareness to the community as a whole. Perhaps with proper handling of the projected women's rights club, the students may begin to feel pride in attending a girls' school. They may begin to look at the positive aspects of being women among women, developing their own leadership capabilities.

The course will be offered again next spring with basically the same format; the number of students will be limited to about ten to allow for fuller participation by all. I'm not saying the course wouldn't work with forty students, but unless the students are in small groups, the shyer ones will not express themselves. And that's one of the course purposes!

It would be fascinating to conduct a "Female-Male Roles II" class with an equal number of boys from a nearby school. If this can't be arranged, one or two panels with peer group males seems essential. But I would not bring in a panel of boys until after the students have gained initial knowledge about the subject. Only with such background could the female students interact with the males in a worthwhile way.

Although many students would like to see the course expanded to sixteen weeks, eight weeks of formal structure is enough to make them aware without boring them. Those interested will continue reading on their own and some are organizing the women's rights club. At the end of the eight weeks, we got into a personal, individual type of thinking and discussion which can be continued by the students on their own without the classroom structure. I think any classroom tends to take on the flavor of the teacher and the majority of the students. I became somewhat radicalized along the way, and I'm sure I lost my objectivity on some of the issues. The vocal students were pushing for most aspects of the feminist movement. This tended to isolate those who held more conservative, traditional views of women's roles. Unfortunately, these girls happen to be the ones who did not speak up in class.

This course was most like the anthropology ones I've taught in which the topic of cultural differences gets one into talking about sexual matters without necessarily relating it to oneself personally. Probably the teacher who has taught anthropology will find it easy to teach courses about female-male roles. But again, the greatest necessity for this kind of course is the teacher's ability to relate to the students.

The Course: The Larger Curriculum

This course could be integral to the larger curriculum at Ellis. Our social studies program has been changed from chronological history to specific discipline areas such as anthropology, economics and political science. We're trying to teach the methods of attacking problems. The primary focus is on the theory of the discipline, concepts of problem-solving, the vocabulary. When we come to a specific area like Female-Male Roles, the students' background in Cultural Anthropology (a required course), Psychology, Sociology (electives) gives them an opportunity to use knowledge gained from a specific discipline in an interdisciplinary way.

Problems

The lack of materials for research was the only problem. The few parents I talked with about the course thought it was great. In a public school in a conservative community, one might run into difficulties, but it would be difficult for anyone, male or female, to tear apart *Feminism* by Schneir; and as far as the cultural reports went, one's on reasonably safe ground by using groups outside the United States.

Examples of Test Questions

Read all the quotes. Choose three to discuss.
1. "Confined then in cages like the feathered race, they have nothing to do but plume themselves, and stalk with mock majesty from perch to perch."—Mary Wollstonecraft
2. "Men themselves are debased by the ignorance and legal inferiority of their wives and daughters."—Frances Wright
3. "But when a woman shows she is able to live without you, [the male] then your vain power gives way to fury."—George Sand
4. "Rule by obedience and by submission away, or in other words study to be a hypocrite, pretend to submit, but gain your point."—Grimké
5. "But when woman can enter the lists with you and make money for herself, she will marry you only for deep and earnest affection."—Lucy Stone
6. "Now my belief is that this poet who never wrote a word and was buried at the crossroads still lives. She lives in you and in me, and in many other women who are not here tonight, for they are washing up the dishes and putting the children to bed."—Virginia Woolf
7. "Everywhere woman must pay for her right to exist with sex favors."—Emma Goldman
8. "But let her beware how she permits her husband to be her conscience-keeper."—Grimké
9. "My friend, what is a man's idea of womanliness?"—Elizabeth Cady Stanton

10. "And woman should stand beside man as the comrade of his soul, not the servant of his body."—Charlotte Perkins Gilman
11. "A free man is a noble being; a free woman is a contemptible being."—Tennessee Claflin
12. Helmer: "But no man sacrifices his honor, even for one he loves." Nora: "Millions of women have done so."—Henrik Ibsen

From your notes list how various cultures solve the following "problems" in female-male roles. Give at least two good examples for each item.
1. Preparation for the role child will play.
2. Methods of and reasons for mate selection.
3. Division of labor within family.
4. Decision-making for family unit.
5. Sexual relations outside of marriage.
6. Responsibility for economic and social welfare of children.
7. Death of mate.

Ginger Denecke-Hackett
Social Studies
Aloha High School
Beaverton, Oreg./1972-73

HER STORY — THE PROBLEMS OF WOMEN IN CONTEMPORARY AMERICA

In this course we will provide opportunities for students of both sexes to examine their potential as human beings freed from sexual stereotypes. The contribution of women to all areas of human endeavor will be examined to provide a basis for feminine pride. Special emphasis will be placed on the future life-roles women will assume in our society in an effort to anticipate the problems involved.

I. Following are the possible units of study in this course. Those marked with an asterisk will be covered by all the students, but since the course is only one semester long, the others will be available for the students to choose from. The last alternative will be available for all women in the course if they have the time and feel the need. I will try to convey my commitment and involvement in the course and thereby help spark an interest in consciousness-raising.

   A. History of American women.
* B. Nature-nurture debate. (Is human behavior, especially sex-role behavior, determined by genetic makeup or is it learned through environmental conditioning?)
* C. Socialization of women (the establishment of sex-role stereotypes).
   D. Women and the law.
   E. What is the American woman like? (Demographic characteristics)
   F. The psychology of women (self-fulfilling prophecy).
   G. Women and work and education.
* H. Role-analysis of women as wives, mothers and sexual objects.
   I. Women and literature and mass media.
* J. Women and their bodies.
   K. Life styles of American women:
      1. Black women and other minority women
      2. Lower-class women (*Below Stairs,* Margaret Powell)
      3. Middle- and upper-class women (*Washington Square,* Henry James)
* L. Women's liberation (what's in it for men?).
* M. Marriage and the family.
* N. Prospects for change (what can we do?).
   O. Consciousness-raising group.

II. For this course I have a list of high priority objectives both for myself and for my students. I hope to keep these in mind as I formulate the assignments and activities in this class, and will check back periodically to see that the activities are compatible with these priorities.

   A. Good interpersonal communication.

B. A high degree of candor and openness shown by teacher in communicating with students and hopefully by students as well.

C. High interest and involvement shown by teacher.

D. High regard by teachers and students for individual interests and abilities which will be realized by designing activities allowing students to pursue their interests and accomplish objectives according to their abilities.

E. High emphasis on critical thinking skills and opportunities for making real change in the community.

F. Increased awareness on part of all students of the oppression of women and the fact that we are all non-conscious sexists.

G. Understanding of liberation in terms of freeing *all* people from narrowly defined roles which don't allow them to fulfill potential as humans.

H. A conscious effort will be made on the part of the teacher to break down the barriers which often exist between women teachers and women students. (Consciousness-raising group is one means of doing this.)

III. Evaluation of student performance will be based on:

A. Attendance (if the student attends regularly, he/she will pass).

B. Self-evaluation (the student will contract to do particular activities and then evaluate his/her performance in these activities).

C. Teacher-evaluation of activities.

Sex-Role Stereotypes Unit (approximately three weeks)

Objectives:

1. Students will examine the sex-role stereotypes that exist in our culture.
2. Students will collect examples of these stereotypes as they are portrayed through the media.
3. Students may, for a project, create a media slide show on sex-role stereotypes to present to other classes.
4. Students will discuss the makeup of sex roles they have learned through family, school and other institutions.
5. From their reflections, students will identify specific ways they as individuals or groups can begin to break down sex-role stereotypes as they exist in school, family and community.
6. Students may, for a project, act as change agents to break down these barriers to the fulfillment of human potential in the Aloha community.
7. Students will use critical thinking skills to analyze the readings.
8. Students will discuss the quality of communication within their groups.

Readings:

1. "Women Today: The Public Images," pp. 15-22, in *The American Woman* (American Education Publications Unit Book).
2. "The Invisible Bar," pp. 40-60, in *Born Female* by Caroline Bird.
3. "The Creation and the Fall," pp. 4-7; "The Womanly Image: Character Assassination Through the Ages," pp. 49-56; "On Playboys and Bunnies," pp. 65-66, in *Up Against the Wall, Mother,* edited by Elsie Adams and Mary Louise Briscoe.
4. "The Stereotype," pp. 51-60, in *The Female Eunuch* by Germaine Greer.

5. "The Happy Housewife Heroine," pp. 28-61, in *The Feminine Mystique* by Betty Friedan.
6. "Woman, and that Includes Man, of Course," adapted from Theodora Wells. (Available from Wells Christie Associates, Box 3392, Beverly Hills, Calif. 90211.)

Activities:

1. With crayon and newsprint the students will draw a picture of their mothers, listing underneath the roles they see their mothers in. Then they will do the same with their fathers. The drawings should then be pinned on the wall and the following questions discussed:
   a. Do you notice any similarities in drawings? Words?
   b. What kinds of roles are the women shown in? Men?
   c. What do you intend to do when you grow up?
   d. How many girls are taking science, auto mechanics, computor science, etc.?
   e. How many boys cook, wash, iron at home? How many boys are taking Bachelor Home Economics?
   f. Who has the 'inside jobs'? Outside jobs? How about your parents?

2. Ask students to write down all the words they can think of associated with the opposite sex. The lists should then be compiled and dittoed off or written on the board. (It will probably turn out, if the class is open enough, that the words associated with men are generally thought of as positive qualities in this society and those associated with women are often negative and/or have sexual connotation.) Organize students into small buzz groups (four persons or less) to discuss the significance of these findings. They might address themselves to the following questions:
   a. What do these findings show you about how we view men and women in this society?
   b. What are some sources of these images that you can think of?
   c. What if any differences exist in the way our culture views men and women and the way other cultures do? Can you cite examples? What about subcultures within our society?

   Ask students to report their group's conclusions to the rest of the class, then continue discussion in the large group. Teacher should summarize the groups' findings at the end of class. The negative images of women should be apparent.

   At this point it would be appropriate either to replicate the Broverman experiment done at the Worcester State Hospital in Massachusetts (if it can be done effectively with the same results), or at least to have the teacher describe the experiment to the students. (See Florence Howe, "Sexual Stereotypes Start Early," *Saturday Review,* October 16, 1971, for a description of the experiment.)

3. Assign students the selections from *Up Against the Wall, Mother* listed in the "Readings" section. Along with their reading, pass out "Know Your Enemy: A Sampling of Sexist Quotes" and ask students to identify the sources (pp. 31-36 in *Sisterhood Is Powerful*). Each selection should be critically analyzed by the students. The following questions might be included in the discussion:
   a. To what do you attribute the difference in the two accounts of the creation?
   b. What attitudes are revealed about women in each of the two accounts of the creation?

c. What other stories or myths do you know which portray woman as the bringer of evil or destruction?

d. How have the Jewish and Christian faiths formalized in law and ceremony the role of women as portrayed in the Old Testament?

e. Since the Bible portrays woman as man's helper and temptress, do you feel that this is woman's natural state and should therefore be maintained?

f. What does the famous quote by Freud, "anatomy is destiny," refer to?

g. In your own experience, what examples can you cite which show unthinking acceptance of female stereotypes?

h. What value judgments are implied by the terms "Playboy" and "Bunny"?

i. Examine *Playboy* for evidence of a role for women that is different than that of a Bunny.

4. Play a tape of record cuts like "Just like a Woman" by Bob Dylan, " Look at that Stupid Girl" by the Stones, "Miss Black America" by Curtis Mayfield and "Where You Lead" by Carol King. Replay each song, asking the students to analyze the nature of women portrayed. Questions such as the following might be asked:

a. Do you think Dylan sees women trained into their roles or are these roles innate?

b. Could we assume that Joanie Mitchell might sing a similar song with the line "he breaks just like a little boy"?

c. Do you think it's harmless for words such as "Look at that Stupid Girl" to be heard again and again in relation to girls?

d. What is the hip culture's view of girls? The black culture's view?

e. Can you think of examples where a man sings of following the woman to the ends of the earth?

Ask students to bring in examples of TV or magazine ads to refute or substantiate the image portrayed in these record cuts.

5. Assign "Women Today: The Public Images." The following questions might be asked about the reading:

a. What influence do you think the image of teen-age girls presented by advertising has on preteens?

b. What does the episode of "All in the Family" show about Archie and Edith's relative positions?

c. How does *Love Story* show how our image of women might be colored by romantic images? Are the actions of the heroine in *Love Story* natural and consistent? Would it have been natural for the hero to give up his interests to put her through three years of graduate school?

6. Ask the students to choose from the four following readings (see "Readings" above) and bring their analyses back to the rest of the class:

a. "The Invisible Bar," *Born Female.*

b. "The Stereotype," *Female Eunuch.*

c. "The Girl," *Female Eunuch.*

d. "The Happy Housewife Heroine," *The Feminine Mystique.*

7. Ask clinical psychologist, Muriel Lozak, to talk to the class about the oppression of narrowly defined roles for both men and women. Students should have thought through questions to ask the speaker and/or a set of specific questions should be given them to answer based on the speaker's talk.

8. Students will read and discuss on a feeling basis, "Woman, and that Includes Man, of Course" by Theodora Wells.

9. Students will brainstorm ideas about how they can act as change agents in their school and community to break down the stereotyped role definitions that exist. Then they should formulate action plans to put their ideas to work.

Susan Klaw, Barbara Gates and Adria Reich
The Group School
Cambridge, Mass/1975-76

WOMEN AND WORK

"Women and Work" is one of ten thematic units of a comprehensive high school curriculum directed at young working class women, which will be published by The Feminist Press in 1976. The curriculum has been developed over a period of five years by teachers and students at The Group School, a certified, alternative high school serving students from low-income families in Cambridge, Massachusetts. What appears here are segments of a draft of the "Women and Work" unit. Drawing from the comments of cooperating teachers and youth workers who have tested the curriculum this fall, the authors are currently making additions and revisions to the manuscript.

The final published curriculum will be usable as a whole, or in many combinations of parts. Units, or sections of units, could be integrated into English, history, psychology, anthropology, career education, or health courses. Several of the longer units, like "Women and Work," could stand by themselves as entire semester courses. The first two units of the curriculum, "Messages from Society," and "Early Socialization," contain basic consciousness-raising activities. The next three units follow issues of "Growing Up Female" through the life cycle, from childhood, to adolescence, to adulthood. "Sexuality" presents a methodology for handling personal concerns of young women— their appearance, their bodies, their developing sexuality. "Women and Work" and "Women Organizing Themselves" combine historical material with explorations of current socio-economic conditions and institutions. "Mean Streets" focuses on the particular psychological and sociological concerns of young women in trouble, and includes specific explorations of relevant institutions and agencies. "Women's News" directs students to consider the range of current issues of concern to women.

Introduction

One of the long-range goals in working with low income young women is to give them tools to take control of their futures. The ability to enjoy successful work experiences is a source of psychological as well as financial strength. First, young women need a sense of the possibilities and limitations of the work world. It's important to give young women space to explore different jobs, as well as their own and other women's attitudes towards work, before they have to start working full-time. Since many won't go on to further schooling, and will be looking for full-time work upon graduation, this space should be provided in high school.

Nine out of ten women in America work at some point in their lives. Despite recent legislation which prohibits discrimination against women in wages and hiring, an earning gap between men and women not only exists, but has been growing wider. In 1955, full-time women workers earned 63.9 percent of men's salaries, while in 1971 they earned only 59.5 percent as much. Even so, for working class women, where the earning gap is widest, the pay is often the only attraction of working. The jobs available to them, in a typing pool, an assembly line, a department store, or as telephone operator, are tedious, routine and dead end. Furthermore, blue-collar women workers are most vulnerable during times of depression. In August 1973, 7.1 percent of women in blue-collar jobs were unemployed, compared to 4 percent of men. One of the reasons for the vulnerability of blue-collar women workers is that only one out of seven belong to unions, although union women earn $1,500 a year more than their non-union counter-parts.[1]

That working class women are exploited makes the topic of women and work a delicate one to raise with our students. On the one hand we want them to understand the ways in which poor women are exploited, since without awareness, resistance to exploitation is impossible. But given the students' lack of aggressiveness, self-confidence and skills, all of which stem from growing up poor and female in America, they are likely to get only those jobs which are most exploitive of women. We don't want to be discouraging, because many already feel that it's going to be impossible for them to get a job or to like their work.

Our unit on "Women and Work" is designed with this conflict in mind. Our approach explores the different kinds of work done by working class women and the advantages and disadvantages of those jobs. To do this, we rely heavily on first-hand accounts by women workers, including struggles to change working conditions. Activities in which students gain personal insights are intermingled with ones in which they gain socio-logical/political understandings. Conscious of the fact that our students may aspire to jobs in which a woman's sexuality is used in an exploitive way, like a cocktail waitress, airline stewardess or secretary, we don't condemn those jobs. Instead we help students evaluate the differences between the real work in the stewardess' job, evacuating pas-sengers, for example, and the exploitive parts, having to be young, attractive and single to be hired.

Section I: Introduction to Women and Work

This introductory section is designed to help students discover patterns in relation to women and work, and thus give them a framework for the examination of specific kinds of work which follows in other sections. In the first activity students list and compare jobs currently done by women and men. In the second, they look at the work the women in their families have done over time by making a family work history chart. The two activities are also intended to introduce students to the approach used throughout the unit in which the topic, "Women and Work," is looked at in both sociological and personal terms.

Activity Number One: Listing Jobs done by Men and Women
When you compare the work that women and men do in our society, you find that the work women do tends to have less status, to require less training and to be more poorly paid. When women and men do identical work, their jobs are sometimes given different titles to allow employers to pay female employees less. The purpose of having students list and compare jobs normally done by women and men, and then look at a chart of pay scales, is to allow them to see some of these patterns.

In a first class, it's good for a group to work together on something. The structure of this exercise, thus, is to have students generate the list of jobs together. The teacher makes two columns on the board—women's jobs and men's jobs—and asks students to name all the jobs they can think of. Valuable debate will arise. One student will want to put "cab driver" in the men's column, while another will argue, "There are plenty of lady cab drivers in Cambridge!" The teacher should let the class decide what's going to go where. You can help by posing a question like, "Are most cab drivers men, or is it about equal?" In the process of arriving at some consensus, students realize two equally important facts about work: most jobs are done primarily by men, or primarily by women; however, at the same time, there are few jobs which are exclusively male or female.

The completed list can be used in several ways. Students can look for differences in the kinds of jobs women have versus the kinds of jobs men have. They'll make such distinctions as "Men have to go to school more," "Women work more with kids," "Men fix things." In order to point out that even within the same field men have the jobs with more status and power, the teacher can isolate jobs in the same profession—nurse/doctor, elementary school teacher/college professor—and get students to consider the differences when men and women work in the same field. Asking students which, if any, of the women's jobs depend on a woman's appearance introduces the notion of sexual exploitation which is developed in later activities. Model, prostitute, actress, airline stewardess will be named; sometimes students will mention secretary and waitress as well. In contrast, they are unlikely to find that any of the men's jobs depend on appearance.

The listing exercise is followed by giving students copies of a chart to examine which shows, among other things, differences in pay scale for women and men doing similar work. We use it because it documents a crucial fact about women's work—inequity in pay—which students haven't been able to observe from the lists they've generated. Originally published in *Ms.,* this particular chart is good because it's easy to read. As it may be difficult to get hold of, we've reprinted the part of it which includes data on working class jobs (see pages 116-117).

Students will respond indignantly to the chart and want to know how people get away with paying women less for equal work. That's a complicated question, and you will have to decide how much you want to get into it.

We point out that many employers are primarily concerned with profit, and thus prefer to keep salaries low. Employers rationalize the inequity between women's and men's salaries by assuming that women who work are not the primary supporters of the family, that the money they earn is extra spending money. Our students can see, just on the basis of their own families, that this is a false assumption since their mothers are often the only ones to bring money home. We mention that, although the Equal Pay Act of 1963 makes it illegal to pay men more than women for the same work, one way employers get around this, as the chart shows, is by calling a job "Administrative Assistant" if a man is doing it, and "Executive Secretary" if a woman is doing it. We also draw on what students who have worked know from personal experience. If you really need a job, you'll take it regardless of the pay; you don't have much choice. Also, you may not realize you're being discriminated against because, unless there's a union which sets and publicizes pay scales, you probably don't know what other workers around you are getting paid. A good way to end this lesson is to ask any students who are working to try and find out what men working alongside them are earning, and to report back to the class.

Activity Number Two: Charting Your Family Work History

In the previous activity, students examined the economic and social position of contemporary women in the work world. Here they consider women's work in both personal and historical terms by charting their family work histories, starting with themselves and going back as many generations as they can. The form we hand out looks
like this:

Family work history

Generation	*Women: jobs held*	*Men: jobs held*
Great-grandparents (great-great aunts, uncles, great-grandparents)		
Grandparents (grandmothers, grandfathers, great-aunts, great-uncles)		
Parents (mother, father, aunts, uncles)		
Your generation (you, sisters, brothers, cousins)		

Although the activity focuses on the work women in their families have done, we include male relatives for comparative purposes, and because it's interesting for students
to get a fuller picture of their families. The chart we originally used listed specific
relatives—grandmother, grandfather, mother, father, etc. We realized later that the
chart had the potential of making a student who was missing a parent, or who couldn't
find out anything about her grandmother, feel bad. In the revised family work form
above, therefore, the focus is on as many members as possible of a given generation.

In giving out and explaining the charts, the teacher should stress two things: (1) students aren't expected to know the answers right off, that the purpose of the activity
is to try to find out as much as they can about the work their relatives have done; and
(2) that being a housewife is a job and should be included in their list. Students are
asked to start with their own generation and fill in as much as they can in class. The
teacher can then help students figure out ways to get the rest of the information—sitting
down with a grandmother, calling an uncle, talking to their parents, etc. We usually give
them a week to try and complete the charts.

Not being able to finish the chart at one sitting has certain advantages. The rest of the
first class and maybe the next can be spent with students comparing notes about the
jobs they or their friends have had. Our students have done such work as saleswork,

(continued on page 118)

Job Title	Employer	Data	Male Salary	Female Salary
First Level Management	Bell Systems	Average salary of employees in 30 districts	$14,169	$11,194
Executive Trainee	Retail chain store	1971 Wharton MBA	$14,000	$12,000
Staff Writer	American Medical Association	Male: 6 months experience Female: 5 years experience	$13,000	$13,000
Academic Librarian	University of California, Berkeley	20 years experience (median salary)	$12,570	$ 8,745
Male: County Agricultural Agent Female: County Home Economist	U. S. Dept. of Agriculture Extension Service	Salary: National average	$11,678	$ 9,743
Male: Head Grocery Clerk Female: Head Bakery Clerk	Giant Foods	Salaries	$196.72 per week	$142.60 per week
Male: "Administrative Assistant" Female: "Executive Secretary"	Eastman Kodak Co.	Starting salaries: High school graduates, 2 years technical schooling	$181 per week	$126 per week
Station Installer	Pacific Telephone & Telegraph Co., San Francisco	Male: Promoted after 72 months as Frameman (1971) Female: Promoted after 72 months as Operator (1971)	$156.50 per week	$124.00 per week
Male: Waiter, full-course meals Female: Waitress, full-course meals	Restaurants and hotels	1970 U. S. Average, includes salary and tips	$3.80 per hour	$2.85 per hour

Job	Employer	Basis	Female	Male
Male: "Janitor" Female: "Maid" (similar duties except less vacuuming and more coffee-cup washing)	Lawyers Cooperative Publishing Co., Rochester, N. Y.	Starting salaries	$87.50 per week	$150.00 per week
Payroll Clerk	Offices	Average salary in all metropolitan areas (released February 1971)	$117.00 per week	$147.50 per week
Order Clerk	Offices	Average salary in all metropolitan areas (released February 1971)	$106.00 per week	$139.50 per week
Male: Stock Clerk I Female: Secretary I	City of South Bend, Ind.	Salaries	$ 5,452	$ 6,439
Male: University-wide Mail Clerk I Female: Library Assistant I	University of California, Berkeley	Male: High school graduate Female: College graduate	$ 5,484	$ 6,360
Retail Salesclerk	Loveman's, Montgomery, Ala.	Average salary for employees with more than 8 years experience (1971)	$2.00 per hour, no commission	$2.57 per hour, 2% commission
Messengers	Offices	Average salary in all metropolitan areas (released February 1971)	$87 per week	$94 per week
Male: Line Assigner Female: Plant Service Clerk	Pacific Telephone & Telegraph Co., San Francisco	Same duties according to U. S. court ruling, 1970	$78 to $109.50 per week	$90 to $156.50 per week

(continued from page 115)

clerical work, factory work, cleaning office buildings. But they often feel there's nothing to say about their jobs, beyond the fact that they're "boring." Often they won't talk about their jobs because they feel inadequate about their performance, or ashamed of the job. Interestingly, in looking back over four years worth of students' writings, we were unable to find a single poem or story by a girl which mentioned work either directly or indirectly. When the teacher tries to draw them out though, students will get more analytical about both the positive and negative aspects of their jobs. One student remarked, "The more I think about it (she was doing clerical work at the time), the more I realize how bad things are at work . . . my time is never my own. I am told exactly what to do, when and how, and if I don't, then that's it." Another student described the pressures of working on an assembly line, how fast you had to go all day long, and the fact that all day you only got two ten-minute breaks, plus a half-hour lunch. The positive feelings expressed stem from the benefits of having a job, rather than from the particular job itself. The fact that working makes them feel independent and adult, and helps them meet new people emerges in such comments as, "I can't always be dependent on my father, I need money for my own stuff"; "I'm old enough now to have a job"; "I like it 'cause I get to meet lots of other kids there."

Our students seldom know much about even their parents' work, and thus the process of filling in the chart can be an eye-opening experience for them. It's important when they've finished to allow space for them to share what they've found out, especially about what the women in their grandparents' and parents' generations have done. One student discovered that her grandmother had left Nova Scotia because it wasn't considered proper for a woman to work there. Another reported that her grandmother had emigrated from Italy and worked in the textile mills in Lawrence, Massachusetts. Another brought out the fact that her mother had held two jobs for the last fifteen years. "I never really knew what she did before," she confessed.

When personal anecdotes have run out, the class makes a huge group chart of the work done by the women in their families. The teacher should make out a chart, similar in format to the individual charts, beforehand, and then students can work together, filling in the data, using different colored magic markers for different generations. When the larger chart is put on the wall, the class can look for patterns.

One important lesson we all learned is that the students' female relatives have always brought money into the family, be it through jobs, through welfare, or sometimes a combination of the two. Another thing the composite chart revealed is that there is little or no upward mobility in the families of our students. In many cases, grandmothers and mothers did the same kind of work our students do. This is in contrast to the men, who often reveal a pattern of downward mobility. Grandfathers were carpenters, longshoremen, fishermen, cooks. As those trades declined, fathers entered the job market as unskilled factory workers.

In discussing the work charts, we want students to feel pride in the work both the women and the men in their families have done. This often involves reiterating that housework and raising kids is work, and hard work at that. One way to look at the welfare system is to see it as a recognition that women should be paid for raising their families. We stress that the jobs available to working class people, and women in particular, have been and continue to be limited. It's necessary to point out that the causes of poverty lie more in powerful economic and social forces, like the elimination of blue-collar jobs in Cambridge as manufacturing has given way to research and development firms, than in personal misfortune.

Section II: Factory Work and Factory Organizing—Then and Now

We devote a section in this unit to factory work because since the nineteenth century, factories have been a major source of both jobs and exploitation for working class women. In the early 1800s, the only occupations open to women were factory work, sewing, teaching or domestic work.[2] In those factories women often worked fourteen to seventeen hours a day, for about $1.50 a week.[3] The hours have gotten shorter, but the exploitation of women continues. For the country as a whole in 1971 there was a forty-one percent gap between the earnings of male and female assembly line workers.[4] Women tend to do the most debilitating jobs and have little chance for promotion.[5] Gains have and are being made, however, through union organizing and most recently, through new women's caucuses within unions designed to promote concerns of special interest to women, such as equal pay, training opportunities, day care, maternity leaves.

Activities in this unit are intended to give students a sense of working conditions for women in nineteenth- and twentieth-century factories, as well as a sense of how women have struggled to change those conditions. Students start by reading first-hand accounts of factory work in the 1840s. Immediate contrast and comparison is then made by interviewing women currently working in factories. They can learn something about union organizing, then and now, by reading from "Mother" Mary Jones' autobiography and then talking to a woman currently involved in union organizing.

Activity Number Three: Reading about Factory Work in the Nineteenth Century
This activity involves reading and discussing two short passages about the lives of women who did factory work in the nineteenth century. The main reading is a chapter on "Women and Work" (pp. 17-25) in *Bread and Roses* by Milton Meltzer. We chose it because it is short, geared towards high school students, and uses first-hand accounts like the following ones to document the appalling conditions that women worked under:

> "The machines go like mad all day, because the faster you work, the more money you get. Sometimes in my haste I get my finger caught and the needle goes right through it. It goes so quick, though, that it does not hurt much. I bind my finger up with a piece of cotton and go on working. We all have accidents like that . . . . All the time we are working, the boss walks around examining the finished garments and making us do them again if they are not just right. So we have to be careful as well as swift. . . .
>
> "An ad in a Long Island paper called for a woman to sew on buttons. With glad heart I went, for what could I do better . . . .
>
> "After making a satisfactory sample I was told that the price was two cents for a gross; no thread supplied. Bewildered, I made some mental multiplication, but I could not think of more than sixty cents for thirty gross of buttons. Of this I subtracted five cents for cotton and thirty cents for car fare, which left a total of twenty five cents earnings.

"However, I was elated at being of some help, and set to work as soon as I reached home. It took me one whole week to mount the 4,320 buttons, and when I delivered them, using my last five cents for car fare, I was told that only ten gross were mounted properly; that all I could get was thirty cents, and would I call next Saturday."

The companion reading is a one-page section from *The American Woman: Who Was She?*, edited by Anne Firor Scott, called "The Home Lives of Factory Women" (p. 19). It's a valuable supplement because it describes what happened to women when the long day in the mill was over: they began the cooking, cleaning, washing and mending for their families. Their work went on past midnight, while the men were asleep, after an evening spent in smoking, drinking, talking union politics with cronies in barrooms, or placidly nodding at home over a newspaper.

It's good to begin the class with visuals, to help make the readings come alive. *The Revolt of the American Woman* by Oliver Jenson contains photographs of nineteenth-century factory workers and workplaces. Ideally, the teacher can have slides made of some of these pictures and project them, along with contrasting slides of middle class or rich women, who weren't allowed to work at all. If you don't have access to facilities for making slides, you can just pass around the pictures for students to examine.

Students can read and discuss the material in one class. More time spent now will probably bore the group. The teacher should be prepared to answer questions, because students will be amazed and even disbelieving when they read about working conditions in 1860. "Why did women put up with it?" "Weren't there unions?" "What could you do, earning $1.56 a week?" etc. You will want to do some extra reading beyond both Meltzer's and Scott's books. You might also get students to draw parallels with today's conditions. Two things we point out, if they don't emerge in the discussion, are that women were paid less than men in the nineteenth century also (referring back to the chart students looked at in the opening activity), and that lots of women today also do two full-time jobs, one at work and one at home. It's not as important to focus on the differences in working conditions, because those will come out in the next activity, when students interview women they know who are working in factories.

Activity Number Four: Interviewing Women Who Work in Factories
To compare factory work in the nineteenth century with factory work in the 1970s, students here interview women currently working in factories. The goals are to see in what ways working conditions have changed and to give students a basis broader than personal experience from which to consider the problems and benefits of factory work for women.

A good way to start is to have any student who has worked in a factory describe her experience to the class. This serves the double purpose of helping other students think about how they might like factory work, and also suggesting topics to cover in the interviews. The teacher can then ask the group for questions and write them on the board.

We vividly remember a story told by one student. She was working in a factory in Cambridge where women were paid on a piece work basis, and where there were quotas on each type of machine. She'd get put on one machine, but as soon as she got good enough at it to reach the quota, she'd get transferred to another machine. The result was that she constantly felt inadequate and incompetent. What she didn't realize was that the employer didn't want her to get too good on a machine, because she'd start producing over the quota and they'd have to pay her more.

The interview form our students generated included questions about pay, hours, holidays, sick leave. Other questions were less factual: Are women treated differently from men in your factory? Do the supervisors flirt with you? Is there a union? Would you want one? Why do you work there? Do you like it? What would make it better?

When they've worked out the questionnaire, students decide who they are going to interview. We usually have each student do one interview. The majority of them should be with women currently working in factories, but it will add to the subsequent discussion if several students interview grandmothers or other older women they know about factory work in the early 1900s. In a small group, results from the interviews can be compared by having students each report. With more than six or seven students, you'll probably want to put the results up on a chart so that all can remember the various responses.

Our students found generally that women they talked to were indifferent about their jobs. They sometimes enjoyed the sociability of the work, but found it boring nevertheless. The overriding reason for working was money, often more than they could earn in other unskilled jobs. Of the ten women interviewed by one class, eight didn't belong to unions and seven of the eight didn't care one way or the other. A few felt that the men in their factories got the pleasanter jobs, defined as ones that they could move around in.

Students were surprised about the pay. As one said, "I never realized I could make more money in a factory than at a register at Zayre's (a large department store)." They also were confused about the lack of union participation, a confusion which may have stemmed from other discussions in the Group School about how important unions had been in improving working conditions. We pointed out that six out of seven working women today are not union members, and that, although increasing numbers of women are joining unions, union leadership is still almost entirely male.[6]

A good follow-up to the interviews is an article called "Women in Factories," written by Jean Tepperman, and printed in the anthology *Sisterhood Is Powerful.* It's a relatively brief description of the working conditions and attitudes of women in two factories in the Chicago area. We've used the reading to raise for discussion some of the ways in which women are discriminated against in factories—no chance for promotion, more tedious jobs, less responsibility, less pay—which may not have emerged through the student interviews. The article also contains a brief but interesting section on women's attitudes toward unions.

Activity Number Five: Union Organizing, Then and Now
How did nineteenth century working conditions change? How can women factory workers today improve their jobs? These are two of the questions addressed in this activity. Students read an excerpt from the autobiography of "Mother" Mary Jones and then talk to a woman currently involved in labor unions. In both cases, the issues are presented in the context of an individual woman writing or speaking about her work.

We do this because the personal angle makes the same issues more interesting to students (something especially important when you're teaching history) and because it provides them with positive female role models.

"Mother" Mary Jones was one of the most remarkable figures in American labor history. In 1880, she changed her life completely when she left her work as a seamstress to become a full-time union organizer. She traveled from the coal mines of West Virginia to the copper mines of Colorado, helping to organize and sustain strikes. She was a master at dramatizing issues and planning effective strategies. To protest child labor in the Pennsylvania textile mills in 1903, for example, she organized a march of maimed, mutilated children of the mill, who traveled from Pennsylvania to visit President Roosevelt in Washington, with a stop along the way at Wall Street to see Morgan. The statement—picked up and publicized nationally—was that "Philadelphia mansions were built on the broken bones, the quivering breasts and the drooping heads of children." Shortly afterward, the Pennsylvania legislature passed a law which kept all children under fourteen out of the factories.

A twenty-page excerpt from "Mother" Mary Jones' autobiography is available in *Growing Up Female in America: Ten Lives,* edited by Eve Merriam. Because the excerpt already contains just the highlights of her career as organizer, we use it in its entirety. Our discussion in class centers around Mother Jones' organizing techniques and personality. Questions could also be asked to get at ways in which the companies tried to break strikes and prevent unions. We've found that even those students normally uninterested in history will enjoy the reading. As one student said, "Mother Jones, she's dynamite!"

The second half of this activity exposes students to a woman currently involved in union organizing. One way to do this is to tour a unionized plant and then, immediately afterward, talk with a female union leader about her work. Such a trip nicely integrates questions of factory conditions, union organizing, and jobs women have, but it may be hard to arrange. The teacher can contact unions connected with major industries in the area and see whether they have a woman organizer in the union who would be willing to talk to the class. The next step is to find out whether any of the plants the union is connected with normally give tours, and to see whether it's possible to schedule the tour and talk on the same morning or afternoon.

An alternative to the trip is to invite as speaker in the classroom a woman who is either doing factory organizing or involved in an organizing drive in her workplace.

We invited a speaker because the mother of one of the students in the class was working at Cambion, a factory in North Cambridge that was finally being organized after several previously unsuccessful attempts. The mother wasn't one of the organizers, but had gotten involved and was supporting the union. In class, she talked about conditions at the factory, how she felt about the union, and how the organizers had gone about organizing union elections. She also brought with her two letters which the company had been circulating among the workers to try to discourage them from joining the union. Among other things, the letters contained "red-baiting," pairing unions with communism, and the threat that, if the union came in, the company might be forced to move from the area. We talked about how that wasn't necessarily an empty threat: many companies did in fact move to non-union areas to save labor costs. Based on the number of questions students asked, we knew the class had been successful. One student reported back later that she had gone home and talked to her mother about whether anybody was trying to get a union started where she worked.

Section III: Examination of Jobs Commonly Done by Women

This section focuses on jobs other than factory work which are commonly done by working class women. The goal is to help students think about the pros and cons of jobs they may want to do, or may find themselves doing. With this goal in mind, the activities alternate between ones in which students explore various kinds of work, as they did with factory work, and ones in which they think more personally about work they could do, or would want to do, and how they would handle various job situations.

The section begins with a series of activities on housework, emphasized because it is already so much a part of our students' lives and will undoubtedly continue to be so. Students start by making a housework collage and discussing their feelings about housework. They then calculate the monetary value of all the work a housewife does and consider whether she should be paid a salary. The assumption underlying all activities is that housework is real, hard work which is undervalued in the society.

The next activities are more personal. Students see a range of office jobs they might be able to get through visiting a large company which hires a number of clerical workers, including students right out of high school. Some of the disadvantages of office work are then raised through a speaker who is involved in organizing office workers to change certain aspects of their jobs. Students then read a series of case studies involving on-the-job sexism and discuss ways they might handle those situations on a day to day basis.

The section ends with suggestions of ways that Studs Terkel's book *Working* can be used with students.

Activity Number Six: Housework Collage
An enjoyable way to begin to look at housework as work is to have students make a housework collage from pictures and ads in magazines. While clipping and pasting pictures, students' attitudes about and experiences with housework have space to surface in an informal setting.

This activity can easily be done in one class. The teacher brings in a pile of magazines and instructs students to look through them, clipping pictures or word slogans which have to do with any aspect of being a housewife or doing housework. After twenty minutes or so, students will have plenty of pictures and can begin pasting them up in a collage.

As students are working on the collage, informal comments will go around the room about how they always have to do this at home, or how much they hate to do that. Or they'll react to the pictures they're cutting out—"Look at the way she's serving everyone!" "If we only had a dishwasher." The teacher should encourage anecdotes, and add her own, without trying to turn it into a formal discussion.

When the finished collage is up on the wall, it will speak for itself. Housework involves many different tasks: a woman's work is never done.

Activity Number Seven: The Value of Housewives
"What do you do?"
"Nothing, I'm just a housewife."
The purpose of this activity is to examine that "just" which so many of us have internalized, and to build English and job skills. Students start out by generating together a chart modeled on one published by the Chase Manhattan Bank in 1972. The outline of the chart, which the teacher should put up on the board, is:

What's a wife worth?

Job	*Hours per week*	*Rate per hour*	*Value per week*
Total hours:			Total value:

The bank's survey records the work of middle class women. After students have made their own chart—reflecting their families' lives—we compare the two.

Before filling in the columns, students list all the tasks a housewife does—mending, caring for children, etc. Students then rename each task on this list as a job outside the home: for example, mending becomes the work of a seamstress, etc.

When the "job" column of tbe chart has been filled in, each student calculates the "Hours per Week." To fill in "Rate per Hours," the teacher should draw on students' information and on the Chase Manhattan Bank figures, explaining that these were for 1972 and might be slightly higher now. Multiplying "Hours" by "Rate" concludes the chart-making and students can then calculate the total "Value per Week."

The students will be most interested in and shocked by the total hours per week a housewife works and what she would be paid for that work weekly outside the home. One of our students noted that her mother received less from welfare per month than she was worth, according to the chart, per week. Another said, "You know, I never realized how many different things my mother did." At some point the teacher might ask, "Why do women say, I'm just a housewife'?"

When students have had a chance to make observations about their chart, we show them the one published by the bank so that they may compare upper middle class housewives with working class housewives (see page 125). Our class' chart showed women spending more time both on dishwashing and taking care of children. The bank's chart suggests that these women had dishwashers and some ability to pay for child care. The jobs of gardener and chauffeur were not listed by our class, but a new job was added—going to school or court when your child is in trouble.

Activity Number Eight: Trip to a Large Company, The Range of Office Jobs
When our students think about jobs for themselves, office work may seem a possibility, but one that's comparable to having a profession. They view it with the same feelings of inadequacy and anxiety that a college-educated, middle class woman feels when she considers being an editor or lawyer. The purpose of this activity, in which students

What's a wife worth?[7]

Job	Hours per week	Rate per hour	Value per week
Nursemaid	44.5	$2.00	$ 89.00
Housekeeper	17.5	3.25	56.88
Cook	13.1	3.25	42.58
Dishwasher	6.2	2.00	12.40
Laundress	5.9	2.50	14.75
Food buyer	3.3	2.50	11.55
Gardener	2.3	3.00	6.90
Chauffeur	2.0	3.25	6.50
Maintenance man	1.7	3.00	5.10
Seamstress	1.3	3.25	4.22
Dietician	1.2	4.50	5.40
Practical nurse	.6	3.75	2.25
Total	99.6		$257.53

tour a large company that recruits students out of high school and talk to someone in personnel about clerical jobs, is to show students that office work is something they can do if they want to and that job options are available to them.

To set up the trip, the teacher should contact any of the large businesses, banks or insurance companies in the area which hire many clerical workers. If they recruit students from high schools, they're likely to have someone working in personnel who regularly talks to student groups.

We visited the Prudential Insurance Company in Boston and would recommend it. Students saw a large typing pool, keypunch operators, secretaries with their own offices, women doing bookkeeping; and they talked with a woman who was the head of personnel. Unfortunately, we weren't able to talk to any of the workers. Students were impressed by the benefits explained to them, especially the company-arranged, low-price tours to Europe, and the low-priced restaurant for employees right in the building. They remarked that many of the women working there looked about their own age and wore nice clothes.

The trip strongly affected one student in particular. When she saw the typing pool of fifteen women, she said, "I can do that!" Although she was learning to type in school, she had never really believed that she could get a job with her skill, except in some small firm in her neighborhood. The idea of being able to get a job in which she would get "dressed up," go downtown every day, go out for lunch, was very exciting to her. It gave her new confidence in herself.

Activity Number Nine: Speaker, Organizing Office Workers
If it can be arranged, we suggest following the trip with a speaker who is involved in some

facet of organizing office workers. In this way some of the problems connected with office work, such as absence of job descriptions, lack of security, little hope for promotion, or no unions, can be raised in the context of women struggling to solve those problems.

The speaker should be encouraged to share with students what she and other women in her office or company are doing and why. Ideally some time should be set aside afterwards for students to reflect on the issues raised. You might want to have them compare some of the things the speaker said about office workers and office work with what they had learned from the personnel representative.

Activity Number Ten: Jobs Commonly Done by Women
Studs Terkel's *Working,* a collection of interviews with over 100 people who talk about what they do all day and how they feel about it, provides rich material for examining jobs commonly done by women. The book is both fascinating and informative and provides an alternative to speakers. Now available in paperback, we suggest that sections from it be used in the "Woman and Work" unit and that the whole book be given to students to read. Our purpose here is to discuss an approach to using the book and to recommend certain excerpts.

We choose interviews by working class women, doing jobs our students might someday have or might fantasize about having. One major goal in choosing excerpts is to help students see both the real work parts of jobs, like typing for a secretary, which women doing them have a right to be proud of, and the exploitive parts, like making coffee, which many women resent. Another goal is to help students look more closely at jobs which on the surface seem very ordinary or very glamorous.

Many of the interviews are short enough to read in class, but are interesting enough that students would probably read them at home. Depending on time, the teacher might want to use from two to four excerpts with the class. Our approach to discussing a given account is to have students think about how the person feels about her work and why, the pros and cons of the job, and how the students think they would like those jobs.

Writing assignments can help students think through these issues, or can be used to tie together previous activities on housework and office work with whatever sections from *Working* students read. Possible assignments are:

1. Imagine you're a stewardess (hooker, waitress, etc.). Describe a typical day in your life and your feelings as you go through the day.
2. Write a conversation between two friends, one who wants to be a waitress (daycare worker, telephone operator, etc.) and the other who has strong feelings, either in favor of or against her decision.
3. If you could choose between being a housewife, a secretary or an airline stewardess (model, prostitute, etc.) which would you choose and why. Include what the job is like and what the advantages or disadvantages would be for you personally.

Almost all the interviews with women raise for discussion general questions about sexual exploitation or prestige. Sections we particularly recommend concern the Executive Secretary, the Hooker and the Airline Stewardess. The executive secretary identifies herself totally with the man she works for:

"I feel like I'm sharing somewhat the business life of the men. So I think I'm much happier as the secretary of an executive than I would be in some woman's field, where perhaps I could make more money. But it wouldn't be an extension of successful executive. I'm perfectly happy in my status."

The hooker sees her work as a game in which she has control:

"As a bright assertive woman I had no power. As a cold, manipulative hustler, I had a lot. I knew I was playing a role. Most women are taught to become what they act. All I did was act out the reality of American womanhood."

The airline stewardess acknowledges the fact that her job got her out of a small town in Nebraska and has allowed her to travel, but resents the way she is treated by the airline:

"They call us professional people, but they talk to us as very young, childishly. They check us all the time on appearance. They check our weight every month. Even though you've been flying for twenty years, they check you and say that's a no-no. Even though there's no room in the coatroom, you're supposed to somehow make room. If you're a pound over, they can take you off flights until you get under."

Other interviews we suggest include the waitress and the supermarket checker, both older women who love their jobs and take pride in the skills they've developed; the bank teller who feels her job is important, but realizes and resents the fact that it doesn't have any prestige; the fashion model who says the work makes you feel like "you're someone else's clothes hanger," but who keeps at it because the pay is so good; the young telephone operator who feels put down at times, but also enjoys the power of being able to tell people to put more money in, or cutting them off; and the ambivalent hospital aide, an eighteen-year-old who says bitterly that she can't stand the patients, feels guilty about her "rotten attitude," but who also obviously cares for her patients and who wants to be a nurse.

Activity Number Eleven: How Would You Respond
Here students explore possible responses to daily sexism on the job and the consequences of those responses. The case studies they read and discuss are all real, coming directly from experiences girls in The Group School have had on their jobs.

We've used the following case studies. The teacher should feel free to add new cases and delete others, with an eye towards making the cases reflect the kinds of work her students do.

1. Judy is applying for a job at an insurance company which involves typing and filing. The personnel manager interviewing her tells her, "We expect all our girls to look attractive. Naturally that means dressing properly. Pantsuits are acceptable, but jeans or slacks without matching tops aren't." He then adds as an afterthought, "You should wear dresses, though, to show off those nice legs of yours."
2. Debby is working nights at Kentucky Fried Chicken. Her job is to stand behind the counter and take orders from customers. Although there are other people in the

kitchen, she is the only one visible to people as they come in. She feels very vulnerable as a girl and is afraid a lot of the time.

3. Donna is working as a waitress at Brigham's. Her supervisor is a man who is constantly flirting with her or bossing her around. He'll do things like standing very close to her, breathing down her neck as she makes a sundae, on the pretext of making sure she's doing it correctly. Or one minute he'll be yelling at her to serve the customers more quickly and the next, he'll be calling her over, putting his arm around her, and asking her whether or not she has a boyfriend.

4. Marie is working at a fancy boutique in Harvard Square and has been going out with the manager. Now she's decided she doesn't really like him, and wants to break up with him, but she still wants the job. After she starts "being busy" whenever he asks her out, he starts making it hard for her to work there. He consistently gives her bad hours—both Friday and Saturday nights for instance—and either ignores her totally or makes nasty comments to her whenever they're both in the store at the same time.

To give students a range of options, the class first reads each case study together and brainstorms about possible responses. When different ways of handling the situation have been listed on the board, the teacher asks students to guess what the consequence might be for each of the responses listed. For instance, the consequence of always moving away from the manager at Brigham's might be that he would yell at you even more. The consequences then also get put on the board, paired with the responses.

Before moving on to the next case, the teacher tells students to make a note to themselves on paper about which response they would choose and why.

Once the group has discussed all the cases, students focus on how they personally would handle the situations by role-playing their responses. We divide students up in pairs for this and tell them that they should do role-plays of how the girl responded in each of the four case studies. We explain that they should take turns being the girl and being the employer or manager whom the girl talks to. When they're the girl, they should choose the response they think they would actually choose. While the pairs are off in different corners of the room, or in different rooms doing their role-plays, the teacher can circulate among them. When they have had a chance to do all four role-plays, we call them back together and each pair shares one of its role-plays with the class.

Section IV: Women in Unusual Jobs

Women have begun to move into fields normally dominated by men. This section of the "Women and Work" unit exposes students to more unusual kinds of work women are now doing. Again, the emphasis is on jobs realistically within the rnage of possibilities for students. The overall goal is to broaden their sense of options for the future.

Activity Number Twelve: What's My Line?
An enjoyable way to learn about unusual jobs that women do is to play a modified version of the TV show "What's My Line?" Three women, each of whom works at a job students don't normally associate with women, come in to "be on the show." Students question them one by one, trying to get enough information from yes/no questions to be able to guess their jobs. Once they've guessed, they talk informally

with each of the women about their work. The game provides a good structure for getting students to think about what a given job is like.

In lining up contestants, we look for women who do a range of unusual jobs. The jobs shouldn't be highly skilled ones, because part of the purpose of the game is to suggest possible job options for students. They also shouldn't be terribly obscure, because the point isn't to stump the students. Jobs that fit this criteria include those from the trades (carpentry, plumbing, printing), a truck driver or cab driver, a mail-person, or a paper girl, a housepainter, a foreman in a factory, a store owner, a woman who has set up her own business. A combination we used once consisted of a printer, a police officer and a cab driver. We explain to contestants beforehand the rationale for the game, how it works, and that we'd like them to talk about their jobs after the guessing part is over.

To be able to play the game in one class period, students need some preparation before-hand. The teacher should explain the procedure a day in advance. Usually, several students are familiar with the TV show and can explain it to the others. We use the following rules: you can only ask yes/no questions; as long as someone gets a yes answer, she can go on asking questions; you can only make a guess when it's your turn. We also tell students that all the contestants will be women who do jobs women don't normally do.

The class hour before the game can be spent preparing questions, since students often are slow to think of yes/no questions on the spot. Generating questions is a valuable process in itself because it makes students think about what distinguishes one job from another—wage vs. salary, self-employed vs. working for someone, etc. The questions we came up with included: Do you work alone? Do you make a product? Do you provide a service? Are you self-employed? Are you paid by the hour? The teacher can make copies of the questions and give them to students when they start playing the game.

During "What's My Line?" the teacher's main job is to watch the time. With three people, you need an hour.

Section V: Defining Job Needs and Expectations

We end this unit on "Women and Work" by encouraging students to think personally about working. Activities are designed to help them define their personal work goals, needs and expectations, the rationale being that before you can start looking for a job, you should know what you want to get out of it. At the end, they're in a better position to review specific jobs covered in the unit, to look through job catalogues, or to meet with a job counselor—all with the goal of finding specific jobs they might want to have.

Activity Number Thirteen: Questionnaire, What Kind of Job do I Want and Why?
Given the urgency of a student from a low income family to earn money, as well as the need to find satisfaction in one's life, it's never too early to think about future work. The structure of this activity is simple: students are given the following questionnaire to fill out and told to take as much time as they need to think about all the questions.

What Kind of Job do I Want and Why?

Personal needs
1. Do I want to do service work? (helping people, waitressing, etc.)
2. Do I want to do physical work?
3. Do I want to do "head" work or office work?
4. Is it important that the job be satisfying or meaningful?
5. Is it important for me to enjoy my work?
6. Is it important to me what other people think of my work?

Mobility needs
1. How long do I want a job for?
2. Do I want on the job training?
3. If training is available, will I accept less money?
4. Do I want the job to lead to something else?

Social needs
1. Do I want to work with people or alone?
2. Do I want to work with people of my own age?
3. Do I want to work for a large company or a small company?

Financial needs
1. How much money do I need? (approximately)
   —rent:
   —food:
   —clothes:
   —entertainment:
   —schooling:
2. Do I need a job where I can earn a lot of money to save or to pay off debts?

Occasionally, a student has said that the questionnaire is irrelevant to her because she is getting married soon and won't need or want a job, or because she has a child and is living on welfare. The teacher should encourage her to answer the questions anyway. You can remind her of the family work tree, which demonstrated that the students' mothers and grandmothers had usually worked. Or you can review other parts of the unit which have shown women either needing or wanting to work outside the home at some point in their lives. Another tack is simply to ask whether she thinks she can count on being supported forever.

A follow-up to the questionnaire should help students think of specific jobs which meet the needs they have defined. A way to begin, which also serves the purpose of reviewing the unit, is to give students a list of all the jobs that have been discussed in the course of the unit and have them look at whether any of those jobs would meet their needs. Ideally, students could then use their questionnaire and that list as the basis for talking with a job counselor about specific jobs.

Notes

1. Nancy Seifer, *Absent from the Majority* (National Project on Ethnic America), pp. 28-33.

2. Claire and Leonard Ingraham, *An Album of Women in American History* (New York: Franklin Watts, Inc., 1973), p. 31.

3. Milton Meltzer, *Bread and Roses* (New York: Random House, 1967), p. 17.

4. Seifer, pp. 34-36.

5. Jean Tepperman, "Women in Factories," in *Sisterhood Is Powerful,* ed. Robin Morgan (New York: Random House, 1970), pp. 117-118.

6. Seifer, p. 33.

7. The chart was published in *Ms.* (July 1972) and also appears in a booklet, "Houseworkers Handbook," available at the New Words Bookstore in Cambridge or from The Women's Center, 46 Pleasant St., Cambridge, Mass. 02139.

Sharon L. Menard
Social Studies
Boulder High School
Boulder, Colo./1974

WOMEN AND THE AMERICAN CULTURE

Background

At Boulder High School, during the last week of the first semester of the junior-level American history course, the students are permitted to select from about twenty mini-courses, including TV Drama, Twentieth-Century American Music, Educational Problems of the 1970's, American Art, Chicano Art and The Automobile. The students select these according to interest and to schedule. The courses last one week, meeting one hour a day.

I was invited by the social studies department to teach a mini-course about Women and the American Culture. This was an outgrowth of my speaking engagements and my work in the school district on the issue of school sexism. The course outline, materials and ideas were a combination of my speeches, materials developed for an inservice training workshop and sources such as the National Education Association.

Purpose

The main purpose of the course was to teach about the American woman, past and present; however, I set some very important secondary goals for this course. I wanted students to understand:

—the need to be open-minded with respect to all people.
—the "softness" of the social sciences when facts or absolutes are difficult to find.
—the need to learn and to understand many different viewpoints.
—the sources of social information and data and where they can be found.
—the need to determine what an authority is, what an authority's qualifications are, and what an authority's bias is.
—the need to support one's own viewpoints and arguments with facts.
—the need to question what one hears or reads.
—the need to examine one's own attitudes with respect to women and sex roles.

Assignments

Individual
1. Student attitude checklist in which students check the things that they would not do and then check the things that they would not have a member of the opposite sex do.
2. Describe a day in your life at age fifty.
3. A self-scoring questionnaire on women and men from *Psychology Today* (July 1971).
4. Course final in which the students choose a book review from a list of eight titles; or write a position paper on any three of eleven quotations.

Group

1. The students were asked to watch TV for an hour and one-half and count the number of women and men that they saw and list what they were doing.
2. The students were given a list of women's names and asked to write a short summary of their contributions to U. S. culture and history.
3. The students were asked to read and summarize orally a report done by the city of Boulder on poverty in Boulder.
4. The students were asked to debate the question: "Will the current feminist movement change the roles of women and men?"

Method

I can tolerate only a minimum of lectures. I find that I learn most from research and work that I have done myself. Also, since the mini-course was to be "independent study," I planned for a maximum of student participation and discussion, within structured situations. The group assignments were designed for class presentation; the individual assignments were designed to help students understand their own attitudes and opinions, compare these with other viewpoints, begin research into facts and opinions about women.

I lectured the first day and part of the second day, but by the second day the students began their own presentations prepared from the list of assignments.

The Class

Twenty-six students enrolled in the course, twenty-five women and one man. One of the regular teachers, a man, also attended the course and a graduate student in social studies education attended as an observer.

First day. We began the class by listing the traits of the "ideal" American woman and man. We did not discuss these lists at this point, but referred back to them in subsequent days when what students learned about women and men did not match their initial descriptions. Women, according to the students, were intelligent, more emotional than men, open-minded, strong, independent, gracious, understanding, sensitive, strong-willed, creative, intuitive. Men were intelligent, emotional (but try to hide it), open-minded, strong, independent, aggressive, understanding, sensitive, strong-willed, progressive, logical. The trait that gave students the most trouble later was "independence." They were not certain when women could be independent (apparently only when a man was not around).

Then I lectured on the history of the American woman, her legal and social status. We discussed traditional history courses and readings and found that women are rarely mentioned and few are listed by name.

Second day. We began with the group report on TV. Students watched TV shows from four different channels, for one and one-half hours. They counted the number of men and women portrayed and listed what these characters were doing. The reports were good. The students observed that TV reinforced sex-role stereotypes with men in main roles and women in supporting roles. They pointed out the number of "rough and tumble" shows with almost no women. (This gave me an opportunity to mention Carolyn Heilbrun's *Saturday Review* article "The Masculine Wilderness of the American

Novel.") The commercials were narrated by men, using women as models and women were most frequently shown with cleaning products. One report included a program about F. Scott Fitzgerald. When the student did not mention Zelda, I asked how she was portrayed. The response was: "Oh, you mean the southern belle." The tone was derisive. So we discussed Zelda, her behavior, reasons for her behavior and her relationship to Scott. I recommended that students read Nancy Milford's *Zelda* to learn more and to see another viewpoint.

For the remainder of the hour I lectured on the economic status of women and the changing roles of women, relying heavily on Department of Labor statistics and the use of flip charts hung up and displayed for the rest of the course.

Third day. We played "What's My Line?" with three local women: a dentist, a minister and a city of Boulder building inspector. The minister had tried three times before she was finally ordained. The time limit to guess her occupation was almost up when one student made a last-ditch effort with, "You aren't a minister, are you?"

The dentist felt that she had had little difficulty in training for and in practicing her profession. Both of her parents had been dentists. The students guessed her occupation easily.

The building inspector was one of three for the city of Boulder. The students were unable to guess her occupation, even with several, very direct hints. When they were told, they were quite fascinated, demanding details about what she did. She was the only one of the three who came from a poor, single-parent black family. She described how her mother, with very little training, struggled to support herself and two daughters, and how she instilled in them the need for education and acquiring job skills that paid well. She also related her battle to obtain an inspector's position in another city after working as a secretary in the inspection department. When she finally was hired, her starting pay was $75 per month less than the men's pay. This caught the interest of the students who then wanted to know if this was still the case. She answered "no," and I explained what it meant to be an equal opportunity employer and what an affirmative action plan was.

Fourth day. I reviewed some of the comments made by the previous day's panel, particularly the experience of the building inspector. Then I gave out the results of the attitude checklist. Of the twenty-three female respondents, the following said that they would not:
1. try to join a boy's club or team (15)
2. pay for a boy on a date (12)
3. smoke a pipe or cigar (10)
4. wear curlers in front of a boy (10)
5. ask a boy out on a date (10)

Of the twenty-three female respondents, the following would not want a boyfriend who:
1. didn't care much about his looks (15)
2. wore cologne or dyed his hair (15)
3. was physically weaker than they (14)
4. spent a lot of time on his looks (12)
5. asked to pay their way on dates (12)
6. made most of the decisions (9)

Students were surprised at the results, but the greatest amazement was registered by a male student-teacher present that day. I heard a noise in the back of the room and looked up to hear this young man exclaim, "Why do you want a man who is stronger than you? So he can beat you up? What's the matter with you?" A debate followed.

The students reported that they had some difficulty in finding several of the "lost women" assigned, using primarily encyclopedias and biographical dictionaries. Women that they could not find included Anne Dudley Bradstreet, Ruth St. Denis, Eliza Spaulding, Patience Lovell Wright, Catherine Green and Rose Schneiderman. They also reported that Leontyne Price and Helen Keller were not in the encyclopedias and that all the information they could find on Mother Jones was that she was a "labor agitator." I recommended that students read two books for further information: Eugenia Andruss' *The Dear-Bought Heritage* and Eve Merriam's *Growing Up Female in America: Ten Lives.*

I gave students copies of *Synopsis of Current Viewpoints: Issue on Women* (December 1973), available from Curriculum Innovations, 501 Lake Forest Ave., Highwood, Ill. 60040. I also distributed a self-scoring questionnaire about women and men from "Woman and Man: A Game," by Carol Tavris and John B. Wexo, in *Psychology Today* (July 1971).

Fifth day. With regard to the "age fifty" assignment, students had imagined themselves as a U. N. translator, artist, fashion designer, teacher, anthropologist, forest ranger, zoologist, doctor and (four) veterinarians.

Then the debate group began with the question "Will the current feminist movement change the roles of women and men?" The pro-side was well done. The students tried to use the information that they had received in the course, primarily laws that will tend to bring about a change in behavior. The con-side was somewhat weaker, lacking in factual argument. One speaker, though, used the rather persuasive argument that, although women "myths" were not supported by fact, they were still widely-assumed to be true. Although change would come, it would be slow and far in the future. After a chance for rebuttal, the whole class joined in active, lively discussion. The biggest point of contention grew around the idea of mothers of young children and infants returning to work. No one suggested the possibility of the father staying home with the children. When I asked about this, several students responded that men don't know what to do with children. They felt that caring for children was innate to women. Of course, many rebuttals came in the wake of that. We took a vote to resolve the question. For "yes" we had one half-raised hand; for "no" I saw flapping elbows, but no hands clearly in the air. I asked how many were abstaining or undecided. Almost all hands were raised.

Evaluation

The course was too brief, though I put as much as humanly possible into one week. The regular teacher was surprised that so much ground could be covered. Of course, I would like to see more time for such a course, primarily used for student discussion and feedback, particularly on the emotional issues.

Joseph Mitchell
Social Studies
Loyola High School
Towson, Md./1972-74

WOMEN IN AMERICAN SOCIETY: A LEARNING ACTIVITIES PACKAGE

Introduction to a Learning Activities Package

Before beginning this program, let us answer the question, "What is a LAP?" A LAP, or Learning Activities Package, is a method for individualizing instruction. It doesn't *teach* you but rather *tells* you where to find information. This means, that instead of working with the rest of your class as a group, most of the time you will be working on your own as an individual. You will cover the same material that you would have covered as a group but there are greater benefits to you as an individual, such as the following:

1. You will be working at your own speed. No one will hold you back. There will be no pressure on you to keep up with any particular pace. When you use a LAP, you make your own pace.
2. You can tailor the program to your own requirements. At the end of a LAP, you should fully understand the material you have covered. However, you may have some knowledge of the material before you begin. Your friend may also know some of the material but not the same material that you know. In a regular class, you and your friend and the rest of the class would have to study all the material presented! However, in using a LAP, you need to study only that material which you do not already know.
3. You select the method you wish to follow in learning. In many sections of this LAP, there is a choice as to what activities can be used to enable you to successfully complete the objectives: different books, films, field trips, interviews, etc. You choose the method which best suits your needs.
4. You can work by yourself *or* with a group. While the program is individualized, you can still perform experiments with other students or have discussion sessions or go on field trips together. In fact, a combination of individual and group work is often the best way to study a topic.

You must agree, some real advantages have been presented. They should be of great benefit and really make your work more enjoyable. But, as the old saying goes, "You never get anything of value for nothing." Your contribution is to accept responsibility. No one will constantly be on your back to make sure you have completed the assignments. However, in one way or another, after you have completed the assignments, your knowledge must be tested. So to assure success, you will find it necessary to get on your own back. Finally, do not forget your teacher! Just because you are working independently, it does not mean that your teacher will not help you. The teacher is there for a definite purpose—to help and guide you. Since you are on your own and have accepted responsibility, you will find times when advice and guidance are necessary. So, why not ask for it? Good luck in this endeavor.

Rationale

The purpose of this LAP is to introduce you to some of the voices in the current phase of a very old movement—the struggle to liberate women from political, social, economic and legal oppression. The first great step in this struggle took place during the middle of the nineteenth century when women fought a long battle that finally achieved for them one of America's most basic rights—the right to vote. It is interesting to note that Afro-Americans (male, of course) had been given the vote almost fifty years earlier than women, and we know how they are still oppressed by American society.

You may wonder why a majority of the population has remained silent for so long. After the vote was won most women expected conditions to change. Only gradually did they come to see that the vote did not touch the most fundamental areas of their lives. In addition, an ideal which glorified motherhood (Betty Friedan calls it "The Feminine Mystique") became part of the American consciousness and women were told by psychiatrists, doctors and magazine editors that only those who conformed to the mystique were complete and normal women.

The current women's movement (sometimes referred to—particularly by the press—as the Women's Liberation Movement) is noteworthy because it has blossomed after a long lull in the struggle. The issues being raised today, however, are the same ones articulated over a hundred years ago. Women are increasingly seeking and finding a role in the world of work and ideas. They are being elected to political office, many with the intention of representing the cause of women's rights. The male-dominated, patriarchal form of family life that has until recently been the norm is coming into serious question. What new life style will emerge is still in doubt, but it will probably be quite different from the old one.

As future voters, husbands, fathers and mature adults (ed. note: Loyola is an all-male high school), you will be called upon to face all the flaws in our present society and hopefully to repair some of them. In order to help you formulate some ideas regarding the relationship between the sexes in the future, this LAP provides an overview of some of the best thinking on the topic and suggests some activities you may initiate on your own. This LAP will require the exercise of your imagination. Try to find out what it *feels* like to be a woman in today's world—how it looks from outside the power base—what frustrations there are as well as what fulfillment is possible.

Perhaps we ought not to assign roles to men and women by sex. Perhaps the liberation of women will result in a corresponding liberation of men—liberation from a stifling definition of what it is to be a man in today's society. Hopefully, the future will allow all of us, regardless of sex, to be human persons first and male and female second.

Pretest Instructions

The purpose of this test you are about to take is to give you the opportunity to assess your feelings about the role of women in American society. It is for your own personal use, and your answers will not be recorded anywhere except on your answer sheets.

The only thing I ask of you is to honestly and objectively answer all of the questions at this time. Then complete all of the activities contained in the LAP. When you have completed all of the activities, take the test again to see if any of your answers have changed as a result of the work you have done. If you wish, we could talk about the results of the tests at our last conference.

Some of the questions in the test might be of a repetitious nature. Ignore that and answer all questions anyway. Also, don't worry if the questions are not in proper numerical order. They were taken from different sources and do not follow any particular order.

The questions for this test were taken from the following sources: "Survey on Women's Liberation," *Redbook* (April 1972), pp. 73-78; "Women's Liberation Survey," *CBS News Poll* (September 8-10, 1970)—a poll of 1,312 people, eighteen years of age and older, taken by telephone.

Pretest Sample

1. Which sex has more advantages or privileges in this society?
   A. Men have many more than women.
   B. Men have more than women.
   C. There are advantages and disadvantages for each sex.
   D. Women have more than men.
   E. Women have many more than men.
2. What is the most effective way for women to overcome discrimination?
   A. By working with men in organized groups.
   B. By working in exclusively female groups.
   C. By working individually to prove their abilities and educate men.
   D. It cannot be overcome under the present system; radical political change must come first.
   E. I do not think there is discrimination against women.
3. What is the *best* way for most women to develop their potential?
   A. By being good wives and mothers only.
   B. By taking jobs that best utilize their feminine skills and qualities, such as nursing or social work.
   C. By taking jobs that most fulfill them as individuals.
   D. By joining women's groups that will develop their consciousness as women.
   E. By combining marriage, motherhood and work.
   F. By combining marriage or a love relationship and work.

Some people believe that personality differences between the sexes are biological in origin; others think that they are learned; others say that there are no differences at all. Which of the statements listed best expresses your viewpoint about the traits in entries 4 through 11?

4. Aggressiveness is:
   A. More common in men, for biological reasons.
   B. More common in men, for cultural reasons.
   C. Equally common in both sexes.
   D. More common in women, for biological reasons.
   E. More common in women, for cultural reasons.
5. A capacity for deep feeling is:
   A. More common in men, for biological reasons.
   B. More common in men, for cultural reasons.
   C. Equally common in both sexes.
   D. More common in women, for biological reasons.
   E. More common in women, for cultural reasons.

6. Independence is:
   A. More common in men, for biological reasons.
   B. More common in men, for cultural reasons.
   C. Equally common in both sexes.
   D. More common in women, for biological reasons.
   E. More common in women, for cultural reasons.
7. Objectivity and rationality are:
   A. More common in men, for biological reasons.
   B. More common in men, for cultural reasons.
   C. Equally common in both sexes.
   D. More common in women, for biological reasons.
   E. More common in women, for cultural reasons.
8. Nurturing capacity is:
   A. More common in men, for biological reasons.
   B. More common in men, for cultural reasons.
   C. Equally common in both sexes.
   D. More common in women, for biological reasons.
   E. More common in women, for cultural reasons.
9. The ability to reason abstractly is:
   A. More common in men, for biological reasons.
   B. More common in men, for cultural reasons.
   C. Equally common in both sexes.
   D. More common in women, for biological reasons.
   E. More common in women, for cultural reasons.
10. Preference for monogamy is:
    A. More common in men, for biological reasons.
    B. More common in men, for cultural reasons.
    C. Equally common in both sexes.
    D. More common in women, for biological reasons.
    E. More common in women, for cultural reasons.
11. Empathy and intuition are:
    A. More common in men, for biological reasons.
    B. More common in men, for cultural reasons.
    C. Equally common in both sexes.
    D. More common in women, for biological reasons.
    E. More common in women, for cultural reasons.

For the following entries, choose one of the statements that best expresses your feelings.

12. The communications media (for example, television and the press) degrade women by portraying them as sex objects or mindless dolls.
    A. Strongly agree.   D. Slightly disagree.
    B. Generally agree.   E. Generally disagree.
    C. Slightly agree.   F. Strongly disagree.

13. Many women who do the same work as their male colleagues earn substantially less money.
    A. Strongly agree. D. Slightly disagree.
    B. Generally agree. E. Generally disagree.
    C. Slightly agree. F. Strongly disagree.
14. Most men do not take women seriously.
    A. Strongly agree. D. Slightly disagree.
    B. Generally agree. E. Generally disagree.
    C. Slightly agree. F. Strongly disagree.
15. If a woman wants to get ahead, there is little to stop her.
    A. Strongly agree. D. Slightly disagree.
    B. Generally agree. E. Generally disagree.
    C. Slightly agree. F. Strongly disagree.
16. I usually find the things men talk about more interesting than the things women talk about.
    A. Strongly agree. D. Slightly disagree.
    B. Generally agree. E. Generally agree.
    C. Slightly agree. F. Strongly disagree.

1. Recently, it was proposed that an "Equal Rights" amendment be added to our Constitution. This amendment would guarantee that women would have all of the rights that men have. Do you favor or oppose adding such an amendment to the Constitution?
    A. Favor the amendment.
    B. Oppose the amendment.
    C. No response.
2. Who would you trust more to be your doctor, a man or a woman?
    A. Would choose a male doctor.
    B. Would choose a female doctor.
    C. Would choose either.
    D. No answer.
    Who would you trust more to be your accountant, a man or a woman?
    A. Would choose a male accountant.
    B. Would choose a female accountant.
    C. Would choose either.
    D. No answer.
    Who would you trust more to be your lawyer, a man or a woman?
    A. Would choose a male lawyer.
    B. Would choose a female lawyer.
    C. Would choose either.
    D. No answer.
3. If you had a daughter who wanted a full-time career—even after she was married—would you encourage her, or not?
    A. Would encourage her.
    B. Would not encourage her.
    C. No answer.

4. Would you favor or oppose setting up child-care centers in your area, that would take care of the children of women who wanted to work during the day?
   A. Favor child-care centers.
   B. Oppose child-care centers.
   C. No answer.
5. If child-care centers were set up in your area, do you think they should be financed by taxes, by the companies that employ the women, or by the women themselves?
   A. Financed by taxes.
   B. Financed by the companies.
   C. Financed by the women who work.
   D. Some combination of all three.
   E. No answer.
6. If both a husband and wife work full-time, do you think that the husband should do as much as the wife does, at least some, or none of the cooking, cleaning, or taking care of the children?
   A. Should do as much.
   B. Should do at least some.
   C. Should do none.
   D. No answer.
7. When married women have full-time jobs outside the home, do you think that their work interferes very much, somewhat, a little, or not at all with their responsibilities at home?
   A. Work interferes very much.
   B. Work interferes somewhat.
   C. Work interferes a little.
   D. No interference at all.
   E. No answer.
8. Would you say that working women generally seem to make better—or worse—mothers than women who don't work outside the home?
   A. Make better mothers.
   B. Make worse mothers.
   C. Equally as good mothers.
   D. No answer.

Part I: Woman's Role in America's Past

Objectives:

—to demonstrate that the women's movement is a serious social, political, economic and intellectual movement, with roots sunk deep in America's past.

—to assess the contributions that women have made to American history and society.

—to analyze the successes and failures of past American women's movements.

—to judge the progress or lack of progress that women have made throughout American history.

Required activity: Read Arthur M. Schlesinger, "The Role of Women in American History," in *Viewpoints in American History* (1922).

Supplemental activities: Choose one of the following activities, complete it, turn it in to your director and move on to the next section.

1. Read one of the following books about women in American history, and write a book report according to prescribed form.
   Flexner, Eleanor, *Century of Struggle: The Woman's Rights Movement in the United States.*
   O'Neill, William, *Everyone Was Brave: A History of Feminism in America.*
   Sinclair, Andrew, *The Emancipation of the American Woman.*
   Smith, Page, *Daughters of the Promised Land: Women in American History.*

2. Write a brief research paper on the first American women's rights convention, held at Seneca Falls, New York in 1848. Consult director for details on how to complete this project.

3. Read one of the following biographies of early feminist leaders, and write a book report according to prescribed form.
   Cromwell, Otelia, *Lucretia Mott.*
   Fauset, Arthur, *Sojourner Truth: God's Faithful Servant.*
   Lerner, Gerda, *The Grimké Sisters of South Carolina: Rebels against Slavery.*
   Lutz, Alma, *Created Equal: A Biography of Elizabeth Cady Stanton.*

4. Write a short research paper on the women's suffrage movement, which culminated with the passage of the 19th amendment to the Constitution in 1919. Consult director for details on how to complete this project.

5. Read the book, *The Ideas of the Woman Suffrage Movement, 1890-1920,* by Aileen Kraditor, and write a book report according to prescribed form.

6. Read one of the biographies of famous suffragists, listed below, and write a book report according to prescribed form.
   Gilman, Charlotte Perkins, *The Living of Charlotte Perkins Gilman.*
   Hayes, Elinor Rice, *Morning Star: A Biography of Lucy Stone.*
   Lutz, Alma, *Susan B. Anthony: Rebel Crusader, and Humanitarian.*

Part II: Why Women's Liberation Today?

Objectives:

—to discover the transition between the suffrage movement of the early twentieth century and the current women's movement.

—to identify the reasons for the revival of the women's movement in the 1960's.

—to compare the past feminist movements with the present one in philosophy and tactics.

Required activities: Read chapters 15, 16 and 17 of Lucy Komisar's *The New Feminism,* and Marlene Dixon's article, "Why Women's Liberation," *Ramparts* (December 1969). After completing the reading assignments, see your director to make arrangements to see the sound/filmstrip, "Feminism as a Radical Movement."

By now you should have a pretty good idea of what the women's movement is all about. Now it's time to put that in writing. Using good English and as much creativity as you can muster, write a 500-word essay on the subject, "Why Women's Liberation?" Turn this in and move on to the next section.

Part III: Psychology, Sociology and Women

Objectives:

—to investigate the charge that women are molded from birth to fit the image society has of them.

—to analyze Freudian psychology's view of women and how women have been affected by this.

Required activities: Read the first five chapters of Lucy Komisar's *The New Feminism.*

Supplemental activities: Read one article from each of the lists below, one on women and psychology, the other on women and sociology. After reading the articles, see your director to arrange a group discussion. Be prepared to discuss the articles you have read as well as to listen to others discuss those that they have read. Once the discussion has been completed, you may move on to the next section.

1. Psychology
   Chesler, Phyllis, "Patient and Patriarch: Women in Psychotherapeutic Relationship," in *Woman in Sexist Society,* ed. Vivian Gornick and Barbara Moran (Basic Books, 1971).
   Friedan, Betty, "The Sexual Solipsism of Sigmund Freud," in *The Feminine Mystique* (Dell, 1963).
   Shainess, Natalie, "A Psychiatrist's View: Images of Woman—Past and Present, Overt and Obscured," in *Sisterhood Is Powerful,* ed. Robin Morgan (Vintage, 1970).
   Weisstein, Naomi, "Psychology Constructs the Female," in *Woman in Sexist Society.*

2. Sociology
   Bardwick, Judith and Douban, Elizabeth, "Ambivalence: The Socialization of Women," in *Woman in Sexist Society.*
   Bem, Sandar and Daryl, "Training the Woman to Know Her Place: The Power of a Non-Conscious Ideology," in *Roles Women Play,* ed. Michele Garskof (Brooks-Cole, 1971).
   Chodorow, Nancy, "Being and Doing: A Cross-Cultural Examination of the Socialization of Males and Females," in *Woman in Sexist Society.*
   Freeman, Jo. "The Social Construction of the Second Sex," in *Roles Women Play.*

Part IV: Woman as Housewife

Objectives:

—to examine Betty Friedan's charge that a "feminine mystique" has brainwashed many women into being housewives and mothers.

—to analyze the housewife's role in society and the amount of dissatisfaction that some women feel in this role.

—to determine what can be done to alleviate the discontent that some housewives feel in their role.

Required activities: Listen to Carly Simon's song, "That's the Way I've Always Heard It Should Be," and read Betty Friedan's "The Problem that Has No Name," chapter I, *The Feminine Mystique.*

Supplemental activities: Complete one of the following projects on the subject of "The American Housewife." Be sure to see your director and tell him of your choice so that he can assist you. Once the project is completed, turn it in and move on to the next section.

1. Do television commercials contribute to the "housewife syndrome?" Watch television for at least two hours a day for one week. (If possible try to do some viewing during the afternoon "soap opera" period. Perhaps we can make a TV set available at school.) Make a list of the commercials indicating the item advertised and the characterization of the women in the commercials. From your findings, draw conclusions in regards to the question listed above.

2. Read Betty Friedan's *The Feminine Mystique,* and write a book report relating its contents to the housewife and her problems.

3. Go through a number of women's magazines (*Redbook, McCall's, Ladies' Home Journal, Better Homes and Garden,* etc.). Cut out the ads which depict women in housewives' roles. Make a collage of your material.

4. How do housewives in your neighborhood feel about their role in society? Make up a brief questionnaire which will attempt to find this out, distribute it, and compile the results, drawing conclusions from the data.

5. Get one copy of two of the following women's magazines: *Redbook, McCall's, Ladies' Home Journal, Family Circle* and *Good Housekeeping.* Read the articles, short stories and fiction, and features contained in the magazine (ignore the advertising; it's covered in another project). Write an analysis of the relationship of the magazines' contents to the "housewife syndrome."

Part V: Woman as Sex Object

Objectives:

—to investigate the charge that many segments of American society treat women as sex objects rather than as persons.

—to analyze the effects that this has specifically on women, and society in general.

Required activity: If the film, "Carnal Knowledge," happens to be playing locally, we will make arrangements to see it, and follow this with a discussion. If it is not showing, another film could be substituted, if appropriate.

Supplemental activities: Choose one of the following projects on the subject, "Woman as Sex Object." Be sure to inform your director as to your choice. Once the project is completed, turn it in and move on to the next section.

1. Read the article, "The Cosmo Girl: A *Playboy* Inversion," in *A World of Her Own,* ed. John Miller (Charles E. Merrill, 1971). Then get a copy of the latest *Cosmopolitan* magazine and analyze its contents (advertising, articles, fiction and general features). Then write a report, relating the contents to the "sex object" theme. The question: Does *Cosmopolitan,* a woman's magazine, perpetuate the sex object theme in American society?

2. "Woman as Sex Object" is a frequent theme in the lyrics of rock music. Do an investigative report on this subject. The following articles from *Ms.* magazine might be helpful: "Women in Rock" (August 1972); "Feminist Rock: No More Ball 'n Chain" (December 1972). Hint—if you're looking for a sexist rock star, try Mick Jagger. Make an audio show of your project by recording it on tape.

3. Is woman's "sex appeal" used to sell products? Investigate this question by getting a copy of one issue of the following magazines: *Playboy, Esquire, Gentlemen's Quarterly.* Write a report on your findings, using samples from the magazines to substantiate your arguments.

4. Read *The Female Eunuch,* by Germaine Greer, and write a report relating its contents to the "sex object" question.

5. "Woman as Sex Object" has been a frequent theme in modern literature. Read one of the following novels and write a report on the development of the female characters as "sex objects."
D. H. Lawrence, *Women in Love.*
——————————, *Lady Chatterley's Lover.*
Norman Mailer, *An American Dream.*

Part VI: Woman as Wage Earner

Objectives:

—to investigate the charges that women wage earners are underpaid, underemployed and promoted less than their male counterparts.

—to analyze the effects of this discrimination on women specifically, and society in general.

Required activities: Read the following materials: (a) "Women in Labor," by Marijean Suezle, in *Perspectives: Women's Liberation,* ed. Michael Adelstein and Jean Pival (St. Martin's Press, 1972); (b) Alice S. Rossi, "Job Discrimination and What Women Can Do About It," in *Liberation Now!* (Dell, 1971) and (c) "Charts and Tables," in *Rebirth of Feminism,* ed. Judith Hale and Ellen Levine (Quadrangle, 1971). After completing this, arrange for a conference with your director to discuss the activities.

Supplemental activities: Choose one of the projects listed below. Be sure to inform your director about your choice. Once the project is completed, turn it in and move on to the next section.

1. Read the book, *Born Female: The High Price of Keeping Women Down,* by Caroline Bird. Write a book report according to prescribed form, relating the book to the objectives listed above.

2. Choose a large business firm in the area and investigate their hiring and promotional practices as far as women are concerned. Before embarking on this project, have a conference with your director so he can help you map strategy. Some possible firms: C & P Telephone Company; Bethlehem Steel; Commercial Credit Corp.; General Electric (Howard County).

3. One big complaint feminists have is the lack of women in professions such as law and medicine. One reason has been the lack of women entering medical and law schools. Take one of the schools listed below and make an in-depth study of its enrollment figures and policies in regards to women. Be sure to see your director before you begin: The Johns Hopkins School of Medicine; University of Maryland Medical School; University of Baltimore Law School; University of Maryland Law School.

4. What problems do women run into when they try to enter the ranks of professional workers? Make a study of this, choosing one occupation or profession. Some possibilities: architecture, broadcasting, science, journalism, advertising. Be sure to consult some of the books in the history department office for some material.

Part VII: Woman and Man—A Simulation Game

Objectives:

—to have some fun, and to prove you can learn something while having fun.

Required activity: Get a copy of the game from your director. As many as eight can play the game at one time. Play the game twice, once in the role of a man and once in the role of a woman. Allow about two hours for each playing of the game. After completing the game, you should have some idea of what an advantage it is to be a man in today's society, and likewise, what a disadvantage it is to be a woman. No assignment here; move on to the next section.

Part VIII: Woman as Literary Artist

Objectives:

—to examine how women have been portrayed in literature.

—to examine the difficulty that women have had in pursuing a writing career in which their works dealt with real women rather than the traditional stereotypes.

—to discover how some modern female writers are breaking out of this cage and are using literature as a medium to promote the cause of womanhood.

Required activities: Read the articles, "Seduced and Abandoned in the New World: The Image of Woman in American Fiction," by Wendy Martin, and "Women Writers and the Double Standard," by Elaine Showalter, in *Woman in Sexist Society.* After completing this, arrange for a discussion with your director to analyze the contents of the articles.

Supplemental activities: Choose one of the novels described below, read it and write a book report according to prescribed form. Be sure to relate the novel to modern feminism as well as provide a critical analysis of the book.

1. Atwood, Margaret, *The Edible Woman.* A young woman about to marry a nice young lawyer finds that as the date of their wedding draws near, she gags on anything she tries to eat. Relief comes only when she bakes a woman-shaped cake, decorates it to resemble herself and sends it off to her fiance. The message—leave her alone to find out who she is and what she wants.

2. Drabble, Margaret, *The Millstone.* The story of Rosamund Stacy, a young intellectual who has a baby, resists all pressures to give the baby up, and becomes a success not only in her work, but in becoming both a woman and a person.

3. Lessing, Doris, *The Golden Notebook.* An autobiographical novel about Anna, a published writer, living in postwar London. She begins to record the events of her life in four notebooks dealing with personal conflicts that drive her close to madness, as well as her attempts to seek independence as a person.

4. ————. *The Summer Before the Dark.* This novel is about a woman in her forties who, in a summer on her own, must redefine her roles of wife and mother.

5. Plath, Sylvia, *The Bell Jar.* An autobiographical novel dealing painfully with the author's increasing alienation from those she knew and her eventual descent into madness, from which she achieved only a tenuous escape.

6. Roiphe, Anne Richardson, *Up the Sandbox.* This novel gives insights into the dilemma of an educated young woman: devotion to husband and children versus desires for a more meaningful life for herself. She alternately imagines herself in "liberating" circumstances and worries about her family's future.

Part IX: Feminism around Baltimore

Objectives:

—to discover the wide variety of feminist activities and organizations in the Greater Baltimore area.

—to visit one of these and write an in-depth report on your findings.

Supplemental activities: Choose one of these activities for your investigation. Remember: a personal visit is necessary to successfully complete the report. Where possible, addresses are provided for your use. Be sure to see your director before you begin.

1. An interview with Alice S. Rossi, Ph.D., Professor of Sociology at Goucher College. Dr. Rossi is also President of Sociologists for Women in Society.

2. A visit to the Maryland Commission on the Status of Women, 1100 N. Eutaw Street, Baltimore.

3. A visit to the Women's Liberation Center, 3028 Greenmount Avenue, Baltimore.

4. A visit to the Women's Law Center, 525 St. Paul's Street, Baltimore.

Part X: Summary and Evaluation

Objectives:

—to analyze the effect that this program has had on you as a person.

—to evaluate the contents of the program itself.

Required activities: See your director and arrange for a private conference. At that time you can discuss anything you wish. Also, any suggestions that you have to improve the program will be greatly appreciated. As a final project, read a short essay by Gloria Steinem, "What It Would Be Like if Women Win," *Time* (August 31, 1970), pp. 22-23. I think it will provide a fitting end to our program.

Part XI: Project

In addition to the activities and assignments contained in the various sections of the LAP, each student is to do a project. It should be based on some aspect of "Women in Society." Below is a list of suggestions. You may choose one of them or you may choose one of your own. In either case, tell your director by December 21st what you will be doing for your project. All projects are due by Friday, January 11, 1974.

1. How do black women feel about the women's liberation movement? Are they in sympathy with it? Are they an active part of the movement? Consult as many sources as you can to substantiate your answers. Be sure to use the *Reader's Guide* to help locate sources.

2. How does the average women feel about the goals and tactics of the women's liberation movement? Consult with your director and begin to draw up a list of questions which would attempt to find this out. Submit the questionnaire to a sampling of your own choosing, compile the results and draw up a report based on your findings.

3. In the Spring of 1972, a new magazine entitled *Ms.* was published, claiming to be "the new magazine for women." Get three copies of the magazine and evaluate its contents: articles, fiction, interviews, advertising. Does it live up to its billing? Write a brief report, analyzing the magazine and its contents.

4. Some people in the women's liberation movement have criticized Sigmund Freud's theories of female psychology, claiming that they reflected his culturally-induced biases against women, rather than any objective, scientific truth. Investigate this charge and write a brief paper, stating the results of your findings.

5. Write a short paper evaluating the educational system in the United States with regard to its socialization of children to sex roles. What are the effects for girls? For boys? What kind of education is needed to produce an adult capable of functioning fully in contemporary society? These are some of the questions you should look into.

6. Few crimes are more heinous than rape; yet oftentimes the victim's suffering extends far beyond the actual crime itself. Police interrogations, long, drawn-out court proceedings, difficulty of proof, and a suspicious and skeptical public—explain why nine out of every ten victims fail to report the crime. Do an investigative report on the crime of rape.

7. Believe it or not, the first novelist was a woman by the name of Aphra Behn, who has been denied recognition for her deeds because of her sex. If you wish to learn more about this fascinating woman, do a brief paper on her.

Lynn Pettit
Physical Education
Folwell Junior High School
Minneapolis, Minn./1972-73

WOMEN IN SOCIETY

Course Outline

I. Introduction to Course
   A. What is the role of "Women in Society"?
   B. Why are we here?
   C. What do you do to get a grade?
   D. Extra credit

II. Women and Work
   A. Class content
      1. Women at work
      2. Women in college
      3. Women on welfare
      4. Women as housewives
   B. Assignment: paper

III. Women in history
   A. Class content
      1. Indian women
      2. Colonial and pioneer women
      3. Southern women
      4. Black women
      5. Suffrage movement
   B. Assignment: no specific assignments here, but extra credit can be earned
      by reading an autobiography or biography of an historical woman

IV. Women and men—physical differences
   A. Class content
      1. Lab situation
      2. Discussion
   B. Assignment: paper

V. Women and society
   A. Class content
      1. Women in books and magazines
      2. Women in TV and radio
      3. Children's toys
      4. Alternatives: how things can change
   B. Assignment:
      1. Research project, to be done in groups (i.e., write a nonsexist children's
         story; visit an elementary school and ask students to draw two pictures

answering—What does a mother do? What does a father do? etc.)
2. Group presentation to class

VI. The women's liberation movement
   A. Class content
      1. Black women
      2. Men's liberation
      3. Women who oppose "liberation"
      4. The Equal Rights Amendment
      5. Day-care centers
   B. Assignment: panel discussions (class time will be given to work on these)

Sample Unit

Women and Work (Students were asked to choose one of the following four topics—
welfare, work, college, housewifery—and complete the assignments in each case)

A. If you are on welfare

1. Read "Welfare Is a Woman's Issue," by Johnnie Tillmon, *Ms.* (Spring 1972) and
   answer the following:
   a. What facts did you learn that you didn't know before?
   b. How did the article make you feel?
   c. What is your opinion of welfare?
   d. Write a general summary of the article.
2. See p. 148 of *Welfare Mothers Speak Out,* Milwaukee County Welfare Rights
   Organization (Norton, 1972).
   a. What is the largest amount paid for basic needs in Minnesota?
   b. How does this compare with other states?
   c. Do you think you could live on this?
3. Summary.
   a. Prepare a statement to take back to the group on what you learned about
      welfare.
   b. How do you feel about what you've learned?
4. For extra credit:
   a. In the book, *Welfare Mothers Speak Out,* read and summarize chapter 1 or 8.
   b. Figure how much it would cost to live, counting rent, food, clothing, etc.,
      and answer whether or not welfare payments are enough to cover these costs.

B. If you are refused a job
1. Read the article, "Heaven Won't Protect the Working Girl," by Louise Bernikow,
   Ms. (Spring 1972).
   a. What facts did you learn that you didn't know before?
   b. How did the article make you feel?
   c. Write a general summary of the article.
2. Read the two pamphlets: *Guidelines on Sex Discrimination in Employment*
   (State of Minnesota Department of Human Rights, State Office Building, St.
   Paul, Minn. 55101) and *How to File a Complaint* (Equal Employment
   Opportunity Commission, 1800 G. St. N.W., Washington, D.C. 20506).

3. Look at Chart 3, in *Guidelines on Sex Discrimination in Employment.*
   a. What kinds of laws does Minnesota have to protect female workers?
   b. How do these compare with other states'?
4. Summary.
   a. Prepare a statement to take back to the group on what you learned about job discrimination.
   b. How do you feel about what you learned?
5. For extra credit:
   a. Read and summarize chapter 9 in *The New Feminism* by Lucy Komisar.
   b. Fill in worksheet on welfare.

C. If you choose to go back to college
   1. How much is tuition? (Look at a college catalogue.)
   2. How can you finance your education?
   3. What would you take your degree in? What do you plan to be when you get out of college?
   4. What's the percentage of women in this field? (Chart number 1)
   5. Read chapter 5 in *The New Feminism* by Lucy Komisar.
      a. What facts did you learn that you didn't know before?
      b. How did the article make you feel?
      c. Write a general summary of the article.
   6. Summary.
      a. Prepare a statement to take back to the group on what you learned about college.
      b. How do you feel about what you've learned?
   7. For extra credit:
      a. How much would it cost you to live while going to school? Consider rent, food, books, clothing, etc.
      b. Is it going to be possible for you to go back to school, as planned?
      c. Read and summarize the article, "A Woman is 58% of a Man," by Teresa Levitin et al., *Psychology Today* (March 1973).

D. If you choose to stay home as a housewife
   1. Read the article, "The Value of Housework: For Love or Money," by Ann C. Scott, *Ms.* (July 1972).
      a. What facts did you learn that you didn't know before?
      b. How did the article make you feel?
      c. Write a general summary of the article.
   2. Plan a week's activities, including household chores, recreational activities and volunteer work. Do you think that the above activities would be enough to keep you satisfied as a useful human being? Write why you do or don't think so.
   3. Summary.
      a. Prepare a general statement to take back to the group on what you learned about being a housewife.
      b. How do you feel about what you learned?
   4. For extra credit: choose another alternative to being a housewife; a. going back to college, or b. getting a job. Pick up one of those worksheets and do some of the activities listed on them.

Bevan Vinton, English
Howard Yank, Social Studies
Roosevelt High School
Portland, Oreg./1974-75

MAN AND WOMAN

Course Description

"Man and Woman" is an exploration of the nature of manhood and womanhood: what it means to be a girl, a woman; what it means to be a boy, a man. In this course we will examine the main elements of the traditional masculine and feminine roles in western civilization. The course will provide students with an opportunity to examine their own developing relationships with their peers and a forum to discuss the development of their own identities. Many sources will be used in looking for answers: literature, history, film and anthropology. The course will be taught by a man and a woman.

Rationale

Given the enormous responsibilities and problems confronting men and women in today's society (financial, parental, occupational, interpersonal), we feel a class which focuses on these issues is essential in order to prepare students properly for the future. We also expect that this course will foster the kind of personal growth essential if individuals are expected to function effectively and responsibly in their personal lives, as well as in their communities. We believe that this course should be offered on an interdepartmental basis. Each student would be scheduled for a two period block of time and would receive 1/2 English credit and 1/2 social studies credit. This arrangement would enable team-teaching methods to be used, as well as provide opportunities for large groups (lecture, film, guest speakers) and small group (discussion, analysis, projects) activities.

Objectives

A. Skill development and processes
1. Each student will be able to demonstrate a tolerance for differences, different values, interests, beliefs. The student will be able to demonstrate this tolerance by permitting these differences to be heard, by developing a willingness to volunteer information and opinions, by responding in a mature manner during class discussions.
2. Each student will be able to respond to literary and nonliterary writing by means of critical analysis for purposes of judging its appropriateness, validity, merit and authenticity.
3. Each student will be able to identify labels and stereotypes.
4. Each student will know that labeling, stereotyping and using cliches preclude thinking, accurate recognition of individual differences and analysis of differing ideas.
5. Each student will be able to read and critically analyze an issue or a problem in a variety of sources which present different views, take different positions, pose different questions and answers, offer additional information, in order to achieve the objectivity, balance and perspective which enable her/him to evaluate and draw conclusions.

6. Each student will be able to skim appropriate materials and will be able to paraphrase the information discovered.
7. Each student will be able to organize written work.
8. Each student will be able to write paragraphs and essays using specifics to support generalizations.
9. Each student will be able to express him/herself in writing.
10. Each student—noting the care given to exactness of statement, documentation, etc.—will be able to assess general probability of accuracy in reporting facts and will be able to indicate logical fallacies in arguments.

B. Content
1. The student will describe the main elements of the traditional masculine and feminine roles in western civilization.
2. The student will examine anthropological data relating to masculine and feminine roles.
3. The student will develop a rationale for the contrasting roles and status of men and women in American society and other differing societies.
4. The student will describe and identify from his/her own experience, the child-raising practices which taught these roles.
5. The student will examine the impact of various child-raising practices on both personal behavior and social patterns and be able to describe and/or identify them.
6. The student will investigate and describe the development of the relative political and economic positions of men and women in American society.
7. The student will examine and describe the impact of the changing status of women in the work force on men, women and children.
8. The student will investigate the role of women in American history and government.
9. The student will determine whether, if one looks at American history and government with the role of women in mind, a different overview of the history of America emerges.
10. The student will examine the images of men and women in literature.
   a. The student will identify aspects of characterization in literature.
   b. The student will recognize the main ideas in selections of literature.
11. The student will examine the role of women in the arts.
12. The student will examine the institutions of marriage and the family—their history, dynamics and present status and trends.
13. The student will examine three alternative styles of family structure, will discuss the advantages and disadvantages of each and will predict likely changes.

14. The student will examine the personal and social impact of parenthood.
15. The student will examine the impact of divorce on partners and their minor children, and will consider constructive responses to this phenomena.
16. The student will examine American law with regard to men and women in various areas: e.g., work, citizenship, marriage and divorce, sexuality, crime, education and sexual behavior.
17. The student will demonstrate awareness of his/her feelings, attitudes and behavior in interpersonal relationships, including the ability to deal with the problems encountered in a marriage situation.

Notes on Contributors

MARTHA BARRETT: 1513 Lynnewood Drive, Havertown, Pennsylvania 19083. "Beginning in 1972, this course has been taught for eight weeks each spring to a class of fifteen students. One outgrowth of the course has been a feminist group averaging twenty-five students (ages 15 to 17) which has met once a week for three years."

MARTHA BEAUCHAMP: 41 Pleasant Street, Marion, Massachusetts 02738. Ms. Beauchamp taught her women's studies course twice at Shanti, a regional alternative high school in Hartford, Connecticut. For the past two years she has been at the Independent Learning Center, an alternative program within Old Rochester Regional High School in Mattapoisett where she teaches Spanish, social studies (including Women's Group) and Biology of Women.

PEGGY BRICK: 190 West Hudson Street, Englewood, New Jersey 07631. "My course was taught to five classes in American Studies during one term." Ms. Brick has developed two other courses—Introduction to Behavioral Science and Behavioral Science Seminar—that include units on sex-role stereotypes and socialization.

DOROTHY BURMAN: 219 East 69 Street, New York, New York 10021. "I find myself interested in developing electives about writers of minority groups that have been overlooked in the usual high school anthologies. One other elective I teach is Modern Jewish American Writers." Ms. Burman has taught her women's studies course to a total of five classes in the past two years.

MARY FONTAINE: Number 54, Street 16, Abasabad, Tehran, Iran. Ms. Fontaine taught her course in Cincinnati, Ohio, then moved to Berkeley, California, and now teaches English in Tehran, Iran.

GINGER DENECKE-HACKETT: 7021 S.W. 33 Street, Portland, Oregon 97219. Ms. Denecke-Hackett's women's studies course has been taught five times. "I am currently a counselor at Newberg High School, Newberg, Oregon, where I am trying to develop a program that can be done in the classroom—or in a group by a counselor— dealing with young women in conflict."

RENEE HAUSMANN: 219 Third Street, S.E., Washington, D.C. 20003. "I am currently teaching in the English Department of Federal City College where I am also co-coordinator of the freshman English program, a Pan-African curriculum. With my colleague, Evelyn Franklin, I have recently formed an educational consulting firm specializing in freshman composition programs that are literature-based. In the summer 1975 issue of the *Journal of English Teaching Techniques,* I published an article entitled 'Jane Austen: A Feminist?' on the teaching of *Emma*." Ms. Hausmann taught Women in the Novel of Character twice at Madeira High School. She also developed a creative writing course called The Artist and Her Work.

LEONARD W. INGRAHAM: College of Education, Arizona State University, Tempe, Arizona 85281. Dr. Ingraham, formerly Director of Social Studies for the New York City public schools, prepared this curriculum as a preliminary edition in 1972-73. It was taught in more than twenty high schools in New York City. Co-author of *An Album of Women in American History* (1972), Dr. Ingraham is now Professor of Social Studies Education.

RENEE KASPER: 596 Waukena Avenue, Oceanside, New York 11572. "After fifteen years of marriage and three children, I entered college at age thirty-five and awakened to the possibilities—or lack of them—that exist for women. I have been teaching Images of Women in Literature for the past two years in a mini-course program . . . and at the end of this school year the course will have been offered nine times. That's more than 250 young people with heightened consciousness."

155

SUSAN KLAW, ADRIA REICH, BARBARA GATES: The Group School, 345 Franklin Street, Cambridge, Massachusetts 02139. Ms. Klaw, Ms. Reich and Ms. Gates have been teaching women's courses at The Group School since 1971. Ms. Klaw also co-directs the Youth Advocacy Program; Ms. Reich is the Academic Coordinator of the school; Ms. Gates is Advisor Coordinator. Together, they are writing a volume describing the working class women's studies curriculum developed at The Group School. The section printed here owes a special debt to Judy Tharinger, the Jobs Coordinator at the school, who taught the unit on Women and Work and invented several of the activities.

MARYA LEVENSON: 23 Rockingham Street, Cambridge, Massachusetts 02138. Ms. Levenson has been teaching ninth-grade ancient history and civics in a public junior high school outside of Boston since 1971. For almost all of that time, she has been developing women's studies courses.

MERLE LEVINE: 3 Gates Way, Sea Cliff, New York 11579. Ms. Levine has been teaching high school women's studies courses since 1971. The curriculum we include was developed during a recent sabbatical leave and then tested with students at The Wheatley School. It is part of a larger text to be published in a student workbook format by Barron's Educational Series later in 1976.

CAROL LINDSAY: 36 Bouton Street, Stamford, Connecticut 06907. "I am a teacher and department chairperson at New Canaan High School in Connecticut. In addition to this course, I have written an American Studies course and another called The Occult in Literature. Woman and Man in Literature was taught three times."

SHARON L. MENARD: 2348 North 107 Street, Lafayette, Colorado 80026. This course has been taught three times. Ms. Menard lectures at various universities, consults on sex-role stereotyping and teaches inservice courses to educators.

BETH MILLSTEIN: 5700 Arlington Avenue, Bronx, New York 10471. Ms. Millstein has been teaching this course at Adlai Stevenson High School, mainly to black and Puerto Rican students, since 1972. She adapted her syllabus from a curriculum by June Chapin.

JOSEPH MITCHELL: 4017 Dee Jay Drive, Ellicott City, Maryland 21043. "I am presently teaching at Oakland Mills High School in Columbia, Maryland. My course was designed for use in an all-male school, but could easily be adapted for use in a coeducational or all-female setting. I have also developed a more individualized program with a wider variety of student choices of materials."

JUNE NAMIAS: Newton North High School, Newtonville, Massachusetts 02160. "I am a teacher and a writer. I have been teaching at various high schools and junior highs since 1962 and for the past seven years at Newton North High School. In 1971, I began teaching a night course, nongraded and untracked, called Women and Society. I have also worked to integrate a feminist perspective into the U.S. history courses and into a course called Individual, Society and History. At present I am on leave and working on a book, *Thru the Golden Door: An Oral History of American Immigration in the Twentieth Century.* I am also a poet and have been published in *Off Our Backs, A Journal of Female Liberation, Furies* and *Quest.*"

ELEANOR NEWIRTH: 51 Longview Road, Port Washington, New York 11050. Ms. Newirth has taught her course three times. "As an off-shoot of my interest in this area, I developed and taught an inservice course to teachers entitled Rediscovering Women in the Social Studies."

LYNN PETTIT: 615 South Hardy Drive #152, Tempe, Arizona 85281. "I am a junior high physical education and health teacher with the Minneapolis Public Schools. I am currently on a study leave from that position, doing graduate work in physical education at Arizona State University. My thesis is concerned with the physiological responses of women to exercise."

KAREN SAGSTETTER: 43 Reservoir Avenue, Rochester, New York 14620. "I have worked on the staff of *Scholastic Teacher,* taught high school English for two and a half years, and am now teaching creative writing at School Without Walls in Rochester. I am also a full-time graduate student at State University of New York/Buffalo." Ms. Sagstetter's course was offered to four sections of students.

BEVAN VINTON: Roosevelt High School, 6941 North Central, Portland, Oregon 97203;
HOWARD YANK: 6105 N.E. 28 Avenue, Portland, Oregon 97211.
Bevan Vinton continues to teach English and social studies at Roosevelt High School.
Howard Yank is now a social studies teacher at Adams High School in Portland.

PATRICIA WINKS: 312 Maple Street, San Francisco, California 94118. Ms. Winks has been teaching
her women's studies course at George Washington High School since 1972.

LOIS F. YATZECK: 1632 North Owaissa Street, Appleton, Wisconsin 54911. "I have taught social
studies at Kaukauna High School since 1970, part-time. I am also the mother of two daughters and
active in church work. I taught Women and History, a nine-week unit, about twelve times. Other
courses I have developed include ones centering on black and white relations, African history, international politics and world religions."

PUBLICATIONS OF THE FEMINIST PRESS'
CLEARINGHOUSE ON WOMEN'S STUDIES

Female Studies VI. Closer to the Ground: Women's Classes, Criticism, Programs—1972. Nancy Hoffman, Cynthia Secor, and Adrian Tinsley, eds., for the Commission on the Status of Women of the Modern Language Association. (1972) Essays on women's studies in the classroom, literary criticism from a feminist perspective, course materials.

Female Studies VII. Going Strong: New Courses/New Programs. Deborah Rosenfelt, ed. (1973) Syllabi for over sixty recent women's studies courses; descriptions of twelve new programs. Introductory essay assessing recent developments in women's studies.

Female Studies IX: Teaching about Women in the Foreign Languages. Sidonie Cassirer, ed., for the Commission on the Status of Women of the Modern Language Association. (1975) Listings and outlines of courses with a focus on women offered by departments of French, Spanish and German in colleges and universities across the country.

Female Studies X: Student Work—Learning to Speak. Deborah Silverton Rosenfelt, ed. (1975) The fruits of some five years of undergraduate women's studies courses on campuses across the country: a first play, a "group autobiography," poems, short stories, papers.

Feminist Resources for Schools and Colleges: A Guide to Curricular Materials. Carol Ahlum and Jacqueline M. Fralley, eds. (1973) A selective guide to curricular materials at every level from the elementary school to the university—for teachers, students, librarians and parents who want to challenge sexism in education and create nonsexist and feminist curriculum.

High School Feminist Studies. Carol Ahlum and Jacqueline Fralley, compilers. Florence Howe, ed. A collection of curricular materials in women's studies for and from the high schools including essays, bibliographies, teaching units.

Nonsexist Curricular Materials for Elementary Schools. Laurie Olsen Johnson, ed. (1974) A collection of materials for the elementary teacher and student, including quizzes, checklists, bibliographies, workbook, model units.

Strong Women. Deborah Silverton Rosenfelt, ed. (1976) Annotated bibliography of widely available paperbacks to help the teacher supplement the male-biased curriculum: anthologies, autobiography, novels, short stories, drama, poetry.

Women in the High School Curriculum: A Review of U.S. History and English Literature Texts. Phyllis Arlow and Merle Froschl. (1975)

Who's Who and Where in Women's Studies. Tamar Berkowitz, Jean Mangi, and Jane Williamson, eds. (1974) Complete directory of women's studies programs, courses and teachers, arranged by institution, department and instructor.

Women's Studies for Teachers and Administrators: A Packet of Inservice Education Materials. Merle Froschl, Florence Howe, and Sharon Kaylen, eds. (1975) Collection of materials—including an hour-long cassette—necessary for organizing inservice education aimed at eliminating sexism in the school.

Women's Studies Newsletter. Quarterly containing articles on new women's studies programs, innovative courses, teaching techniques, curricular materials, book reviews, conference reports, bibliography, job information.

THE FEMINIST PRESS offers alternatives in education and in literature. Founded in 1970, this nonprofit, tax-exempt educational and publishing organization works to eliminate sexual stereotypes in books and schools, providing instead a new (or neglected) literature with a broader vision of human potential.

Our books—high-quality, low-cost paperbacks—include reprints of important works by women writers, feminist biographies of women, and nonsexist children's books.

The Clearinghouse on Women's Studies publishes resource guides, curricular materials, bibliographies, directories, and a newsletter, designed to provide information and support for women's studies at every educational level.

The Curriculum and Inservice Projects research sexism in the schools and explore ways to counter the effects of sex-role stereotyping. They develop supplementary materials for high school English and social studies classrooms, and work with teachers on new methods to help students become their best and freest selves.

Through this work we can begin to recreate the forgotten history of women, begin to create a more humane and equitable society for the future.

For a catalogue of all our publications, write to us. We hope that you will.

THE FEMINIST PRESS
BOX 334
OLD WESTBURY, NEW YORK 11568

The Clearinghouse on Women's Studies